ORDER YOUR BUTTERWORTHS TAX ANNUALS 1999-2000

It's easy to lose your way in the wake of a new Budget and
tax legislation. Butterworths can assist by providing accurat
price. All the titles are leading tax annuals and each comple
Butterworths Tax Annuals 1999-2000 have an unrivalled
professionals for providing clear, concise and thorough expl
individual area of tax. No practitioner should be without ther

GW00707297

Butterworths Tax Annuals Set
Published September 1999
TA99MW

ISBN 0 40692 1 70-9
£150.00 approx

Butterworths Yellow Tax Handbook
"The tax practitioner's bible. Bigger than ever" *Taxation Practitioner*
Published August 1999
BYTH99

ISBN 0 40698 388-7
£45.00 approx

Butterworths Orange Tax Handbook
"Is an invaluable and welcome sight every year" *Taxation*
Published August 1999
BOTH99

ISBN 0 40698 389-5
£41.00 approx

Moores Rowland Yellow Tax Guide 1999-2000
Edited by Colin Davis MA (Cantab), FCA
Published August 1999
MRYT99

ISBN 0 40698 386-0
£47.95 approx

Moores Rowland Orange Tax Guide 1999-2000
Edited by Nigel Eastaway FCA, FCCA, FCMA, FCIS, FTII, MBAE, FHKSA, FTIHK, FOI, TEP, AIIT
Moores Rowland, Chartered Accountants
**"...are invaluable companions to that other pair of fiscal indispensables, Butterworths Yellow and
Orange Tax Handbooks"** *Solicitor's Journal*
Published August 1999
MROT99

ISBN 0 40698 387-9
£47.95 approx

Whillans's Tax Tables 57th Edition
Edited by Sheila Parrington LLB and Gina Antczak ACA ATII
Published April 1999
WTT99

ISBN 0 40698 390-9
£9.95 approx

Whillans's Tax Tables (Revised) 58th Edition
Edited by Sheila Parrington LLB and Gina Antczak ACA ATII
"The publication of these tables twice each year is always a welcome event" *New Law Journal*
Published September 1999
WTT992

ISBN 0 40698 391-7
£9.95 approx

Order your copies of the 1999-2000 editions
TODAY

TO ORDER SIMPLY COMPLETE THE ORDER FORM OVERLEAF

Butterworths

ORDER FORM

Please send this year's and subsequent year's editions of the publications indicated below until countermanded;

Title	Code	Qty	Approx price	Total
Butterworths Tax Annuals Set 1999-2000 ISBN 0 40692 170-9	TA99MW		£150.00 approx	
Butterworths Yellow Tax Handbook 1999-2000 ISBN 0 40698 388-7	BYTH99		£45.00 approx	
Butterworths Orange Tax Handbook 1999-2000 ISBN 0 40698 389-5	BOTH99		£41.00 approx	
Moores Rowland's Yellow Tax Guide 1999-2000 ISBN 0 40698 386-0	MRYT99		£47.95 approx	
Moores Rowland's Orange Tax Guide 1999-2000 ISBN 0 40698 387-9	MROT99		£47.95 approx	
Whillans's Tax Tables 57th Edition ISBN 0 40698 390-9	WTT99		£9.95 approx	
Whillans's Tax Tables (Revised) 58th Edition ISBN 0 40698 391-7	WTT992		£9.95 approx	

SIMPLY COMPLETE AND RETURN THIS CARD - NO STAMP NEEDED

Dominic Rooke-Allden, Butterworths,
Marketing Department, FREEPOST 6983, London, WC2A 1BR
Telephone: 0181 662 2000 or Facsimile: 0181 686 3155

I WOULD LIKE TO PAY (Please tick as appropriate)

☐ using my Butterworths account no. _____

☐ by credit card as follows

 ☐ Mastercard ☐ American Express

 ☐ Barclaycard or other Visa card

My credit card no. is

☐☐☐☐ ☐☐☐☐ ☐☐☐☐ ☐☐☐☐

and its expiry date is _____

☐ with the attached cheque for £ ____
(made payable to Butterworths)

☐ Please supply the above on 21 days' approval

Signed ....

Date ....

MY FIRM / ORGANISATION IS

_____

Address _____

_____

_____ Country _____

Postcode _____ DX _____

VAT Reg No _____

and it has _____ partners/employees

MY DETAILS ARE

Name _____

Job title _____

Telephone number _____

☐ Please keep me informed of other books, journals and information services on this and other related subjects from Butterworths or companies approved by Butterworths.

 **Butterworths**

ℛ A member of the Reed Elsevier plc group

Registered No: 729731 England VAT Registered No: 243 3583 67
NB: Your data may be used for direct marketing purposes by Selected companies

Overseas

Average rates of exchange

Rates for the years ending December 1998 and March 1999 are not available at the time of going to press. (For TA 1988 s 278 purposes, the appropriate rate is the average for the year ended 31 March.)

Average for year ending	31.12.96	31.3.97	31.12.97	31.3.98	31.12.98	31.3.99
Algeria (Dinar)	85·7181	88·6549	95·3397	96·3977		
Argentina (Peso)	1·5609	1·5855	1·6385	1·6432		
Australia ($A)	1·9952	2·0129	2·2087	2·3021		
Austria (Schilling)	16·5372	17·3392	19·9796	20·4914		
Bahrain (Dinar)	0·589	0·5983	0·618	0·6198		
Bangladesh (Taka)	64·3978	66·3433	71·8156	73·2702		
Barbados (BD$)	3·1399	3·1913	3·2969	3·3067		
Belgium (Franc)	48·3809	50·7632	58·5873	60·0947		
Bolivia (Boliviano)	7·9464	8·1664	8·6305	8·736		
Botswana (Pula)	5·1291	5·4936	5·9396	6·0386		
Brazil (Real)	1·5705	1·6232	1·7525	1·7894		
Brunei ($)	2·1949	2·2324	2·4208	2·5236		
Burma (Kyat)	9·178	9·4811	10·2315	10·2881		
Burundi (Franc)	405·1671	403·9885	520·8658	589·9479		
Canada (Can$)	2·1643	2·1936	2·2669	2·3028		
Cayman Islands (CI$)	1·3065	1·3286	1·3583	1·3589		
Chile (Peso)	644·0859	657·2934	687·7897	703·7922		
China (Renminbi Yuan)	12·9393	13·1517	13·5969	13·596		
CIS (Rouble) (Official)	0·9908					
(Market)	7,958·611	8,451·753	9,475·4158			
1.4.97–31.12.97				9,548·9477		
1.1.98–31.3.98				9·9369		
Colombia (Peso)	1,616·58	1,651·973	1,872·778	1,997·295		
Costa Rica (Colon)	321·0629	337·0134	379·4464	389·5695		
Cuba (Peso)			34·1751	35·8312		
1.1.96–30.11.96	1·5484					
1.12.96–31.12.96	31·1923					
1.4.96–30.11.96		1·5541				
1.12.96–31.3.97		31·1678				
Cyprus (£)	0·7253	0·7499	0·8404	0·8559		
Czechoslovakia (Koruna)	42·245	43·4344	51·8142	54·4364		
Denmark (Krone)	9·0577	9·4616	10·8156	11·0912		
Ecuador (Sucre)	4,946·143	5,312·16	6,490·7567	6,850·581		
Egypt (£)	5·3159	5·3971	5·5689	5·591		
El Salvador (Colon)	13·6261	13·8569	14·358	14·3648		
EMS (ECU)	1·2478	1·2911	1·4492	1·4797		
Ethiopia (Birr)	9·1336	9·4883	10·668	10·8539		
Fiji Islands (F$)	2·1868	2·2158	2·3537	2·5122		
Finland (Markka)	7·1751	7·4542	8·5027	8·7589		
France (Franc)	7·9905	8·3433	9·5568	9·7851		
French Cty/Africa (CFA franc)	794·5833	829·7642	952·8192	973·84		
French Pacific Is (CFP franc)	144·5258	150·4152	173·0895	177·1803		
Gambia (Dalasi)	15·3013	15·585	16·3181	16·4068		
Germany (Deutsche mark)	2·3506	2·4642	2·8391	2·912		
Ghana (Cedi)	2,542·721	2,694·739	3,362·86	3,578·286		
Greece (Drachma)	376·2084	389·8525	447·1124	461·9111		
Grenada/Wind. Isles (EC$)	4·2176	4·284	4·4259	4·4389		
Guyana (G$)	217·3761	221·3241	232·4098	234·4382		
Honduras (Lempira)	17·7612	19·0761	21·3249	21·5222		
Hong Kong (HK$)	12·0795	12·2759	12·6824	12·7128		
Hungary (Forint)	231·6071	247·7858	304·2664	319·3189		
Iceland (Krona)	104·1897	107·3178	116·2706	117·6784		
India (Rupee)	55·2826	56·2891	59·5592	61·1163		
Indonesia (Rupiah)	3,634·018	3,723·169	4,731·619	7,726·729		
Iran (Rial)	4,686·156	4,760·009	4,917·584	4,932·109		
Iraq (Dinar)	0·4857	0·4933	0·5097	0·5112		
Irish Republic (Punt)	0·9755	0·9888	1·0814	1·1239		

3

Average rates of exchange — continued

Average for year ending	31.12.96	31.3.97	31.12.97	31.3.98	31.12.98	31.3.99
Israel (Shekel)	4·9887	5·1515	5·6472	5·7802		
Italy (Lira)	2,408·06	2,473·67	2,788·26	2,858·55		
Jamaica (J$)	55·6957	55·2863	56·2463	57·0217		
Japan (Yen)	169·593	178·8762	198·189	201·5651		
Jordan (Dinar)	1·1062	1·1258	1·163	1·167		
Kenya (Shilling)	89·1287	89·3362	96·0346	98·695		
Korea South (Won)	1,248·863	1,300·689	1,512·7625	1,829·133		
Kuwait (Dinar)	0·468	0·4768	0·4974	0·5		
Laos (New Kip)	1,431·731	1,456·261	1,616·78	1,849·443		
Lebanon (£)	2,454·038	2,476·73	2,524·757	2,523·745		
Libya (Dinar)	0·5553	0·5641	0·644	0·6572		
Luxembourg (Franc)	48·3809	50·7632	58·5873	60·0948		
Malawi (Kwacha)	23·9018	24·2698	26·2217	30·098		
Malaysia (Ringgit)	3·9289	3·9661	4·6203	5·2295		
Malta (Pound)	0·5638	0·5813	0·6341	0·6432		
Mauritius (Rupee)	30·7386	31·7472	34·4037	35·6534		
Mexico (Peso)	11·8748	12·2089	13·0057	13·2708		
Morocco (Dirham)	13·038	13·9962	15·5795	15·827		
Nepal (Rupee)	87·7806	89·7057	93·24	94·678		
Netherlands (Guilder)	2·6339	2·7639	3·1952	3·2795		
N'nd Antilles (Guilder)	2·7857	2·8334	2·9303	2·9315		
New Zealand (NZ$)	2·2698	2·2861	2·4827	2·6109		
Nicaragua (Gold Cordoba)	13·0508	13·6574	15·3967	15·8654		
Nigeria (Naira)	34·3652	34·8876	35·9028	35·9815		
Norway (Krone)	10·0835	10·3301	11·594	11·9974		
Oman (Rial Omani)	0·6015	0·611	0·6311	0·633		
Pakistan (Rupee)	56·3789	59·5736	67·3595	69·1708		
Papua New Guinea (Kina)	2·0476	2·0934	2·3387	2·5122		
Paraguay (Guarani)	3,197·293	3,294·955	3,549·4278	3,700·0241		
Peru (New Sol)	3·8302	4·0024	4·3604	4·4355		
Philippines (Peso)	40·9431	41·6537	48·6631	54·6569		
Poland (Zloty)	4·1814	4·437	5·3532	5·5712		
Portugal (Escudo)	240·8921	250·3734	287·0583	295·8785		
Qatar (Riyal)	5·6853	5·7748	5·9676	5·9875		
Romania (Leu)	4,811·369	6,204·511	11,532·98	12,433·58		
Rwanda (R Franc)	399·0622	443·2439	505·5068	520·114		
Saudi Arabia (Riyal)	5·8584	5·9511	6·1483	6·1663		
Seychelles (Rupee)	7·7512	7·914	8·2395	8·2923		
Sierra Leone (Leone)	1,358·974	1,337·208	1,298·899	1,345·217		
Singapore (S$)	2·2125	2·2508	2·4363	2·5424		
Solomon Islands (SI$)	5·4868	5·6318	6·0008	6·4455		
Somali Republic (Shilling)	4,077·322	4,147·178	4,296·9542	4,298·787		
South Africa (Rand)	6·725	7·1191	7·547	7·7471		
Spain/Balic. Isles (Peseta)	197·843	207·5908	239·785	246·1423		
Sri Lanka (Rupee)	86·3735	89·2778	96·6421	98·7092		
Sudan (Dinar)	186·6184	214·1687	244·0676	250·2443		
Surinam (Guilder)	639·3482	648·9861	661·3535	657·9441		
Swaziland (Lilangeni)	5·7303	7·0875	7·5447	7·7058		
Sweden (Krona)	10·4755	10·8837	12·5085	12·8045		
Switzerland (Franc)	1·932	2·0616	2·3751	2·3972		
Syria (Pound)	65·2647	66·4698	66·9719	66·3858		

Average rates of exchange — continued

Average for year ending	31.12.96	31.3.97	31.12.97	31.3.98	31.12.98	31.3.99
Taiwan (New T$)	42·887	43·5986	47·0966	49·4721		
Tanzania (Shilling).........	884·3338	922·4204	1,000·059	1,017·706		
Thailand (Baht)..............	39·6131	40·4954	51·4646	60·0541		
Tonga Islands (Pa Anga)	1·9941	2·0103	2·2	2·2942		
Trinidad and Tobago (TT$)............................	9·1599	9·482	10·1211	10·1684		
Tunisia (Dinar)..............	1·5202	1·582	1·8042	1·854		
Turkey (Lira)..................	128,783·2	152,836·6	251,532·048	295,626·61		
Uganda (New Shilling)..	1,622·468	1,651·004	1,760·402	1,814·281		
United Arab Emirates (Dirham)......................	5·7369	5·8274	6·0205	6·0378		
Uruguay (Peso Uruguayo)	12·4152	13·256	15·4775	16·0205		
USA (US$)	1·5619	1·5866	1·638	1·642		
Venezuela (Bolivar).......			800·7369	818·8615		
1.1.96–21.4.96..........	441·5667					
22.4.96–31.12.96	741·0028					
1.4.96–21.4.96..........		439·8923				
22.4.96–31.3.97..........		749·6244				
Vietnam (Dong)	17,165·53	17,556·35	19,135·658	19,665·03		
Yemen North (Rial).......	198·2838	209·5619	210·8668	208·4937		
Yemen South (Dinar) ...						
1.1.96–31.3.96..........	45·9503					
Zaire Republic (Zaire)..	73,656·37	127,788·8	225,418·1	221,423·4658		
Zambia (Kwacha)..........	1,885·7	2,011·703	2,167·322	2,288·8509		
Zimbabwe (Dollar)........	15·6631	16·5514	20·043	22·6336		

Rates of exchange on year-end dates

	31.12.96	31.3.97	31.12.97	31.3.98	31.12.98	31.3.99
Australia ($A)	2·1546	2·0948	2·5253	2·5252		
Austria (Schilling).........	18·5497	19·2808	20·8157	21·7878		
Belgium (Franc)	54·3586	56·6252	60·9619	63·8841		
Canada (Can$)	2·3456	2·2683	2·3546	2·3815		
Denmark (Krone)..........	10·0948	10·4364	11·2664	11·8053		
France (Franc)	8·8966	9·242	9·8985	10·3753		
Germany (Deutsche mark)	2·6373	2·7395	2·9585	3·0969		
Hong Kong (HK$)	13·2369	12·7239	12·749	12·9749		
Irish Republic (Punt)	1·0111	1·0337	1·1544	1·2324		
Italy (Lira).....................	2,602·03	2,739·27	2,909·06	3,052·58		
Japan (Yen)...................	198·631	203·296	213·937	223·31		
Luxembourg (Franc)	54·3586	56·6252	60·9619	63·8841		
Netherlands (Guilder) ..	2·9601	3·08	3·3356	3·491		
Norway (Krone)	10·9273	10·8338	12·1302	12·7672		
Portugal (Escudo)........	265·679	275·462	302·498	317·152		
South Africa (Rand)	8·0046	7·2585	8·0071	8·4381		
Spain/Balic. Isles (Peseta)	222·597	232·786	250·784	262·93		
Sweden (Krona)............	11·6848	12·3703	13·0552	13·3872		
Switzerland (Franc)	2·2978	2·3655	2·3999	2·5529		
USA (US$)	1·7113	1·642	1·6454	1·6746		

Note: The material on pages 3 to 5 is Crown Copyright.

Double taxation agreements (including protocols and regulations)
Taxes on income and capital gains

Agreements terminated or superseded within the last six years are printed in italic. Amending protocols and exchanges of notes are printed in square brackets. Entry into force after 5.4.70 is indicated in the third column.

Country	SI/SR & O	Entry into force
Antigua & Barbuda	1947/2865	
	[1968/1096]	
Argentina	1997/1777	1.8.97
Armenia†	1986/224	30.1.86
Australia	1968/305	3.10.95
	[1980/707]	21.5.80
	(talks 1997)	
Austria*	1970/1947	17.12.70
	[1979/117]	6.2.79
	[1994/768]	1.12.94
Azerbaijan	*1986/224*	*30.1.86*
	1995/762	3.10.95
Bangladesh	1980/708	8.7.80
Barbados	1970/952	26.6.70
	[1973/2096]	12.12.73
Belarus†	1986/224	30.1.86
	1995/2706	
Belgium*	1987/2053	21.10.89
	(talks 1997)	
Belize	1947/2866	
	[1968/573]	
	[1973/2097]	12.12.73
Bolivia	1995/2707	23.10.95
Bosnia Herzegovina‡	1981/1815	16.9.82
Botswana	1978/183	9.2.78
	(talks 1998)	
Brazil	(talks 1997)	
Brunei	1950/1977	
	[1968/306]	
	[1973/2098]	12.12.73
Bulgaria	1987/2054	28.12.87
Canada§§	1980/709	17.12.80
	[1980/1528]	18.12.80
	[1985/1996]	23.12.85
	1980/780 (dividend)	1.7.80
	[1987/2071]	1.1.88
	1996/1782	30.7.96
Chile	(talks 1998)	
China◊	1984/1826	23.12.84
	[1996/3164]	4.3.97
Colombia	(talks 1994)	
Croatia‡	1981/1815	16.9.82
Cyprus	1975/425	18.3.75
	[1980/1529]	15.12.80
Czech Republic§	1991/2876	20.12.91
Denmark	1980/1960	17.12.80
	[1991/2877]	19.12.91
	[1996/3165]	20.6.97
Ecuador	(text agreed)	
Egypt	1980/1091	23.8.80
Estonia	1994/3207	19.12.94
European Economic Community	(Convention and Directives 90/434/ EEC, 90/435/EEC, 90/436/EEC: see TA 1988 s 815B)	23.7.90
Falkland Islands	*1984/363*	*27.6.84*
	[1992/3206]	*30.12.92*
	1997/2985	18.12.97
Faroe Islands**	*1950/1195*	
	[1961/579]	
	1969/1068	*31.5.71*
	[1971/717]	*31.5.71*
	1973/1326	*19.12.75*
	[1975/2190]	*19.12.75*
Fiji*	1976/1342	17.8.76
Finland	1970/153	
	[1980/710]	25.4.81
	[1985/1997]	20.2.87
	[1991/2878]	23.12.91
	[1996/3166]	8.8.97
France*§§	1968/1869	
	[1973/1328]	6.8.73
	[1987/466]	7.4.87
	[1987/2055]	23.12.87
	(text agreed)	
Gabon	(talks 1986)	
Gambia	1980/1963	5.7.82
Georgia†	1986/224	30.1.86
German Democratic Republic: now part of German Federal Republic		
German Federal Republic*§§	1967/25	
	[1971/874]	1.6.71
	(talks 1994)	(extended to former GDR from 1.1.91)
Ghana (1978 Convention never entered into force)	*1947/2868* *1978/785* 1993/1800	10.8.94
Greece*	1954/142	
Grenada	1949/361	
	[1968/1867]	
Guernsey	1952/1215	
	[1994/3209]	3.1.95
Guyana	1992/3207	18.12.92
Hungary	1978/1056	27.8.78
Iceland	1991/2879	19.12.91
India	*1981/1120*	*21.10.81*
	1993/1801	25.10.93
Indonesia	*1975/2191*	*3.1.76*
	1994/769	14.4.94
Irish Republic*	[1976/2152]	23.12.76
	[1995/764]	21.9.95
	[1998/3151]	23.12.98
Isle of Man	1955/1205	
	[1991/2880]	19.12.91
	[1994/3208]	3.1.95
Israel	1963/616	
	[1971/391]	25.3.71
Italy	1990/2590	31.12.90
Ivory Coast	1987/169	10.2.87
Jamaica	1973/1329	31.12.73
Japan	1970/1948	25.12.70
	[1980/1530]	31.10.80
Jersey	1952/1216	
	[1994/3210]	3.1.95
Jordan	(talks 1999)	
Kazakhstan	*1986/224*	*30.1.86*
	1994/3211	15.7.96
	[1998/2567]	2.11.98
Kenya*	1977/1299	18.10.77
Kiribati	1950/750	
	[1968/309]	
	[1974/1271]	25.7.74
Korea	*1978/786*	*31.5.78*
	1996/3168	30.12.96
Kuwait	(signed 1999)	
Kyrgyzstan†	1986/224	30.1.86
Latvia	1996/3167	30.12.96
Lesotho	*1949/2197*	
	[1968/1868]	
	1997/2986	23.12.97

Double taxation agreements — continued

Country	SI/SR & O	Entry into force
Lithuania§§	(talks 1997)	
Luxembourg*	1968/1100	
	[1980/567]	21.5.80
	[1984/364]	19.3.84
Macedonia‡	1981/1815	16.9.82
Malawi	1956/619	
	[1964/1401]	
	[1968/1101]	
	[1979/302]	14.3.79
Malaysia	1973/1330	13.9.73
	[1987/2056]	26.1.88
	1997/2987	8.7.98
Malta	1962/639	
	[1975/426]	18.3.75
	1995/763	27.3.95
Mauritius*	1981/1121	19.10.81
	[1987/467]	26.10.87
Mexico	1994/3212	15.12.94
Moldova†	1986/224	30.1.86
Mongolia	1996/2598	4.12.96
Montserrat	1947/2869	
	[1968/576]	
Morocco	1991/2881	29.11.90
Myanmar*	1952/751	
Namibia*§§	1962/2352	
	[1962/2788]	
	[1967/1489]	
	[1967/1490]	
	(agreement initialled)	
Netherlands*	1967/1063 (dividend)	
	1980/1961	6.4.81
	[1983/1902]	20.12.90
	[1990/2152]	20.12.90
	(talks 1997)	
New Zealand	1984/365	16.3.84
Nigeria	1987/2057	27.12.87
Norway*§§	1985/1998	20.12.85
	(talks 1997)	
Oman◇◇	1998/2568	9.11.98
Pakistan	1987/2058	8.12.87
Papua New Guinea	1991/2882	20.12.91
Philippines	1978/184	9.2.78
Poland	1978/282	25.2.78
Portugal*	1969/599	
Romania	1977/57	17.1.77
Russian Federation†	1986/224	30.1.86
	1994/3213	18.4.97
St Christopher and Nevis	1947/2872	
Serbia and Montenegro‡	1981/1815	16.9.82

Country	SI/SR & O	Entry into force
Sierra Leone	1947/2873	
	[1968/1104]	
Singapore	1967/483	
	[1978/787]	4.8.78
	1997/2988	19.12.97
Slovakia§	1991/2876	20.12.91
Slovenia‡	1981/1815	16.9.82
Solomon Islands	1950/748	
	[1968/574]	
	[1974/1270]	25.7.74
South Africa*	1969/864	
	(talks 1996)	
Spain	1976/1919	25.11.76
	[1995/765]	26.5.95
Sri Lanka	1980/713	21.5.80
Sudan	1977/1719	25.10.77
Swaziland*	1969/380	
Sweden	1984/366	26.3.84
	(talks 1997)	
Switzerland*	1978/1408	7.10.78
	[1982/714]	18.5.82
	[1994/3215]	19.12.94
Tajikistan†	1986/224	30.1.86
Thailand	1981/1546	20.11.81
Trinidad and Tobago	1983/1903	22.12.83
Tunisia	1984/133	8.2.84
Turkey	1988/932	26.10.88
Turkmenistan†	1986/224	30.1.86
Uganda	1952/1213	
	1993/1802	21.12.93
Ukraine	1986/224	30.1.86
	1993/1803	11.8.93
United Arab Emirates	(text agreed)	
USA	1946/1331 (dividend)	
	[1955/499]	
	[1961/985]	
	[1980/779]	22.5.80
	1980/568	25.4.80
	[1994/1418] (dividend)	16.6.94
	[1996/1781] (dividend)	30.7.96
	(talks 1999)	
Uzbekistan	1986/224	30.1.86
	1994/770	10.6.94
Venezuela	1996/2599	31.12.96
Vietnam	1994/3216	15.12.94
Zambia*	1972/1721	29.3.73
	[1981/1816]	14.1.83
Zimbabwe	1982/1842	11.2.83

Double taxation agreements — continued

Shipping and air transport profits

Country	SI or SR & O	Country	SI or SR & O
Algeria (air)	1984/362	Jordan	1979/300
Argentina	*1949/1435*	Kuwait (air)	1984/1825
Armenia (USSR air)*	1974/1269	Kyrgyzstan (USSR air)*	1974/1269
Bahrain (air)	(text agreed)	Lebanon	1964/278
Belarus (USSR air)*	1974/1269	Moldova (USSR air)*	1974/1269
Brazil	1968/572	Oman (air)**	(text agreed)
Cameroon (air)	1982/1841	Qatar (air)	(text agreed)
China (air)	1981/1119	*Russia (USSR air)*	*1974/1269*
Congo Democratic Republic	1977/1298	Saudi Arabia (air)	1994/767
Ethiopia (air)	1977/1297	Tajikistan (USSR air)*	1974/1269
Georgia (USSR air)*	1974/1269	Turkmenistan (USSR air)*	1974/1269
Hong Kong (air)	1998/2566	United Arab Emirates (air)	(text agreed)
Iran (air)	1960/2419	*USSR (air)*	*1974/1269*

* The Revenue has confirmed that this Arrangement will be treated in the same way as the Convention covering income and capital gains SI 1986/224. See note † on p 7.

** This agreement was not brought into force. See now the comprehensive Agreement, p 7 above.

Taxes on capital

France	1963/1319	South Africa	1979/576
India	1956/998	Sweden	1981/840
Ireland	1978/1107		1989/986
Italy	1968/304	Switzerland	*1957/426*
Netherlands	1980/706		1994/3214
	[1996/730]	USA	1979/1454
Pakistan	1957/1522		

Income arising abroad — Schedule D assessment

	Case IV	Case V		
	Securities	Professions, trades, etc	Pensions	Possessions
NON-RESIDENTS	Exempt	Exempt	Exempt	Exempt
RESIDENTS				
1) **Foreign domicile**	Remittance	Remittance	Remittance	Remittance
2) **UK domicile**				
(a) Non Commonwealth citizen[1]	Arising	Arising	90%[3] arising	Arising
(b) Commonwealth citizen[2]				
(i) ordinarily resident	Arising	Arising	90%[3] arising	Arising
(ii) not ordinarily resident	Remittance	Remittance	Remittance	Remittance

[1] But not citizen of the Republic of Ireland.
[2] Or citizen of the Republic of Ireland.
[3] Pensions paid by the governments of the Federal Republic of Germany or of Austria to victims of Nazi persecution are exempt from 6.4.86. Previously 50% exemption.

Schedule E liability of non-resident employees   see p 69.

Tax-free (FOTRA) securities

Under FA 1996 s 154 interest on certain securities ('FOTRA securities') issued by the Treasury is exempt from tax where the beneficial owner is not ordinarily resident in the UK. Except in the case of 3½% War Loan 1952 or after, the exemption does not apply where the securities are held for the purposes of a trade or business carried on in the UK. From 6 April 1998, FOTRA status has been extended to all government stock on the terms of FA 1996 s 154 ((1998) SWTI 440).

General

Certificates of tax deposit

The Series 7 Prospectus came into operation on 1 October 1993.

From 1 October 1993, certificates are not available for purchase for use against corporation tax liabilities, although certificates purchased before that date can be used before 1 October 1999 and set against all liabilities listed in the schedule to the Series 6 Prospectus.

Certificates are available to individuals, trustees, companies or other persons or bodies for the payment of any taxes or other liabilities listed in the schedule to the Prospectus. Minimum first deposit £2,000; subsequent deposits not less than £500.

Interest is paid without deduction of tax and is assessed under Schedule D Case III. It will only be paid for the first 6 years of a deposit. Under the Series 7 Prospectus a deposit bears interest for the first year at the rate in force at the time of the deposit and for each subsequent year at the rate in force on the anniversary of the deposit. No bonus or interest supplement is payable.

Series 7
Deposits of £100,000 or over: rate varies according to number of months held for in relevant year:

A = under £100,000
B = £100,000 or over

From	Amount	Held for (mths in yr)	Pay't of tax %	Cashed %	From	Amount	Held for (mths in yr)	Pay't of tax %	Cashed %
Series 7 (1.10.93)					31.10.96	A	no limit	2½	1¼
24.11.93	A	no limit	1¾	1		B	under 1	2½	1¼
	B	under 1	1¾	1			1-under 3	5¼	2¾
		1-under 3	4¼	2¼			3-12	5	2½
		3-under 6	4	2	7. 5.97	A	no limit	2¾	1½
		6-under 9	3¾	2		B	under 1	2¾	1½
		9-12	3¾	1¾			1-under 3	5½	2¾
9. 2.94	A	no limit	1½	¾			3-under 6	5¼	2¾
	B	under 1	1½	¾			6-under 9	5½	2¾
		1-under 3	4	2			9-12	5¼	2¾
		3-under 6	3¾	2	9. 6.97	A	no limit	3	1½
		6-under 9	3¾	1¾		B	under 1	3	1½
		9-12	3½	1¾			1-12	5½	2¾
13. 9.94	A	no limit	2	1	11. 7.97	A	no limit	3¼	1¾
	B	under 1	2	1		B	under 1	3¼	1¾
		1-under 6	4¾	2½			1-under 3	6	3
		6-under 9	5	2½			3-under 9	5¾	3
		9-12	5½	2¾			9-12	6	3
8.12.94	A	no limit	2½	1¼	8. 8.97	A	no limit	4½	2¼
	B	under 1	2½	1¼		B	under 1	4½	2¼
		1-under 3	5¼	2¾			1-under 9	6	3
		3-under 6	5½	2¾			9-12	5¾	3
		6-under 9	5¾	3	7.11.97	A	no limit	4	2
		9-12	6	3		B	under 1	4	2
3. 2.95	A	no limit	3	1½			1-under 6	6½	3¼
	B	under 1	3	1½			6-12	6¼	3¼
		1-under 6	5¾	3	5. 6.98	A	no limit	4	2
		6-under 9	6	3		B	under 1	4	2
		9-12	6¼	3¼			1-under 3	6½	3¼
14.12.95	A	no limit	2½	1¼			3-under 9	6¼	3¼
	B	under 1	2½	1¼			9-12	6	3
		1-under 3	5½	2¾	9.10.98	A	no limit	3¾	2
		3-under 9	5	2½		B	under 1	3¾	2
		9-12	4¾	2½			1-under 3	6¼	3¼
19. 1.96	A	no limit	2¾	1½			3-under 6	5¾	3
	B	under 1	2¾	1½			6-under 9	5½	2¾
		1-under 3	5¼	2¾			9-12	5¼	2¾
		3-under 9	4¾	2½	6.11.98	A	no limit	3¼	1¾
		9-12	4½	2¼		B	under 1	3¼	1¾
11. 3.96	A	no limit	2½	1¼			1-under 3	5¾	3
	B	under 1	2½	1¼			3-under 6	5¼	2¾
		1-under 3	5	2½			6-under 9	5	2½
		3-under 9	4¾	2½			9-12	4¾	2½
		9-12	4½	2¼	11.12.98	A	no limit	3¼	1¾
7. 6.96	A	no limit	2¼	1¼		B	under 1	3	1½
	B	under 1	2¼	1¼			1-under 3	5¼	2¾
		1-12	4¾	2½			3-under 6	4¾	2½
							6-under 9	4½	2¼
							9-12	4¼	2¼
					8.1.99	A	no limit	2½	1¼
						B	under 1	2½	1¼
							1-under 3	5	2½
							3-under 6	4½	2¼
							6-12	4	2
					5.2.99	A	no limit	1¾	1
						B	under 1	1¾	1
							1-under 3	4½	2¼
							3-under 6	4	2
							6-12	3¾	2

Due dates of tax

Capital gains tax

From 1996–97:
(TMA 1970 s 59B. There are no provisions for payment on account for capital gains tax.)
Normally 31 January following end of year of assessment.
(See also *Extended due dates* under **Income tax**, below)
Before 1996–97:
Later of *(a)* 1 December following end of year of assessment, and
　　　　 (b) 30 days after issue of notice of assessment.

Corporation tax

Generally (accounting periods ending after 30 September 1993: pay and file and self assessment)
(TMA 1970 s 59D, substituted by FA 1998 Sch 19 para 29 for accounting periods ending after 30 June 1999.)
9 months and 1 day after end of accounting period.
Instalments for larger companies (TMA 1970 s 59E, SI 1998/3175)
(Large: profits exceeding upper relevant maximum amount in force at end of accounting period, subject to certain restrictions: reg 3.)
　　1st instalment: 6 months and 13 days from start of accounting period (or date of final instalment if earlier);
　　(2nd instalment: 3 months after 1st instalment, if length of accounting period allows);
　　(3rd instalment: 3 months after 2nd instalment, if length of accounting period allows);
　　Final instalment: 3 months and 14 days from end of accounting period.
Transitional provisions (reg 4) percentage of total liability payable by instalments for accounting periods ending:
　　after 30 June 1999 but before 1 July 2000: 60%
　　after 30 June 2000 but before 1 July 2001: 72%
　　after 30 June 2001 but before 1 July 2002: 88%
(balance due and payable in accordance with *Generally* above).
Advance corporation tax (abolished from 6 April 1999) (FA 1998 ss 31, 32, Sch 3)
Tax in respect of franked payments to be included in a return is due 14 days after a return period ends.
Return periods end on 31 March, 30 June, 30 September, 31 December and at the end of each accounting period, when not one of the above.
Close companies: tax on loans to participators
Loans etc made in accounting periods ending after 30 March 1996: 9 months and 1 day after the end of the accounting period. Previously 14 days after the end of the accounting period in which the loan was made. To be included in instalment payments for large companies in respect of accounting periods ending after 30 June 1999 (TMA 1970 s 59E(11), see above).

Income tax

From 1997–98:
(1)　*Payment on account* (TMA 1970 s 59A)*
A payment on account is required where a taxpayer was assessed to income tax in respect of the immediately preceding year in an amount exceeding the amount of tax deducted at source in respect of that year (subject to a de minimis limit, see below). This excess is known as the "relevant amount".
The payment on account is made in 2 equal instalments due on –
　　(a)　31 January during the year of assessment, and
　　(b)　31 July in the following year of assessment.
No payments on account are required where–
　　(a)　the aggregate of the relevant amount (see above) and the Class 4 NIC liability for the preceding year is less than £500; or
　　(b)　more than 80% of the taxpayer's income tax and Class 4 NIC liability for the immediately preceding year was met by tax deducted at source.
From 1996–97:
(2)　*Payment of income tax* (TMA 1970 s 59B)
Balance of income tax due for a year of assessment (after deducting payments on account, tax deducted at source and credits in respect of dividends, etc) is due on:
31 January following end of year of assessment (i.e. the first such payment was due on 31 January 1998).
　Extended due dates:
　　(a)　If a taxpayer has given notice of liability within 6 months of the end of the year of assessment (as required by TMA 1970 s 7), but a notice to make a return is not given until after 31 October following the end of the year of assessment, the final payment is not due until 3 months after the notice is given (TMA 1970 s 59B(3)).
　　(b)　If an amended self-assessment is made less than 30 days before the due date (or the extended due date at *(a)* above) the additional tax is payable on or before the day following the end of a 30-day period beginning on the day on which notice of the amendment is given (TMA 1970 s 59B(5)).
　　(c)　If an assessment other than a self-assessment under TMA 1970 s 9 is made, tax payable under the assessment is due on the day following the end of a 30-day period beginning on the day on which notice of the assessment is given (TMA 1970 s 59B(6)).
For partnership businesses commenced before 6 April 1994 where there has been no subsequent deemed cessation and recommencement, each partner's share of the income tax paid for 1996–97 by the partnership was treated for these purposes as if it had been tax deducted at source.
*(*For 1996–97 only:***
(1)　*Payment on account* (TMA 1970 s 59A as amended by FA 1995 Sch 21 para 2)
A payment on account was required where a taxpayer was assessed to income tax in respect of 1995–96 in an amount exceeding the aggregate of (a) the amount of higher-rate tax charged on any income not subject to PAYE or income from which tax had been deducted or was treated as deducted, and which was attributable to the difference between the higher rate and the basic rate (or lower rate in the case of dividend income); (b) tax deducted at source; and (c) the excess of any Schedule E liability over tax deducted under PAYE etc (subject to a de minimis limit, see below). This excess was known as the "relevant amount".
The payment on account was to be made in 2 instalments as follows–
　　(a)　due on 31 January 1997:
　　　　(i)　100% of 1995–96 tax charged under Schedule A and Schedule D Cases III to VI and
　　　　(ii)　50% of the remainder (including Class 4 NIC)
　　excluding tax deducted at source, and
　　(b)　due on 31 July 1997: 50% of the remainder (including Class 4 NIC).
No payments on account were required where the aggregate of the relevant income (see above) and the Class 4 NIC liability for 1995–96 was less than £500.)

** These rules do not apply to partnership businesses commenced before 6 April 1994 where there has been no subsequent deemed cessation and recommencement. For 1996–97, such partnerships were required to pay tax in two instalments on 1 January and 1 July 1997, as under the old rules (see p 12).

Interest on overdue tax see p 13.　　　**Remission of tax** see p 17.
Interest factors see p 16.　　　　　　**Repayment supplement** see p 18.

Inheritance tax (capital transfer tax)

Chargeable transfers other than on death, made between:
6 April and 30 September – 30 April in next year.
1 October and 5 April   – 6 months after end of month in which chargeable transfer is made.

Chargeable events following conditional exemption for heritage etc. property and charge on disposal of trees or underwood before the second death
                              – 6 months after end of month in which chargeable event occurs.

Transfers on death
Earlier of *(a)* 6 months after end of month in which death occurs, and
            (b) delivery of account by personal representatives.

Tax or extra tax becoming payable on death: (1) chargeable transfers and potentially exempt transfers within 7 years of death, or
                                          (2) gifts in excess of £100,000 made to political parties before 15 March 1988 and within 1 year of death: due 6 months after end of month in which death takes place.

Interest on overdue tax

Interest on overdue income tax and capital gains tax

(NB: These rules apply with respect to liabilities for 1996–97 and subsequent years and to liabilities for 1995–96 and earlier years assessed after 5 April 1998. However, for partnerships with trades, etc set up and commenced before 6 April 1994, the previous rules continued to apply for the year 1996–97.)

For payments on account (under TMA 1970 s 59A(2)), tax not postponed pending an appeal (under TMA 1970 s 55) and balancing payments (under TMA 1970 s 59B), interest runs from the due date to the date of payment, on the amount outstanding. For the due date, see pp 10, 11. In respect of payments on account, interest is charged on the difference between the amount that ought to have been paid and the amount actually paid.

For amendments to self-assessments (under TMA 1970 s 9(4)–(6)) and discovery assessments (under TMA 1970 s 29), interest normally runs from the annual filing date for the relevant tax year.

Where a claim made under TMA 1970 s 59A(3) or (4) to reduce payments on account proves to be excessive, an underpayment may arise. In such a case, interest is charged on the difference between the amount actually paid and the amount that ought to have been paid if the claim had been made correctly.

Surcharge on unpaid income tax and capital gains tax (TMA 1970 s 59C, amended by FA 1995 s 109)

Applies from 1996-97, and for assessments for 1995–96 or an earlier year of assessment made after 5 April 1998 (FA 1995 s 109(2)). (Tax taken into account in determining certain other penalties (under TMA 1970 ss 7, 93(5), 95 and 95A) is ignored for the purposes of calculating the surcharge.)

28 days: Where income tax or capital gains tax becomes payable and all or part of it remains unpaid the day following 28 days after the due date, the taxpayer is liable to a surcharge of 5% of the unpaid tax.

6 months: The taxpayer is liable to a further surcharge of 5% on any of the tax remaining unpaid 6 months and 1 day from the due date.

Interest is payable on surcharge from the expiry of 30 days beginning on the day on which the surcharge is imposed until the date of payment. It is charged at the rate applying to overdue income tax and capital gains tax (see p 13).

Interest on overdue corporation tax (accounting periods ending after 30 September 1993)

Interest runs from the due date (see p 10) to the date of payment: TMA 1970 s 87A (wording amended by FA 1994 Sch 19 para 24 and SI 1998/3175 reg 7 for accounting periods ending after 30 June 1999) and ss 59D (substituted from the same date) and 59E (inserted from the same date).

For instalment payments by large companies for accounting periods ending after 30 June 1999, a special rate of interest runs from the due date to the earlier of the date of payment and nine months after the end of the accounting period (after which the normal rate applies). SI 1989/1297 regs 32A and 32B (inserted by SI 1998/3176 reg 6).

Interest on inheritance tax

Interest runs from the due date (see p 11 above) to the date of payment.

Interest on overdue tax — continued

Interest on PAYE and national insurance

Employer's tax and Class 1 national insurance payable under PAYE (1992–93 and future years)	19 April following deduction year to date of payment
(Settlement agreement: Income Tax (Employ-ments) Regulations 1993 Part VI Ch V)	19 October following year to which agreement relates to date of payment
Class 1A national insurance	19 April following year in which contributions due to date of payment
Class 4 national insurance	See p 12

'Old' rules:

Period for which interest runs: default interest charged under TMA 1970 s 88 (*repealed* with effect for assessments in respect of 1996–97 and subsequent years (1997–98 and subsequent years if the taxpayer is a partnership whose trade etc commenced before 6 April 1994), and for assessments in respect of 1995–96 and earlier years where such assessments are made after 5 April 1998.)

Advance corporation tax	Not applicable
Capital gains tax	1 December following end of tax year for which charged to date of payment
Income tax	
Schedule A	1 January in tax year for which charged to date of payment
Schedule C	*1 January in tax year for which charged to date of payment*
Schedule D Cases I, II and V	One-half from 1 January in tax year for which charged; one-half
(foreign trades and professions)	from following 1 July to date of payment
Schedule D Cases III, IV, V	
(other than trades etc), VI	1 January in tax year for which charged to date of payment
Schedule E	1 January in tax year for which charged to date of payment
Higher rate tax	1 December following end of tax year for which charged to date of payment

Period for which interest runs: non-default interest (for partnerships with trades, etc set up and commenced before 6 April 1994, in respect of years before 1997–98, and generally for liabilities in respect of 1995–96 and earlier years assessed before 6 April 1998, only)
(*For due date see pages 10 and 11, above)

Advance corporation tax	Due date* to date of payment
Capital gains tax	See p 12 (below)
Capital transfer tax	Due date* to date of payment
Corporation tax (accounting periods	
ending after 30 September 1993)	Due date to date of payment
Development land tax	3 months after event giving rise to liability to date of payment
Employer's tax and Class 1 national	
insurance payable under PAYE	
(1992–93 and subsequent years)	19 April following deduction year to date of payment
Class 1A national insurance	19 April following year in which contributions due to date of payment
Class 4 national insurance	See p 12 (below)
Income tax	
Schedule A	See p 12 (below)
Schedule C	See p 12 (below)
Schedule D	See p 12 (below)
Schedule E	Due date to date of payment
Higher rate tax	See p 12 (below)
Inheritance tax	Due date* (see above) to date of payment

Capital gains tax, income tax under Schedules A, C, D (for partnerships with trades, etc set up and commenced before 6 April 1994, or liabilities in respect of 1995–96 and earlier years assessed before 6 April 1998, only)

Interest runs from due date for payment (see pp 10, 11) until paid *UNLESS* the assessment is under appeal *and* an application is made to postpone the tax (*or* if additional tax not charged by the assessment is found payable on appeal), when the interest runs from the *later* of—
    (a) the original due date (see column *(a)* below), and
    (b) the *earlier* of— (i) the date on which the tax actually becomes due (see column *(b)* (i) below), and
                      (ii) the date given in TMA 1970 s 86(4) Table (see column *(b)* (ii) below).

Tax	*(a)*	*(b)*(i)		*(b)*(ii)
		(1)	(2)	
	Original due date	*Tax not postponed*	*Tax postponed but payable or additional tax determined payable*	*Date given in TMA 1970 s 86(4) Table*
Capital gains tax	1 December following y of a†	Due date *(a)*, or 30 days after the determination of the postponement application, if later	Due date *(a)*, or 30 days after issue of notice of total tax due, if later	1 June after end of *next* y of a
Higher rate tax				
Schedule A Schedule D Cases III (except public/ foreign dividends) IV, V (other than trades, professions), VI	1 January in y of a†	As above	As above	1 July following y of a
Schedule C Schedule D Case III (public/foreign dividends etc)	30 days from issue of notice of assessment	30 days after determination of postponement application	30 days after issue of notice of total tax due	6 months after due date *(a)*
Schedule D Cases I,II (including Class 4 national insurance contributions), V (foreign trades, professions)	2 equal instalments: 1 Jan in y of a† and 1 July following y of a†	Each instalment: appropriate due date *(a)*, or 30 days after determination of application, if later	Each instalment: appropriate due date *(a)*, or 30 days after issue of notice of total tax due, if later	1 July following y of a

† Or 30 days after issue of notice of assessment, if later; not applicable for the purposes of column *(b)* (i) or (ii).

Prescribed rate

	Rate	Period
(1) **Generally:** Income tax (including PAYE due from employer) (before 31 January 1997); capital gains tax (before 31 January 1997); corporation tax (for accounting periods ending before 1 October 1993). Before 31 January 1997, the rates shown also applied to advance corporation tax; development land tax; Class 1, 1A and 4 national insurance contributions; income tax on company payments; petroleum revenue tax (including advance petroleum revenue tax); stamp duty reserve tax	6.25% 7% 6·25% 5·5% 6·25% 7% 7·75% 9·25% 10% 10·75% 11·5% 12·25% 13% 12·25% 11·5% 10·75% 9·75% 7·75% 8·25% 9% 8·25% 9% 9·5% 8·5% 11% 8% 12% 9% 6% 4% 3%	6 February 1996–30 January 1997 6 March 1995–5 February 1996 6 October 1994–5 March 1995 6 January 1994–5 October 1994 6 March 1993–5 January 1994 6 December 1992–5 March 1993 6 November 1992–5 December 1992 6 October 1991–5 November 1992 6 July 1991–5 October 1991 6 May 1991–5 July 1991 6 March 1991–5 May 1991 6 November 1990–5 March 1991 6 November 1989–5 November 1990 6 July 1989–5 November 1989 6 January 1989–5 July 1989 6 October 1988–5 January 1989 6 August 1988–5 October 1988 6 May 1988–5 August 1988 6 December 1987–5 May 1988 6 September 1987–5 December 1987 6 June 1987–5 September 1987 6 April 1987–5 June 1987 6 November 1986–5 April 1987 6 August 1986–5 November 1986 1 May 1985–5 August 1986 1 December 1982–30 April 1985 1 January 1980–30 November 1982 1 July 1974–31 December 1979 19 April 1969–30 June 1974[1] 19 April 1967–18 April 1969 before 19 April 1967
(2) **Income tax, capital gains tax and Class 1, 1A and 4 national insurance contributions:** from 31 January 1997 (SI 1989/1297; SI 1996/3187)	7.5% 8.5% 9.5% 8.5%	from 6 March 1999 6 January 1999–5 March 1999 6 August 1997–5 January 1999 31 January 1997–5 August 1997
(3) **Corporation tax self assessment:** (accounting periods ending after 30 June 1999) (a) Instalment payments (except where tax still unpaid nine months after end of accounting period) (b) Payments other than instalment payments (or for instalment payments still unpaid nine months after end of accounting period)	 7.5% 8% 8.25% 7.5%	 from 15 February 1999 18 January 1999–14 February 1999 17 January 1999–17 January 1999 from 6 March 1999
(4) **Corporation tax pay and file:** (accounting periods ending after 30 September 1993)	5.75% 6.5% 7.5% 6.25% 7% 6·25% 5·5% 6·25%	from 6 March 1999 6 January 1999–5 March 1999 6 August 1997–5 January 1999 6 February 1996–5 August 1997 6 March 1995–5 February 1996 6 October 1994–5 March 1995 6 January 1994–5 October 1994 1 October 1993–5 January 1994
(5) **Advance corporation tax, development land tax, income tax on company payments, petroleum revenue tax** (including **advance petroleum revenue tax**) and **stamp duty reserve tax:** from 31 January 1997	5.75% 6.5% 7.25% 6.25%	from 6 March 1999 6 January 1999–5 March 1999 6 August 1997–5 January 1999 31 January 1997–5 August 1997
(6) **Inheritance tax** and **capital transfer tax:** The rates for periods before 16 December 1986 applied *unless* the transfer was one listed at (7) below	4% 5% 4% 5% 6% 8% 9% 10% 11% 9% 8% 6% 8% 11% 8% 12% 9%	from 6 March 1999 6 October 1994–5 March 1999 6 January 1994–5 October 1994 6 December 1992–5 January 1994 6 November 1992–5 December 1992 6 July 1991–5 November 1992 6 May 1991–5 July 1991 6 March 1991–5 May 1991 6 July 1989–5 March 1991 6 October 1988–5 July 1989 6 August 1988–5 October 1988 6 June 1987–5 August 1988 16 December 1986–5 June 1987 1 May 1985–15 December 1986 1 December 1982–30 April 1985 1 January 1980–30 November 1982 before 1 January 1980

Prescribed rate – continued

	Rate	Period
(7) **Inheritance tax:** chargeable transfers on death or potentially exempt transfers **Capital transfer tax:** chargeable transfers on death only	9% 6% 9% 6%	1 May 1985–15 December 1986 1 December 1982–30 April 1985 1 January 1980–30 November 1982 before 1 January 1980

[1] The rate of default interest charged under TMA 1970 s 88 for 19 April 1969–30 June 1974 was 4%.

Interest factors table

The following table may be used to estimate interest on overdue tax (TMA 1970 s 86). It may also be used to estimate repayment supplements (see p 16) for periods beginning after June 1974 and before 31 January 1997 only. For the purposes of the repayment supplement, the amount multiplied is the repayment. (For repayment supplement for later periods, see p 16.) The table may also be used to estimate the amount of interest due under the former TMA 1970 s 88 on tax lost due to taxpayer's fault. For periods **before** 31 January 1997, the table may also be used for advance corporation tax and development land tax.

The table cannot be used to estimate interest on corporation tax overpaid under Pay and File, to which a different interest rate applies (see p 17).

Calculations of interest on unpaid tax changed from a monthly to a **daily** basis from **6 April 1998** for tax years 1996-97 onwards and for assessments for 1995-96 and before raised after 5 April 1998 (under TMA 1970 s 86 and FA 1995 s 110(2)). The Revenue will not publish monthly factor tables after 5 April 1999.

Interest factors are given as at 1st of the month. To calculate the interest, multiply the basic amount of tax due by the difference between the factors for the dates involved.

	Jan	Feb	Mar	Apr	May	June	July	Aug	Sept	Oct	Nov	Dec
1965	·840	·8425	·845	·8475	·850	·8525	·855	·8575	·860	·8625	·865	·8675
1966	·870	·8725	·875	·8775	·880	·8825	·885	·8875	·890	·8925	·895	·8975
1967	·900	·9025	·905	·9075	·910	·9133	·9167	·920	·9233	·9267	·930	·9333
1968	·9367	·940	·9433	·9467	·950	·9533	·9567	·960	·9633	·9667	·970	·9733
1969	·9767	·980	·9833	·9867	·990	·9933	·9967	1·000	1·0033	1·0067	1·010	1·0133
1970	1·0167	1·020	1·0233	1·0267	1·030	1·0333	1·0367	1·040	1·0433	1·0467	1·050	1·0533
1971	1·0567	1·060	1·0633	1·0667	1·070	1·0733	1·0767	1·080	1·0833	1·0867	1·090	1·0933
1972	1·0967	1·100	1·1033	1·1067	1·110	1·1133	1·1167	1·120	1·1233	1·1267	1·130	1·1333
1973	1·1367	1·140	1·1433	1·1467	1·150	1·1533	1·1567	1·160	1·1633	1·1667	1·170	1·1733
1974	1·1767	1·180	1·1833	1·1867	1·190	1·1933	1·197	1·2045	1·212	1·2195	1·227	1·2345
1975	1·242	1·2495	1·257	1·2645	1·272	1·2795	1·287	1·2945	1·302	1·3095	1·317	1·3245
1976	1·332	1·3395	1·347	1·3545	1·362	1·3695	1·377	1·3845	1·392	1·3995	1·407	1·4145
1977	1·422	1·4295	1·437	1·4445	1·452	1·4595	1·467	1·4745	1·482	1·4895	1·497	1·5045
1978	1·512	1·5195	1·527	1·5345	1·542	1·5495	1·557	1·5645	1·572	1·5795	1·587	1·5945
1979	1·602	1·6095	1·617	1·6245	1·632	1·6395	1·647	1·6545	1·662	1·6695	1·677	1·6845
1980	1·692	1·702	1·712	1·722	1·732	1·742	1·752	1·762	1·772	1·782	1·792	1·802
1981	1·812	1·822	1·832	1·842	1·852	1·862	1·872	1·882	1·892	1·902	1·912	1·922
1982	1·932	1·942	1·952	1·962	1·972	1·982	1·992	2·002	2·012	2·022	2·032	2·042
1983	2·0487	2·0553	2·062	2·0687	2·0753	2·082	2·0887	2·0953	2·102	2·1087	2·1153	2·122
1984	2·1287	2·1353	2·142	2·1487	2·1553	2·162	2·1687	2·1753	2·182	2·1887	2·1953	2·202
1985	2·2087	2·2153	2·222	2·2287	2·2353	2·2445	2·2537	2·2628	2·2720	2·2812	2·2903	2·2995
1986	2·3087	2·3178	2·327	2·3362	2·3453	2·3545	2·3637	2·3728	2·3799	2·3870	2·3940	2·4019
1987	2·4098	2·4178	2·4257	2·4336	2·4411	2·4486	2·4555	2·4624	2·4693	2·4768	2·4843	2·4918
1988	2·4987	2·5056	2·5125	2·5193	2·5262	2·5327	2·5391	2·5456	2·5537	2·5618	2·5708	2·5797
1989	2·5887	2·5983	2·6079	2·6175	2·6271	2·6367	2·6462	2·6564	2·6666	2·6768	2·6871	2·6979
1990	2·7088	2·7196	2·7304	2·7413	2·7521	2·7629	2·7738	2·7846	2·7954	2·8063	2·8171	2·8273
1991	2·8375	2·8477	2·8579	2·8675	2·8771	2·8861	2·8950	2·9033	2·9116	2·9200	2·9277	2·9354
1992	2·9431	2·9508	2·9585	2·9663	2·9740	2·9817	2·9894	2·9971	3·0048	3·0125	3·0202	3·0267
1993	3·0326	3·0384	3·0442	3·0494	3·0546	3·0598	3·0650	3·0702	3·0755	3·0807	3·0859	3·0911
1994	3·0963	3·1009	3·1055	3·1101	3·1147	3·1193	3·1238	3·1284	3·1330	3·1376	3·1428	3·1480
1995	3·1532	3·1584	3·1636	3·1694	3·1753	3·1811	3·1869	3·1928	3·1986	3·2044	3·2103	3·2161
1996	3·2219	3·2278	3·2330	3·2382	3·2434	3·2486	3·2538	3·2591	3·2643	3·2695	3·2747	3·2799
1997	3·2851	3·2903	3·2974	3·3045	3·3116	3·3186	3·3257	3·3328	3·3407	3·3486	3·3565	3·3644
1998	3·3723	3·3803	3·3882	3·3961	3·4040	3·4119	3·4198	3·4278	3·4357	3·4436	3·4515	3·4594
1999	3·4673	3·4744	3·4815	3·4878*	3·4940*	3·5003*	3·5065*	3·5128*	3·5290*	3·5253*	3·5315*	3·5378*
2000	3·5440*	3·5503*	3·5565*	3·5628*	3·5690*	3·5753*	3·5815*	3·5878*	3·5940*	3·6003*	3·6065*	3·6128*
2001	3·6190*	3·6253*	3·6315*									

* Presuming rate remains at 7·5%.

Supplementary table of interest factors on 1st of month

	Jan	Apr	July		Jan	Apr	July
1937	·000	·0075	·015	**1951**	·420	·4275	·435
1938	·030	·0375	·045	**1952**	·450	·4575	·465
1939	·060	·0675	·075	**1953**	·480	·4875	·495
1940	·090	·0975	·105	**1954**	·510	·5175	·525
1941	·120	·1275	·135	**1955**	·540	·5475	·555
1942	·150	·1575	·165	**1956**	·570	·5775	·585
1943	·180	·1875	·195	**1957**	·600	·6075	·615
1944	·210	·2175	·225	**1958**	·630	·6375	·645
1945	·240	·2475	·255	**1959**	·660	·6675	·675
1946	·270	·2775	·285	**1960**	·690	·6975	·705
1947	·300	·3075	·315	**1961**	·720	·7275	·735
1948	·330	·3375	·345	**1962**	·750	·7575	·765
1949	·360	·3675	·375	**1963**	·780	·7875	·795
1950	·390	·3975	·405	**1964**	·810	·8175	·825

Remission of tax

By concession, arrears of tax may be waived if they result from the Revenue's failure to make proper and timely use of information supplied by the taxpayer or, where it affects the taxpayer's coding, by his or her employer. From 26 April 1994 the concession also applies to information supplied by the DSS affecting the taxpayer's entitlement to a retirement or widow's pension (see Concession A19). The concession only applies where the taxpayer could reasonably have believed that his or her affairs were in order and (unless the circumstances are exceptional) where the taxpayer is notified of the arrears more than 12 months after the end of the tax year in which the Revenue received the information indicating that more tax was due.

Before 11 March 1996, the proportion of arrears which could be remitted was determined by a scale according to the taxpayer's income.

Date of notification of arrears	Taxpayer's gross income*	Proportion remitted
17 February 1993–10 March 1996	£15,500 or below	Whole
	Above £15,500 but not above £18,000	3/4
	Above £18,000 but not above £22,000	1/2
	Above £22,000 but not above £26,000	1/4
	Above £26,000 but not above £40,000	1/10
	Above £40,000	None

Repayment supplement

Calculated as simple interest on the amount of tax repaid. The supplement is tax free. The interest factors table on p 14 can be used to estimate repayment supplements for periods beginning after June 1974 and before 31 January 1997; for the purposes of the repayment supplement, the amount multiplied is the repayment. (From 31 January 1997 the rate is determined under SI 1989/1297 as amended by SI 1996/3187, see below.)

These rates apply also to overpaid Class 1, 1A and 4 national insurance contributions but not to overpaid corporation tax for accounting periods ending after 30 September 1993 (see p 17).

Period to which supplement relates	Rate
from 6 March 1999	3%
6 January 1999–5 March 1999	4%
6 August 1997–5 January 1999	4·75%
6 February 1997–5 August 1997	4%
6 February 1996–5 February 1997	6·25%
6 March 1995–5 February 1996	7%
6 October 1994–5 March 1995	6·25%
6 January 1994–5 October 1994	5·5%
6 March 1993–5 January 1994	6·25%
6 December 1992–5 March 1993	7%
6 November 1992–5 December 1992	7·75%
6 October 1991–5 November 1992	9·25%
6 July 1991–5 October 1991	10%
6 May 1991–5 July 1991	10·75%
6 March 1991–5 May 1991	11·5%
6 November 1990–5 March 1991	12·25%
6 November 1989–5 November 1990	13%
6 July 1989–5 November 1989	12·25%
6 January 1989–5 July 1989	11·5%
6 October 1988–5 January 1989	10·75%
6 August 1988–5 October 1988	9·75%
6 May 1988–5 August 1988	7·75%
6 December 1987–5 May 1988	8·25%
6 September 1987–5 December 1987	9%
6 June 1987–5 September 1987	8·25%
6 April 1987–5 June 1987	9%
6 November 1986–5 April 1987	9·5%
6 August 1986–5 November 1986	8·5%
6 May 1985–5 August 1986	11%
6 December 1982–5 May 1985	8%
6 January 1980–5 December 1982	12%
6 April 1974–5 January 1980	9%
Before 6 April 1974	6%

Interest factors from January 1997 (for earlier periods see p 16)

	Jan	Feb	Mar	Apr	May	June	July	Aug	Sept	Oct	Nov	Dec
1997	3·2851	3·2903	3·2937	3·2970	3·3003	3·3037	3·3070	3·3103	3·3143	3·3182	3·3222	3·3261
1998	3·3301	3·3340	3·3380	3·3419	3·3459	3·3498	3·3538	3·3578	3·3618	3·3657	3·3697	3·3736
1999	3·3776	3·3809	3·3842	3·3867*	3·3892*	3·3917*	3·3942*	3·3967*	3·3992*	3·4017*	3·4042*	3·4067*
2000	3·4092*	3·4117*	3·4142*	3·4167*	3·4192*	3·4217*	3·4242*	3·4267*	3·4292*	3·4317*	3·4342*	3·4367*
2001	3·4392*	3·4417*	3·4442*									

* Presuming rate remains at 3%

The calculation of repayment supplement changed from a monthly to a **daily** basis from **31 January 1998** for tax years from 1996-97 (except for 1996-97 partnership assessments). The Revenue will not publish monthly factor tables after 5 April 1999.

'New' rules:

Income tax (TA 1988 s 824; FA 1997 s 92)

From 1996–97 (1997–98 for partnerships whose trade, profession or business commenced before 6 April 1994) repayment supplement applies to:

(a) amounts paid on account of income tax
(b) income tax paid by or on behalf of an individual
(c) surcharges on late payments of tax
(d) penalties incurred by an individual under any provision of TMA 1970

but excluding amounts paid in excess of the statutory maximum the taxpayer is required to pay.

Except for tax deducted at source, the repayment supplement runs *from* the date on which the tax, penalty or surcharge was paid *to* the date on which the order for repayment is issued. For tax deducted at source, repayment supplement runs from 31 January after the end of the tax year for which the tax was deducted.

Capital gains tax (TCGA 1992 s 283; FA 1997 s 92)

From 1996–97 repayment supplement runs *from* the date on which the tax was paid *to* the date on which the order for repayment is issued.

Individuals, personal representatives and trusts. (Before 1996–97, or before 1997–98 for partnerships whose trade, profession or business commenced before 6 April 1994.)

Repayments of IT, surtax or CGT made over 12 months after year of assessment to which repayment relates. Calculated *from* later of

(a) end of year of assessment following that for which repayment is made, and

(b) end of year of assessment in which overpayment of tax was made,

to end of tax month in which repayment order issued (TA 1988 s 824 as originally enacted).

Interest on tax overpaid (companies: accounting periods ending after 30 September 1993 and before 1 July 1999) (TA 1988 s 826)

These provisions are amended for accounting periods ending after 30 June 1999, to which corporation tax self-assessment applies. Advance corporation tax is abolished from 6 April 1999 (FA 1998 ss 31, 32, SI 1999/358).

Repayments of corporation tax, repayments of ACT in respect of foreign income dividends, repayments of income tax in respect of payments received, and payments of tax credits in respect of franked investment income received, made after the material date.

Calculated *from* the material date *to* the date the repayment order is issued.

For corporation tax, the material date is the later of

(a) the date on which the tax was paid and

(b) the date on which the tax became, or would have become, due and payable – generally, nine months and one day after the end of the accounting period.

For ACT, the material date is the date on which corporation tax for the accounting period in which the distribution was made became, or would have become, due and payable – generally, nine months and one day after the end of the accounting period.

For repayments of income tax in respect of payments received and payments of tax credits in respect of franked investment income received, the material date is the date on which corporation tax for the accounting period in which the payments or the franked investment income were received became, or would have become, due and payable. Again, this is generally nine months and one day after the end of the accounting period.

This rule is qualified in instances where there is a carry-back of surplus ACT or a carry-back of trading losses for more than 12 months.

Surplus ACT (s 826(7) repealed for accounting periods beginning on or after 6 April 1999 by FA 1998 Sch 3)

Where there is in any accounting period ('the later period') an amount of surplus ACT and a claim is made under TA 1988 s 239(3) to carry this surplus ACT back to an earlier accounting period ('the earlier period'), then interest on any repayment of corporation tax for the earlier period (or of income tax on a payment received in the earlier period) resulting from the claim under s 239(3) begins to run only after the date on which the corporation tax for the *later* period (the period in which the surplus ACT arose) became due and payable.

This rule is in itself subject to modification where the surplus ACT arises because of a trading loss carried back (see below).

A similar rule (s 826(7C)) applies to the carry-back of a non-trading deficit on a company's loan relationships as applies to the carry-back of surplus ACT.

Trading losses carried back for more than 12 months (s 826(7A, 7B))

Where a claim is made under TA 1988 s 393A(1) to set off a loss incurred in a later period against the profits of an earlier period not falling within the 12 months immediately preceding the later period, and

(a) a repayment of corporation tax in respect of that earlier period or a repayment of income tax in respect of a payment received in the earlier period; or

(b) following a claim under TA 1988 s 242 to include surplus franked investment income in profits available for set-off, a payment of the whole or part of the tax credit comprised in franked investment income of the earlier period,

is made, interest in respect of that part of the repayment due to the claim under TA 1988 s 393A(1) or TA 1988 s 242 (so far as it relates to the claim under s 393A(1)) begins to run only after the date on which the corporation tax in respect of the later period (the lossmaking period) became, or would have become, due and payable.

Carry-back of trading loss giving rise to carry-back of surplus ACT (s 826(7AA) repealed for accounting periods beginning on or after 6 April 1999 by FA 1998 Sch 3)

Where

(a) a trading loss carried back under s 393A(1) from a later period ('the lossmaking period') gives rise to an amount of surplus ACT, and that surplus ACT is then carried back under s 239(3) to a still-earlier period and

(b) as a result a repayment of corporation tax for the still-earlier period (or of income tax on a payment received in the still-earlier period) falls to be made

then interest on those repayments begins to run only after the date on which the corporation tax for the *lossmaking period* became due and payable.

A similar rule (s 826(7CA)) applies to the carry-back of surplus ACT following the carry-back of a non-trading deficit on a company's loan relationships.

Rates	
from 6 March 1999	2.75%
6 January 1999–5 March 1999	3.25%
6 August 1997–5 January 1999	4%
6 February 1996–5 August 1997	3.25%
6 March 1995–5 February 1996	4%
6 October 1994–5 March 1995	3.25%
6 January 1994–5 October 1994	2·5%
1 October 1993–5 January 1994	3·25%

Corporation tax for accounting periods ending after 30 June 1999

SI 1989/1297 regs 3BA and 3BB (inserted by SI 1998/3176 reg 8)

For instalment payments by large companies and early payments by other companies, a special rate of interest runs from the date the excess arises (but not earlier than the due date of the first instalment) to the earlier of the date the repayment order is issued and nine months after the end of the accounting period after which the normal rate of interest applies.

Rates on overpaid instalment payments and on corporation tax paid early (but not due by instalments):

from 15 February 1999	5.25%
18 January 1999–14 February 1999	5.75%
7 January 1999–17 January 1999	6%

Rates on overpaid corporation tax in respect of periods after normal due date (SI 1989/1297 reg 3BB):

from 6 March 1999	4%

Penalties

A) Personal tax returns: offences by taxpayers

Offence	Penalty
Failure to give notice of chargeability to income or capital gains tax within 6 months from end of year of assessment (TMA 1970 s 7).	Amount not exceeding tax assessed (either self-assessed under TMA 1970 s 9 or under a TMA 1970 s 29 'discovery' assessment) for that year and not paid before 1 February following that year.
(From 1996–97) Failure to comply with notice requiring return for income tax or capital gains tax (TMA 1970 s 93).	(a) Initial penalty of £100; and (b) upon direction by Commissioners, further penalty not exceeding £60 for each day on which failure continues after notification of direction; (c) if failure continues after six months following filing date, and no application for a direction under (b) has been made, a further penalty of £100. (d) In addition, if failure continues after first anniversary of filing date, and there would have been a liability to tax shown in the return, a penalty not exceeding the liability that would have been shown in the return. (e) If the taxpayer can prove that the liability to tax shown in the return would not have exceeded a particular amount, the sum of penalties under (a) and (c) above are not to exceed that amount.
(From 1996–97) Failure to comply with notice requiring partnership return (TMA 1970 s 93A).	(a) Initial penalty on each 'relevant partner' of £100; and (b) upon direction by Commissioners, further penalty on each relevant partner not exceeding £60 for each day on which failure continues after notification to representative partner of direction; (c) if failure continues after six months following filing date, and no application for a direction under (b) has been made, a further penalty on each relevant partner of £100. NB: A 'relevant partner' is any person who was a partner at any time during the period for which the return is required.
Fraudulently or negligently delivering incorrect return or accounts or making an incorrect statement in connection with a claim for an allowance, deduction or relief (TMA 1970 s 95).	Penalty not exceeding the difference between the amount payable under the return etc and the amount which would have been payable if the return etc had been correct.
(From 1996–97) Fraudulently or negligently delivering incorrect partnership return or accounts or making an incorrect statement or declaration in connection with such a return (TMA 1970 s 95A).	Penalty on each relevant partner not exceeding the difference between the amount payable by him or her under the return, etc and the amount that would have been payable by him or her if the return, etc had been correct. For the meaning of 'relevant partner', see under TMA 1970 s 93A above.

B) Corporation tax returns under pay and file and corporation tax self assessment

Offence	Penalty
Pay and file (accounting periods ending before 1 July 1999)	
Failure to give notice of chargeability to corporation tax within 12 months after end of accounting period (TMA 1970 s 10).	Penalty not exceeding amount of tax unpaid 12 months after end of accounting period (after set-off of income tax credits).
Failure to comply with notice requiring return for corporation tax (TMA 1970 s 94).	(a) If return is delivered within 3 months of due date – £100 (£500 in respect of default for third consecutive period); (b) if return is delivered more than 3 months after due date – £200 (£1,000 in respect of default for third consecutive period); and (c) if return is delivered between 18 months and 2 years after end of return period – an additional penalty of 10% of tax unpaid at end of 18-month period; (d) if return is delivered more than 2 years after end of return period – an additional penalty of 20% of tax unpaid at end of 18-month period.
Fraudulently or negligently delivering incorrect return or accounts or making an incorrect statement in connection with a claim for an allowance, deduction or relief (TMA 1970 s 96).	Penalty not exceeding the difference between the amount payable under the return etc and the amount which would have been payable if the return etc had been correct.

B) Corporation tax returns under pay and file and corporation tax self assessment (contd.)

Offence	Penalty
Self assessment (accounting periods ending on or after 1 July 1999)	*(For the restriction of penalties where multiple tax-related penalties are payable in respect of the same accounting period see FA 1998 Sch 18 para 90)*
Failure to give notice of chargeability to corporation tax within 12 months after end of accounting period (FA 1998 Sch 18 para 2).	Penalty not exceeding amount of tax payable for that accounting period remaining unpaid 12 months after end of accounting period (taking no account of relief deferred under TA 1988 s 419(4A)).
Failure to deliver a comapny tax return by the filing date (FA 1998 Sch 18 paras 17, 18).	*Flat-rate penalties* (Unless FA 1998 Sch 18 para 19 (excuse for late delivery of returns) applies) (a) If return is delivered within 3 months of the filing date: £100 (£500 for third successive failure); (b) in any other case: £200 (1,000 for third successive failure); (the increased penalties under (a) and (b) apply with modifications where the first or second period ends before 1 July 1999 (para 17(4)). *Tax-related penalties* (c) If return is delivered between 18 months (or the filing date, if later) and 2 years after the end of the return period: an additional penalty of 10% of the unpaid tax; (d) If return delivered more than 2 years after the end of the return period: an additional penalty of 20% of the unpaid tax. (In determining the amount of unpaid tax no account is taken of relief deferred under TA 1970 s 419(4A)).
Fraudulently or negligently delivering a company tax return which is incorrect (FA 1998 Sch 18 para 20).	An amount not exceeding the amount of tax understated (taking no account of relief deferred under TA 1988 s 419(4A)).
On discovering that a company tax return delivered by it (neither fraudulently nor negligently) is incorrect, a company does not remedy the error wihout reasonable delay (FA 1998 Sch 18 para 20).	An amount not exceeding the amount of tax understated (taking no account of relief deferred under TA 1988 s 419(4A)).
Fraudulently or negligently making an incorrect return, statement or declaration in connection with a claim for any tax allowance, deduction or relief, or submitting any incorrect accounts in connection with the ascertainment of the company's tax liability (FA 1998 Sch 18 para 89).	Penalty not exceeding the amount of tax understated (excluding relief deferred under TA 1988 s 419(4A)).

C) PAYE returns

Offence	Penalty
Failure to submit return P9D or P11D (benefits in kind) by due date (6 June following tax year 1995–96; 6 July following subsequent tax years) (TMA 1970 s 98 (1)).	(a) An initial penalty not exceeding £300; and (b) a continuing penalty not exceeding £60 for each day on which the failure continues after imposition of the initial penalty.
Fraudulently or negligently submitting incorrect return P9D or P11D (TMA 1970 s 98(2)).	Penalty not exceeding £3,000.
Failure to submit returns P14 (individual end of year summary), P35 (annual return), P38 or P38A (supplementary returns for employees not on P35) by due date (19 May following tax year) (TMA 1970 s 98A).	(a) First 12 months: penalty of £100 for each 50 employees (or part thereof) for each month the failure continues; (b) failures exceeding 12 months: a penalty not exceeding the amount of PAYE or NIC due and unpaid at 19 April following year of assessment. (For late 1995–96 returns, the Revenue will normally limit the amount of the penalty to the total of the tax and NIC that should be reported on the return or to £100, whichever is greater: Revenue Press Release dated 14 June 1996.)
Fraudulently or negligently submitting incorrect form P14, P35, P38 or P38A (TMA 1970 s 98A).	Penalty not exceeding the difference between the amount payable under the return and the amount which would have been payable if the return had been correct.

D) Special returns of information

Offence	Penalty
Failure to comply with a notice to deliver a return or other document, furnish particulars or make anything available for inspection under any of the provisions listed in column 1 of the table in TMA 1970 s 98.	(a) An initial penalty not exceeding £300 (£3,000 for failure to comply with TA 1988 s 765A(2)(a) or (b)); and (b) a continuing penalty not exceeding £60 (£600 for failure to comply with TA 1988 s 765A(2)(a) or (b)) for each day on which the failure continues after imposition of the initial penalty.
Failure to comply with requirement to furnish information, give certificates or produce documents or records under any of the provisions listed in column 2 of the table in TMA 1970 s 98.	(a) An initial penalty not exceeding £300; and (b) a continuing penalty not exceeding £60 for each day on which the failure continues after imposition of the initial penalty.
Fraudulently or negligently delivering any incorrect document, information etc required under any of the provisions listed in column 1 or 2 of the table in TMA 1970 s 98.	Penalty not exceeding £3,000.
(Accounting periods ending after 30 June 1999). Failure of a company to produce documents, etc., for the purposes of an enquiry (FA 1998 Sch 18 para 29). (It was announced in the 1999 Budget that penalties will be introduced for failure to provide information required under regulations concerning payment of corporation tax by instalments.)	(a) £50; (b) If failure continues after imposition of penalty under (a), an additional penalty for each day the failure continues, not exceeding: (i) £30 if determined by the Revenue under TMA 1970 s 100; and (ii) £150 if determined by the Commissioners under TMA 1970 s 100C.

E) Other offences by taxpayers, agents etc

Offence	Penalty
Failure to retain records as required by TMA 1970 s 12B(1) (TMA 1970 s 12B(5)).	Penalty not exceeding £3,000.
Falsification of documents (TMA 1970 s 20BB).	On summary conviction, a fine not exceeding the statutory maximum (£5,000); on conviction on indictment, imprisonment for a term not exceeding 2 years or a fine or both.
Failure to produce documents required under TMA 1970 s 19A (power to enquire into self-assessment return, etc) (TMA 1970 s 97AA).	(a) Initial penalty of £50; and (b) further penalty not exceeding £30 (where penalty determined by officer of Board) or £150 (where penalty determined by Commissioners) for each day on which failure continues after imposition of initial penalty.
Offences in connection with the supply of information regarding European Economic Interest Groupings—	
(i) failure to supply information	An initial penalty not exceeding £300 per member of the Grouping at the time of failure and after direction by the Commissioners a continuing penalty not exceeding £60 per member of the Grouping at the end of the day for each day on which the failure continues after notification of the direction.
(ii) fraudulent or negligent delivery of an incorrect return, accounts or statement. (TMA 1970 s 98B).	Not exceeding £3,000 for each member of the Grouping at the time of delivery.
Assisting in the delivery of incorrect returns, accounts or information (TMA 1970 s 99).	Not exceeding £3,000.
Fraudulently or negligently giving a certificate of non-liability to income tax for the purposes of receiving interest gross on a bank or building society account, or failing to comply with an undertaking given in such a certificate (TMA 1970 s 99A).	Not exceeding £3,000.
Refusal to allow a deduction of income tax authorised by the Taxes Acts (TMA 1970 s 106).	£50.
Obstruction of officer of the Board in inspection of property to ascertain its market value (TMA 1970 s 111).	Not exceeding level 1 on the standard scale.

E) Other offences by taxpayers, agents etc (cont.)

Offence	Penalty
Issue by a company of a certificate of approval for enterprise investment scheme relief fraudulently or negligently or without the authority of the inspector (TA 1988 s 306(6)).	Not exceeding £3,000.
False statement to obtain relief for payments to secure a retirement annuity, a purchased life annuity or under a personal pension scheme (TA 1988 ss 619(7), 653, 658(5)).	Not exceeding £3,000.
Creation or transfer of shares or debentures in a non-resident subsidiary company without the consent of HM Treasury (TA 1988 s 766).	On conviction on indictment— (a) imprisonment for not more than 2 years or a fine, or both; or (b) in the case of a UK company, a fine not exceeding the greater of— (i) £10,000; or (ii) three times the tax payable by the company attributable to income and gains arising in the previous 36 months.
Failure by a Lloyd's syndicate's managing agent to comply with notice requiring return of syndicate's profit or loss (FA 1993 Sch 19 para 2(3), (4)).	£60 for each 50 members of syndicate (or part thereof) for each day the failure continues.
Delivery by a Lloyd's syndicate's managing agent fraudulently or negligently of an incorrect return of syndicate profits (FA 1993 Sch 19 para 2(5)).	Not exceeding £3,000 for each member of the syndicate.
Obstructing, molesting or hindering an officer or other person employed in relation to inland revenue in the execution of his duty (Inland Revenue Regulation Act 1890 s 11).	Level 3 on the standard scale.
(Accounting periods ending after 30 June 1999). Deliberately or recklessly failing to pay corporation tax due in respect of total liability of company for accounting period, or fraudulently or negligently making claim for repayment (TMA 1970 s 59E(4); S1 1998/3175 reg 13).	Penalty not exceeding twice amount of interest charged under S1 1998/3175 reg 7.
(Accounting periods ending after 30 June 1999) Failure of a company to keep and preserve records (other than those only required for claims, etc., or dividend vouchers and certificates of income tax deducted where other evidence is available) (FA 1998 Sch 18 para 23).	Penalty not exceeding £3,000.

F) Standard scale penalties under Criminal Justice Act[1]

Level	Amount	
	1.5.84–30.9.92 £	From 1.10.92 £
1	50	200
2	100	500
3	400	1,000
4	1,000	2,500
5 (statutory maximum)	2,000	5,000

[1] Criminal Justice Act 1982 s 37.

Mitigation of penalties

The Board has discretion to mitigate or entirely remit any penalty or to stay or compound any penalty proceedings (TMA 1970 s 102).

Interest on penalties

From 1996–97 penalties under TMA 1970 Parts II (ss 7–12B), IV (ss 28A–43B), VA (ss 59A–59D) and X (ss 93–107) carry interest at the prescribed rate (see p 13): TMA 1970 103A. Surcharges on unpaid income tax and capital gains tax carry interest under TMA 1970 s 59C (with effect from 9 March 1998, by virtue of SI 1998/310). As regards corporation tax, the provisions apply for accounting periods ending on or after 1 July 1999.

Time limits for claims and elections: 1999–2000

The information in the tables below was originally derived from Tax Digest No 108 "Time limits for claims and elections" (Spring 1992) published by the Institute of Chartered Accountants in England and Wales.

From 1996–97: Whenever possible, a claim or election must be made on the tax return or by an amendment to the return (TMA 1970 s 42 and FA 1998 Sch 18 paras 9, 10, 67 and 79). Exceptions to this general rule are dealt with in TMA 1970 Sch 1A.

Except where another period is expressly prescribed, a claim for relief in respect of income tax and capital gains tax must be made within five years from the 31 January following the year of assessment to which it relates (TMA 1970 s 43(1) as amended). The time limit for claims by companies remains at six years from the end of the accounting period to which it relates (TMA 1970 s 43(1) (b) and, for accounting periods ending after 1 July 1999, FA 1998 Sch 18 para 55).

The tables below set out exceptions to the general limits.

Unless otherwise specified, for income tax and capital gains tax, two-year time limits run from the 31 January in the year of assessment (see FA 1996 s 128). For companies the time limit runs from the end of the accounting period to which the claim relates (TMA 1970 s 43(1) (b), FA 1998 Sch 18 para 55).

Before 1996–97: Except where a longer or shorter period was expressly prescribed, a claim for relief had to be made within six years of the end of the chargeable period to which it related (TMA 1970 s 43(1) as originally enacted).

Income and corporation tax

Claim	Time limit
Sums received in respect of a furnished letting to be assessed under Schedule A to the extent of the rental element (not generally applicable for income tax from 1995–96) (TA 1988 s 15(2)). (Of no application, generally, after 31 March 1998.)	*2 years from end of chargeable period.*
Land managed as one estate at 5 April 1963 – new owner entitled to include notional rent in respect of parts not let and to claim expenses as if those parts were let at a full rent. Applies throughout that person's ownership (TA 1988 s 26(3)). (Of no application for income tax purposes on or after 6 April 2001 or for corporation tax purposes, for accounting periods beginning on or after 1 April 2001.)	12 months after the end of the first year of assessment or accounting period for which the claimant was entitled to claim or such further time as the Board may allow.
Capital allowances on machinery or plant used for the maintenance, repair or management of let property. Applies to all future periods (not generally applicable for income tax from 1995–96 and repealed altogether for income tax for 1997-98 and subsequent years, and for corporation tax for accounting periods ending after 31 March 1997) (TA 1988 s 32(5), (6)).	*Before the date when the assessment in respect of the net income from the property for the year becomes final and conclusive.*
Relief for gifts of plant and machinery to educational establishments (TA 1988 s 84(3), (3A)).	First anniversary of 31 January next following year of assessment in the basis period of which the gift was made (income tax); 2 years from end of accounting period in which the gift was made (corporation tax).
Averaging relief to be available to a person carrying on a trade of farming or market gardening (TA 1988 s 96(8) as amended).	12 months after 31 January next following end of second year which enters into the averaging calculation.
Herd basis to apply (TA 1988 s 97, Sch 5 para 2 as amended).	12 months from 31 January next following first year of assessment for which profits computed by reference to period in which herd was kept (income tax); 12 months from 31 January next following year of assessment in which fell the end of the first period of account in which herd was kept (partnerships); 2 years from end of first accounting period in which herd was kept (corporation tax).
Work in progress at date of discontinuance of profession or vocation to be valued at actual cost (TA 1988 s 101(2), (2A)).	First anniversary of 31 January next following year of assessment in which discontinuance occurred (income tax); 2 years from end of accounting period in which discontinuance occurred (corporation tax).
Post cessation receipts to be charged as if received on the date of discontinuance or change of basis of computation (TA 1988 s 108 as amended).	One year from 31 January following end of year of assessment in which sum received.
Change in persons carrying on a trade, profession or vocation in partnership not to be treated as a discontinuance (not applicable to partnerships commenced after 5 April 1994 or, from 1997–98, to partnerships commenced on or before that date) (TA 1988 s 113(2)).	*2 years from date of partnership change.*
Tax arising upon the exercise of a share option to be payable by instalments, provided the option was acquired prior to 6 April 1984 (TA 1988 s 137(1)(d), (3)).	60 days after the end of the year in which the exercise occurs.

Claim	Time limit
Election by employee for alternative method to be applied in calculating the cash equivalent of the benefit obtained from a loan (TA 1988 s 160, Sch 7 para 5 as amended).	12 months from 31 January next following year of assessment.
Relief to be given for expenses incurred wholly, exclusively and necessarily in the performance of the duties of an office or employment (TA 1988 s 198(1)).	The date on which the assessment becomes final and conclusive.
Certain subscriptions etc to be deducted from the emoluments of an office or employment (TA 1988 s 201(1)).	The date on which the assessment becomes final and conclusive.
Inspector to be required to issue a return (before 1996-97 an assessment) under Schedule E (TA 1988 s 205(4)).	5 years after 31 October next following year of assessment.
Surplus ACT paid to be carried back for offset against corporation tax liabilities for accounting periods beginning within six years prior to the period of payment (TA 1988 s 239(3)) (repealed with respect to accounting periods beginning after 5 April 1999).	*2 years.*
Surplus franked investment income to be treated as profits chargeable to corporation tax for offset against trading losses and capital allowances (TA 1988 s 242) (Repealed generally with effect for accounting periods beginning after 1 July 1997.)	*2 years.*
Interest and other payments to be treated as group income. Before 6 April 1999, applies also to dividends. Applies until revoked but the company making the payments may give notice to the collector of taxes that it is not to apply to specific payments (TA 1988 ss 247, 248).	3 months prior to date of payment but if the inspector notifies his or her acceptance of the election within three months the election is effective from the date of notification.
Income from jointly owned property to be assessed on husband and wife in unequal shares (TA 1988 s 282B(2)).	Effective from date of declaration.
Relief to be given for the enterprise investment scheme (TA 1988 s 306(1) as amended).	Not earlier than 4 months after the company commences its qualifying activity and no later than fifth anniversary of 31 January next following year of assessment.
Certain expenses to be deducted from the emoluments of a clergyman (TA 1988 s 332(3)).	The date on which the assessment becomes final and conclusive.
Loss sustained in a trade, profession or vocation to be set against other income of the year or the last preceding year. Extended to certain pre-trading expenditure by TA 1988 s 401 (TA 1988 s 380(1) as substituted).	12 months from 31 January next following year of assessment in which loss arose.
Loss sustained in the first 4 years of a new trade, profession or vocation to be offset against other income arising in the 3 years immediately preceding the year of loss. Extended to certain pre-trading expenditure by TA 1988 s 401 (TA 1988 s 381(1)).	First anniversary of 31 January next following year of assessment in which loss sustained.
Loss sustained by a company in a trade in an accounting period ending after 31 March 1991 to be offset against— (a) profits of that accounting period; (b) profits of the preceding three years for losses arising in accounting periods ending before 2 July 1997 and profits of the preceding one year for losses arising in subsequent accounting periods. Extended to certain pre-trading expenditure by TA 1988 s 401 (TA 1988 s 393A(1) (2A)).	2 years or such further period as Board may allow.
Group relief to be given for accounting periods ending after 30 September 1993 and before 1 July 1999. The surrendering company must consent to the claim (TA 1988 s 412, Sch 17A para 2).	2 years after the end of the surrendering company's accounting period or the date on which the relevant assessment becomes final, whichever is later.
Group relief to be given for accounting periods ending after 30 June 1999. The surrendering company must consent to the claim (FA 1998 Sch 18 paras 66 to 77)	The last of: (a) 1 year from the filing date of the claimant company's return for the accounting period for which the claim is made; (b) 30 days after the end of an enquiry into the return; (c) if the Revenue amend the return after an enquiry, 30 days after issue of notice of amendment; (d) if an appeal is made against the amendment, 30 days after the determination of the appeal; (or such later time as the Revenue may allow).

Claim	Time limit
Relief for non-trading deficits on loan relationships in a company in an accounting period ending after 31 March 1996 to be claimed by: (a) offset against profits of the same period; (b) group relief; (c) offset against post 31 March 1996 profits of earlier accounting periods (as for trading losses above); or (d) offset against non-trading profits for the next accounting period, and so on. (FA 1996, s 83)	2 years or such further period as Board may allow.
Averaging treatment to be applied in determining the number of days on which holiday accommodation is let (TA 1988 s 504(6), (6A)).	First anniversary of 31 January next following year of assessment in which accommodation let (income tax); 2 years from end of accounting period in which accommodation let (corporation tax).
UK resident in receipt of a capital sum from the sale of patent rights to be charged to tax for period of receipt (TA 1988 s 524(2), (2A)).	First anniversary of 31 January next following year of assessment in which sum received (income tax); 2 years from end of accounting period in which sum received (corporation tax).
Non-resident in receipt of a capital sum on the sale of non-UK patent rights to be charged to tax as if the sum was received over a period of 6 years (TA 1988 s 524(4) as amended).	First anniversary of 31 January next following year of assessment in which sum is paid.
Consideration for know-how sold together with a trade or part of a trade not to be treated as a payment for goodwill. Time limit runs from the date of the disposal. Both purchaser and vendor must elect (TA 1988 s 531(3)).	2 years.
Certain sums received by an author in respect of the assignment of a copyright to be assessed as if received over a period of up to 3 years (TA 1988 s 534(1), (5) as amended).	1 year from 31 January next following the latest year of assessment in which payment receivable.
Spreading claim made under TA 1988 s 535(1) in respect of sums received by author more than 10 years after first publication of the work to be recalculated on the death of the author or the discontinuance of his or her profession (TA 1988 s 535(8A)).	1 year from 31 January next following year of assessment in which payment receivable.
Sums received by a designer for the assignment of rights in a design to be assessed as if received over a period of up to 3 years (TA 1988 s 537A(5), (5A) as amended).	1 year from 31 January next following the latest year of assessment in which payment receivable.
Loss on disposal by an investment company of shares in a qualifying trading company to be offset against other income of the period of loss or the preceding accounting period (TA 1988 s 573(2)).	2 years.
Loss on disposal by an individual of shares in a qualifying trading company to be offset against other income of the year of loss or the last preceding year (TA 1988 s 574(1) as substituted).	1 year from 31 January next following year of assessment in which loss incurred.
Unremittable overseas income to be excluded from assessment (TA 1988 s 584(2), (6) (as substituted)).	1 year from 31 January next following year of assessment in which income arises (income tax); 2 years from end of accounting period in which income arises (corporation tax).
Relief to be given in respect of a qualifying premium paid under a retirement annuity contract entered into before 1 July 1988 for the immediately preceding year of assessment (or the year before that if no net relevant earnings in the immediately preceding year) (TA 1988 s 619(4) as amended).	31 January next following year of assessment in which premium paid.
Unused relief to be available against a qualifying premium paid under a retirement annuity contract entered into before 1 July 1988 where an assessment becomes final and conclusive more than 6 years after the year to which it relates (TA 1988 s 625(3)).	6 months from the date when the assessment becomes final.
Relief to be given against relevant earnings from Lloyd's underwriting activities in respect of a qualifying premium paid in the next year but two under an approved contract entered into before 1 July 1988 (repealed from 1997–98) (TA 1988 s 627(1), (3)).	*Before the end of the year of assessment in which the premium is paid.*
Relief to be given against relevant earnings from Lloyd's underwriting activities in respect of a contribution paid under approved personal pension arrangements in the next year of assessment but two (repealed from 1997–98) (TA 1988 s 641(2), (4) as amended).	*31 January next following year of assessment in which contributions paid.*

Claim	Time limit
Relief to be given in respect of a contribution paid under approved personal pension arrangements for the immediately preceding year of assessment (or the year before that if no net relevant earnings in the immediately preceding year) (TA 1988 s 641(1), (4) as amended).	31 January next following year of assessment in which contributions paid.
Unused relief to be available for relief against a contribution paid under approved personal pension arrangements where an assessment to tax for a year of assessment becomes final and conclusive more than 6 years after the end of that year (TA 1988 s 642(4)).	6 months from the date when the assessment for the year in question becomes final and conclusive.
Income arising to trustees of maintenance funds for historic buildings not to be treated as the income of the settlor (TA 1988 s 691(2), (4) as amended).	First anniversary of 31 January next following year of assessment to which it relates.
Income of a beneficiary to be adjusted for past years on completion of the administration of a deceased's estate (TA 1988 s 700(1), (3) as amended).	3 years from 31 January next following year of assessment in which the administration is completed.
Controlled foreign company to be deemed not to have made a specified claim (TA 1988 ss 747, 753(4), Sch 24 para 4). (New provisions apply in respect of self-assessment for accounting periods ending after 30 June 1999. (FA 1998, Sch 17)).	60 days from issue of notice of direction.
Controlled foreign company to be deemed to be subject to a direction for an earlier period in which a loss was incurred (TA 1988 s 747, Sch 24 para 9). (New provisions apply in respect of self-assessment for accounting periods ending after 30 June 1999. (FA 1998, Sch 17)).	60 days from issue of direction.
Relief for maintenance payments made under obligations entered into before 15 March 1988 as if the obligation had been entered into after that date (FA 1988 s 39).	First anniversary of 31 January next following first year of assessment for which it is to have effect.
Emoluments to be taxed only in the year of receipt (FA 1989 s 38(6) and SP1/92).	5 April 1991 or (at Board's discretion) 3 months after the issue of a Schedule E assessment for 1988–89 or 1989–90.
Adjustment of employer's Schedule D calculation for emoluments paid subsequently, but within 9 months of the end of the employer's period of account (FA 1989 s 43(5)).	2 years from end of period of account.
Unrelieved trading losses to be set against capital gains (FA 1991 s 72, TA 1988 s 380(1)).	12 months from 31 January next following year of assessment in which loss sustained.
Claim for relief by a trader etc for gifts in kind to low-income countries under the Millennium Gift Aid scheme (FA 1998 s 47(6)).	First anniversary of 31 January next following year of assessment in the basis period of which the gift is made (income tax); 2 years from end of accounting period in which the gift is made (corporation tax).
Capital allowances	
Grant of a long lease of a building to be treated as a sale of the relevant interest by the lessor. Both lessor and lessee must elect (CAA 1990 s 11(1), (3)).	2 years from the date when the lease takes effect.
Part or all of the total of plant and machinery first-year allowances to be disclaimed (CAA 1990 ss 22(7), 140(3), Sch A1 para 7).	Required allowance claimed in tax return (income tax);[2] Required allowance claimed in return (corporation tax).
Part or all of the total of plant and machinery writing down allowances to be disclaimed (CAA 1990 s 24(3), 140 (3), Sch A1 para (7)).	Required allowance claimed in tax return (income tax);[2] Required allowance claimed in return (corporation tax).
Writing down allowance to be available where first year allowance not claimed (CAA 1990 s 25(3) as amended, (3A)).	First anniversary of 31 January next following year of assessment in which ends chargeable period related to incurring of expenditure (income tax);[1] 2 years from end of chargeable period related to incurring of expenditure (corporation tax).

Claim	Time limit
Part or all of a first year allowance in respect of expenditure on a ship to be postponed to a later period (CAA 1990 s 30(1) as amended, (1A)).	First anniversary of 31 January next following year of assessment in which period of account ends (income tax);[1] 2 years from end of accounting period for which allowance made (corporation tax).
Part or all of a postponed first year allowance in respect of expenditure on a ship to be given in a later period (CAA 1990 ss 30(2), 140(3), Sch A1 para 7). (Now provisions apply in respect of self-assessment for companies for accounting periods ending after 30 June 1999.)	Claim to be made in return (income tax and corporation tax)[2]
Capital allowances to be given in respect of expenditure on machinery or plant used for the maintenance, repair or management of let property. Applies to all future periods (TA 1988 s 32(5)). (Does not generally apply to income tax from the year 1994–95 and repealed altogether for income tax for 1997-98 and subsequent years, and for corporation tax for accounting periods ending after 31 March 1997.)	*Before the date on which the assessment for the period becomes final and conclusive.*
Part or all of a writing down allowance in respect of expenditure incurred after 13 March 1984 on a ship to be postponed to a later period (CAA 1990 s 31(3) as amended, (3A)).	First anniversary of 31 January next following year of assessment in which chargeable period ends (income tax);[1] 2 years from end of chargeable period (corporation tax).
Allowances postponed under CAA 1990 s 31(3) to be treated as writing-down allowances for a subsequent period (CAA 1990 ss 31(4), 140(3), Sch A1 para 7). (Now provisions apply in respect of self-assessment for companies for accounting periods ending after 30 June 1999).	Claim to be made in return (income tax and corporation tax)[2]
Single ship trade treatment not to apply to the whole or part of the expenditure (CAA 1990 s 33 (1) as amended, (5A)).	First anniversary of 31 January next following year of assessment in which chargeable period ends (income tax);[1] 2 years from end of chargeable period (corporation tax).
Machinery or plant to be treated as a short life asset (CAA 1990 s 37(2) as amended, (2A)).	First anniversary of 31 January next following year of assessment in which chargeable period ends (income tax);[1] 2 years from end of chargeable period (corporation tax).
Transfer of short life asset to a connected person to be treated as taking place at tax written down value (CAA 1990 s 37(9)).	2 years from end of chargeable period in which disposal occurred.
Machinery or plant which becomes a fixture and is subject to an equipment lease to be treated as belonging to equipment lessor. Election to be made by both lessor and lessee but not permitted if they are connected persons (CAA 1990 s 53 (2) as amended, (2A)).	First anniversary of 31 January next following year of assessment in which chargeable period ends (income tax);[1] 2 years from end of chargeable period (corporation tax).
Machinery or plant which has become a fixture on land which is subsequently let to be treated as belonging to lessee. Election to be made by both lessor and lessee but not permitted if they are connected persons (CAA 1990 s 55).	2 years from date on which lease takes effect.
Oilfield abandonment expenditure to be deductible in relation to a ring fence trade (CAA 1990 s 62A(4), (5)).	2 years from end of chargeable period related to incurring of expenditure.
Expenditure on production or acquisition of films etc to be reallocated (CAA 1990 s 68(5) as amended, (5A)).	First anniversary of 31 January next following year of assessment in which relevant period ends (income tax); 2 years from end of relevant period (corporation tax).[1]
Succession to a trade between connected persons to be ignored in computing capital allowances (CAA 1990 s 77(3)).	2 years from the date of the succession.

Claim	Time limit
Acquisition of relevant interest in capital expenditure on agricultural land and buildings to be treated as a balancing event (CAA 1990 s 129(2) as amended).	First anniversary of 31 January next following year of assessment in which chargeable period ends (income tax);[1] 2 years from end of chargeable period (corporation tax).
Claim for income tax capital allowances made in taxing the trade (CAA 1990 s 140(3)).	Claim to be made in return.
Capital allowances given by way of discharge or repayment of tax and offset against income of the specified class: the excess of such allowances to be set against other income of the year and the immediately succeeding year (CAA 1990 s 141(3) as amended). (Repealed with effect from 1997-98.)	*First anniversary of 31 January next following year of assessment.[1]*
Excess of corporation tax capital allowances given by discharge or repayment of tax over the relevant class of income to be set against the profits of that period and the immediately preceding period (CAA 1990 s 145(3)).	2 years.
Claims, amended claims and withdrawals of claims in respect of corporation tax capital allowances for accounting periods ending after 30 September 1993 and before 1 July 1999 (CAA 1990 s 145A, Sch A1 paras 2, 3). (New provisions apply for self-assessment by companies for accounting periods ending after 30 June 1999, see below.)	The latest of — (a) two years after the end of the accounting period; (b) the date on which the company's corporation tax assessment for the period becomes final; and (c) the date on which the determination of the company's losses or the amount available for group relief for the accounting period becomes final.
(Accounting periods ending after 30 June 1999). A claim for capital allowances (FA 1998 Sch 18 para 82).	The last of: (a) 1 year from the filing date of the claimant company's return for the accounting period for which the claim is made; (b) 30 days after the end of an enquiry into the return; (c) if the Revenue amend the return after an enquiry, 30 days after issue of notice of amendment; (d) if an appeal is made against the amendment, 30 days after the determination of the appeal; (or such later time as the Revenue may allow).
Disposal and acquisition of property between persons one of which controls the other or which are under common control to be treated as made at the lower of open market value and tax written down value (CAA 1990 s 158(1)).	2 years from the date of the disposal.

[1] For the purposes of income tax, applies from 1997–98 in respect of trades, etc set up and commenced before 6 April 1994 and from 1996–97 for trades etc commenced after 5 April 1994: see FA 1996 s 135(3), Sch 21.

[2] An amended claim may be made in an amended return, the normal time limit for which is the first anniversary of 31 January next following the year of assessment in which the chargeable period ends.

Capital gains

Claim	Time limit
Loss to be allowed where the value of an asset has become negligible (TCGA 1992 s 24(2)).	Year for which loss to be allowed, or up to 2 years after the end of that year if the value is still negligible when claim made.
Events occurring prior to 31 March 1982 to be ignored in computing gains arising after 5 April 1988 (TCGA 1992 s 35 (5), (6) as amended).	First anniversary of 31 January next following year of assessment in which disposal made (capital gains tax) or 2 years after end of accounting period in which disposal made (corporation tax).
Variation or disclaimer of the terms of a will or intestacy, made within two years of the death, to be treated as effected by the deceased (TCGA 1992 s 62(6), (7)).	6 months after instrument of variation or disclaimer effected or such longer time as the Board may allow.
Postponement of charge on deemed disposal of assets where a subsidiary company ceases to be resident in the UK (TCGA 1992 s 187(1)).	2 years from date of ceasing to be resident in UK.

Claim	Time limit
Determination of main residence for principal private residence exemption (TCGA 1992 s 222(5)(a)).	2 years from the beginning of the period for which a determination requires to be made, ie the date of acquisition of a second or further residence, but provided that an initial notice has been given within the time limit it may subsequently be varied at any time and the notice of variation may have effect from up to 2 years prior to the date on which it is made.
Rollover relief on disposal of shares to trustees of qualifying employee share ownership trust (TCGA 1992 s 229(1)).	2 years from date of acquisition of replacement assets.
Losses on certain loans to traders to be allowed as capital losses (TCGA 1992 s 253(3)).	The loss is treated as accruing on the date that the claim is made, or at an earlier date, which is: (a) no more than 2 years before the beginning of the year of assessment in which the claim is made (capital gains tax) or (b) no earlier than the first day of the earliest accounting period ending no more than 2 years before the date of the claim.
Losses arising from payments by guarantor of certain irrecoverable loans to traders to be allowed as capital losses at time of claim or 'earlier time' (TCGA 1992 s 253(4), (4A)).	Fifth anniversary of 31 January next following year of assessment in which payment made (capital gains tax); 6 years after end of accounting period in which the payment was made (corporation tax: TCGA 1992 s 253(4A), FA 1996 s 135(2): accounting periods ending after 30 June 1999).
Tax to be paid by instalments where the consideration is payable over a period and undue hardship would otherwise be suffered (TCGA 1992 s 280).	Date of payment of tax.
Halving of postponed charges, or held over or rolled over gains, on disposals of assets acquired after 31 March 1982 (but before 6 April 1988) from a person who acquired (or is deemed to have acquired) them before 31 March 1982 (TCGA 1992 Sch 4 para 9).	First anniversary of 31 January next following year of assessment in which disposal (or other event) occurred (capital gains tax); 2 years from the end of the accounting period in which the disposal (or other event) occurred, or such longer time as the Board may allow (corporation tax).
Gain on a disposal of an asset held at 6 April 1965 to be computed as if the asset had been acquired on that date. An election once made is irrevocable (TCGA 1992 Sch 2 para 17).	First anniversary of 31 January next following year of assessment in which disposal made (capital gains tax); 2 years from end of accounting period in which disposal made (corporation tax); or such further time as the Board may by notice allow.
Quoted ordinary (and participating preference) shares and units in certain unit trusts held (or deemed to have been held) at 6 April 1965 to be pooled at their 6 April 1965 values for disposals after 5 April 1985 (31 March 1985 for companies) or 19 March 1968, as the case may be (TCGA 1992 s 109(4), (5), Sch 2 paras 4(2), (11) as amended, 5).	First anniversary of 31 January next following year of assessment in which first relevant disposal made (capital gains tax); 2 years from end of accounting period in which first relevant disposal made (corporation tax); or such further time as the Board may allow.
Retirement relief generally. Relief must be claimed unless due by reason of a disposal made by an individual aged 50 or over; reorganisation provisions of TCGA 1992 s 126 *et seq* not to apply; relief to be given in respect of certain capital distributions; spouse's period of ownership to be aggregated with that of person making the disposal (TCGA 1992 Sch 6 as amended paras 2, 5, 12,16). (To be phased out from 6 April 1999 and not available for disposals after 5 April 2003 (FA 1998 s 140).)	First anniversary of 31 January next following year of assessment.

Exchanges

Recognised stock exchanges

The following is a list of countries with exchanges which have been designated as recognised stock exchanges under TA 1988 s 841. Unless otherwise specified, any stock exchange (or options exchange) in a country listed below is a recognised stock exchange for the purposes of TA 1988 s 841, provided it is recognised under the law of the country concerned relating to stock exchanges.

Country	Effective date
Australia	14 December 1970
Australian Stock Exchange and its stock exchange subsidiaries	22 September 1988
Austria	14 December 1970
Belgium	14 December 1970
Brazil	
Rio de Janeiro	17 August 1995
São Paulo	20 December 1995
Canada	
Any stock exchange prescribed for the purposes of the Canadian Income Tax Act	14 December 1970
China	
Hong Kong	6 April 1971
Denmark	
Copenhagen Stock Exchange	14 December 1970
Finland	
Helsinki Stock Exchange	14 December 1970
France	14 December 1970
Germany	16 August 1971
Greece	
Athens Stock Exchange	14 June 1993
Irish Republic	14 December 1970
Italy	3 May 1972
Japan	14 December 1970
Korea	10 October 1994
Luxembourg	29 February 1972
Malaysia	
Kuala Lumpur Stock Exchange	10 October 1994
Mexico	10 October 1994
Netherlands	14 December 1970
New Zealand	
New Zealand Stock Exchange	22 September 1988
Norway	14 December 1970
Portugal	29 February 1972
Singapore	
Singapore Stock Exchange	30 June 1977
South Africa	
Johannesburg Stock Exchange	14 December 1970
Spain	16 August 1971
Sri Lanka	
Colombo Stock Exchange	29 February 1972
Sweden	
Stockholm Stock Exchange	16 July 1985
Switzerland	
Swiss Stock Exchange	30 June 1977
Thailand	10 October 1994
United Kingdom	6 April 1965
United States	
Any stock exchange registered with the Securities and Exchange Commission as a national securities exchange[1]	14 December 1970
Nasdaq Stock Market[2]	10 March 1992

[1] The term "national securities exchange" does not include any local exchanges registered with the Securities and Exchange Commission.

[2] As maintained through the facilities of the National Association of Securities Dealers Inc and its subsidiaries.

Recognised futures exchanges

The following is a list of exchanges which have been designated as recognised futures exchanges under TCGA 1992 s 288(6). By concession, the UK exchanges designated before the end of 1985 can be treated as having been designated with effect from 6 April 1985.

Country	Effective date
Australia	
Sydney Futures Exchange	31 October 1988
Canada	
Montreal Exchange	29 July 1987
China	
Hong Kong Futures Exchange	15 December 1987
Sweden	
OM Stockholm	18 March 1992
United Kingdom	
International Petroleum Exchange of London	6 August 1985
London Commodity Exchange	18 March 1992
London Gold Market	12 December 1985
London International Financial Futures and Options	
Exchange	18 March 1992
London Metal Exchange	6 August 1985
London Silver Market	12 December 1985
London Wool Terminal Market	6 August 1985
OMLX	18 March 1992
United States	
Chicago Board of Trade	24 April 1987
Chicago Mercantile Exchange	19 December 1986
Citrus Associates of the New York Cotton Exchange	25 August 1988
Coffee, Sugar and Cocoa Exchange, New York	15 December 1987
Commodity Exchange	25 August 1988
Mid America Commodity Exchange	29 July 1987
New York Cotton Exchange	25 August 1988
New York Mercantile Exchange	19 December 1986
Philadelphia Board of Trade	19 December 1986

Recognised clearing systems

The following is a list of systems for clearing quoted Eurobonds or relevant foreign securities which have been designated as recognised clearing systems under TA 1988 s 841A(2) (formerly TA 1988 s 124(6)).

Country	Effective date
Belgium	
Euro-clear	26 July 1984
Luxembourg	
Cedel	26 July 1984
United Kingdom	
Bank of England European Settlements Office	16 August 1993
First Chicago Clearing Centre	14 October 1988
London Clearing House	22 March 1992
United States	
The Depository Trust Co	18 July 1995

Recognised investment exchanges

The following exchange has been designated as a recognised investment exchange (under the Financial Services Act 1986 s 37(3)) for the purposes of TA 1988 s 841(3).

Country	Effective date
United Kingdom	
London International Financial Futures Exchange	
(Administration and Management) (LIFFE (A&M))	22 March 1992

Applications for clearances and approvals

Clearance application	Address
Share exchanges (TCGA 1992 s 138)	Inland Revenue, Capital and Valuation Division, Room 107, Sapphire House, 550 Streetsbrook Road, Solihull, West Midlands B91 1QU

Clearance application	Address
Transfer of assets on company reconstruction (TCGA 1992 s 139(5))	Inland Revenue, Capital and Valuation Division, Room 107, Sapphire House, 550 Streetsbrook Road, Solihull, West Midlands B91 1QU
Transfer of long term insurance business (TCGA 1992 s 139(5), TA 1988 s 444A)	Inland Revenue, Insurance Group, Room 130, New Wing, Somerset House, London WC2R 1LB
Demergers (TA 1988 s 215)	Inland Revenue, Company Tax Division, Room 28, New Wing, Somerset House, London WC2R 1LB
Company purchase of own shares (TA 1988 s 225)	Inland Revenue, Company Tax Division (Purchase of Own Shares), Room 28, New Wing, Somerset House, London WC2R 1LB
Transactions in securities (TA 1988 s 707)	Inland Revenue, Section 2, Room 336, Third Floor, South West Wing, Bush House, Strand, London WC2B 4QN

Approval application	Address
Employee share ownership trusts (FA 1989 Sch 5)	Inland Revenue, Business Profits Division (Employee Share Schemes), Room 111A, New Wing, Somerset House, Strand, London WC2R 1LB
Employee share schemes (TA 1988 Sch 9 para 1)	Inland Revenue, Savings and Investment Division (Employee Share Schemes), New Wing, Somerset House, London WC2R 1LB
Occupational pension schemes (TA 1988 s 604)	Pension Schemes Office, Yorke House, PO Box 62, Castle Meadow Road, Nottingham NG2 1BG
Professional bodies (relief for subscriptions) (TA 1988 s 201)	Inland Revenue, Insurance and Specialist Division (Schedule E), Sapphire House, 550 Streetsbrook Road, Solihull, West Midlands B91 1QU
Profit-related pay schemes (TA 1988 s 176)	Inland Revenue, Profit-Related Pay Office, St Mungo's Road, Cumbernauld, Glasgow G70 5TR

Inland Revenue explanatory pamphlets

Tax Bulletin: published six times a year. Available only on annual subscription from Business Profits Division, Room 426, 22 Kingsway, London WC2B 6NR (0171 438 7700).

Copies of the pamphlets listed below are obtainable from the offices of HM Inspectors of Taxes, or from Tax Enquiry Centres, with the exception of

IR12 (loose-leaf): available by subscription to the PSO mailing list: SR Communications plc, Unit 9, Deptford Trading Estate, Blackhorse Road, London SE8 5JH (Helpline: 0171 463 8167)

IR67 and CGT reform – the 1998 Finance Act: Inland Revenue Library, Room 28, New Wing, Somerset House, Strand, London WC2R 1LB (IR67: £5.20; CGT reform: £5)

IR83: IR Information Centre, South West Wing, Bush House, Strand, London WC2B 4RD (0171 438 7772)

PRP2: Profit-Related Pay Unit, Inland Revenue Accounts Office, St Mungo's Road, Cumbernauld, Glasgow G67 1YZ (01236 783043, e-mail: wtrenwith.it.smr@gtnet.gov.uk

Inheritance tax: CTO: (England and Wales) Ferrers House, PO Box 38, Castle Meadow Road, Nottingham NG2 1BB (0115 974 2400)

(Scotland) Mulberry House, 16 Picardy Place, Edinburgh EH1 3NB (0131 556 8511)

(Northern Ireland) Dorchester House, 52–58 Great Victoria Street, Belfast BT2 7QL (01232 315556)

IR76, IR120 (You and the Pensions Schemes Office), PSO1: Pension Schemes Office, Yorke House, PO Box 62, Castle Meadow Road, Nottingham NG2 1BG (0115 974 1670).

IR120: Braille and audio cassette versions must be ordered and will be sent through the post or, together with clear print version, are obtainable from the RNIB on 01345 023153.

The charities publications are available from FICO, St. John's House, Merton Road, Bootle, Merseyside L69 9BB (0151 472 6106); CB series is available from FICO (Scotland), Trinity Park House, South Trinity Road, Edinburgh EH5 3SD (0131 551 8127).

Digest of DT agreements is available from FICO, Fitz Roy House, PO Box 46, Nottingham NG2 1BD (0115 974 2000).

Business Economic Notes are obtainable by post from the Inland Revenue Library, Room 28, New Wing, Somerset House, Strand, London WC2R 1LB (price £2.00 per booklet BEN 23-26, £1.50 for earlier booklets — post free) or by calling at the Information Centre (address as above).

The SO series is available from local stamp offices, by phoning 01903 701280, or from (England and Wales) The Stamp Office, Room 57, East Block, Barrington Road, Worthing BN12 4SE (01903 508930); (Scotland) The Stamp Office (Scotland), Mulberry House, 16 Picardy Place, Edinburgh EH1 3NF (0131 556 8998); (Northern Ireland) The Stamp Office, Dorchester House, 52-58 Great Victoria Street, Belfast BT2 7QE (01232 314614).

The Collection Series is available from local collection offices. Collection 4 (England and Wales) from Enforcement Office, Durrington Bridge House, Barrington Road, Worthing, West Sussex BN12 4SE; Collection 3 and 4 (Scotland) from Enforcement Section, Meldrum House, 15 Drumsheugh Gardens, Edinburgh EH3 7UN; Collection 3 and 4 (N Ireland) from Belfast 2 (Enforcement) 4th Floor, Olivetree House, 23 Fountain Street, Belfast BT1 5ET.

Self-assessment: SAT1 (£7.50) and SAT2 (£5) available from Inland Revenue Library, Room 28, New Wing, Somerset House, Strand, London WC2R 1LB.

Self-assessment generally: Orderline 0645 000404; fax 0645 000604; e-mail saorderline.ir@gtnet.gov.uk; PO Box 37, St Austell, Cornwall PL25 5YN. (SA/BK5 from Orderline only.) Information also available on the Internet at: www.inlandrevenue.gov.uk/sa/ and general advice on the Helpline 0645 000444.

Special Compliance Office (COP8, COP9, IR120): Special Compliance Office, Angel Court, 199 Borough High Street, London SE1 1HZ (0171 234 3708).

IR 120 – You and the Enforcement Office: Customer Service Manager, IR, Enforcement Office, Durrington Bridge House, Barrington Road, Worthing, West Sussex BN12 4SE.

The AO series is available from The Adjudicator's Office, Haymarket House, 28 Haymarket, London SW1Y 4SP.

Material for schools from The Inland Revenue Education Service, PO Box 10, Wetherby, West Yorkshire LS23 7EH (01937 840238; fax 01937 845381)

A number of publications are available on the internet at: www.inlandrevenue.gov.uk

Pamphlet	Date Supp	Title
IR List	1998	Catalogue of leaflets and booklets
IR 1	1996 (1997,8)	Extra-statutory concessions
IR 6	1994	Double taxation relief for companies
IR 12	1995	Practice notes on the approval of occupational pension schemes
IR 14/15	1997	Construction industry tax deduction scheme
IR 14/15 (CIS)	1998	Construction industry scheme
IR 16	1997	Share acquisitions by directors and employees – explanatory notes
IR 20	1996	Residents and non-residents – liability to tax in the UK
IR 33	1992	Income tax and school leavers
IR 34	1996	Pay As You Earn
IR 37	1995	Appeals against tax
IR 40	1997	Construction industry – Conditions for getting a subcontractor's tax certificate
IR 40 (CIS)	1998	Construction industry Scheme: conditions for getting a subcontractor's tax certificate
IR 41	1996	Income tax and jobseekers
IR 42	1992	Lay-offs and short-time work
IR 45	1997	What to do about tax when someone dies
IR 46	1997	Clubs, societies and voluntary associations
IR 56/NI39	1995	Employed or self-employed? A guide for tax and national insurance
IR 60	1997	Income tax and students

Inland Revenue explanatory pamphlets — continued

Pamphlet	Date	Supp	Title
IR 64	1993		Giving to charity. How businesses can get tax relief
IR 65	1993		Giving to charity. How individuals can get tax relief
IR 67	1986		(1988) Capital taxation and the national heritage
IR 68	1990		Accrued income scheme. Taxing securities on transfer
IR 69	1996		Expenses payments: forms P11D. How to save yourself work
IR 72	1995		Investigations: the examination of business accounts
IR 73	1994		Inland Revenue investigations: how settlements are negotiated
IR 75	1987		Tax reliefs for charities
IR 76	1991		Personal pension schemes – Guidance notes
IR 78	1991		Personal pensions: a guide for tax
IR 80	1998		Income tax and married couples
IR 83	1990		Independent taxation – a guide for tax practitioners
IR 87	1997		Letting and your home. Including the 'Rent a Room' scheme and letting your previous home when you live elsewhere
IR 88	1989		Capital tax relief for national heritage property – how to make a claim
IR 89	1998		Personal equity plans (PEPs) – a guide for potential investors
IR 90	1998		Tax allowances and reliefs
IR 91	1995		A guide for widows and widowers
IR 92	1995		A guide for one-parent families
IR 93	1997		Separation, divorce and maintenance payments
IR 95	1996		Approved profit-sharing schemes – an outline for employees
IR 96	1996		Approved profit-sharing schemes – explanatory notes
IR 97	1996		Approved SAYE share option schemes – an outline for employees
IR 98	1996		Approved SAYE share option schemes – explanatory notes
IR 101	1996		Approved company share option plans – an outline for employees
IR 102	1996		Approved company share option plans – explanatory notes
IR 109	1997		Employer compliance reviews and negotiations
IR 110	1999		A guide for people with savings
IR 113	1994		Gift aid: A guide for donors and charities
IR 114	1998		TESSA: Tax free interest for taxpayers
IR 115	1992		Tax and childcare
IR 116	1997		Guide for subcontractors with tax certificates
IR 117	1997		A subcontractor's guide to the deduction scheme
IR 119	1997		Tax relief for vocational training
IR 120	1994 (1998)		You and the Inland Revenue (Tax, Collection and Accounts Offices). Versions are available in Bengali, Braille, Chinese, Greek, Gujarati, Hindi, Punjabi, Turkish, Urdu, Vietnamese and Welsh, clear print and audio cassettes
	1995		You and the Inland Revenue (Special Compliance Office)
	1996		You and the Inland Revenue (Financial Intermediaries and Claims Office)
	1998		You and the Pension Schemes Office
	1993		You and the Enforcement Office
	1995		You and the Capital Taxes Office
IR 121	1998		Income tax and pensioners
IR 122	1997		Volunteer drivers
IR 123	1996		Mortgage interest relief – buying your home
IR 125	1996		Using your own car for work
IR 126	1995		Corporation tax pay and file: a general guide
IR 128	1993		Corporation tax pay and file: company leaflet
IR 129	1995		Occupational pension schemes: an introduction
IR 131	1996 (1997,8)		Inland Revenue Statements of Practice
IR 132	1993		Taxation of company cars from 6 April 1994 – employers' guide
IR 133	1993		Income tax and company cars from 6 April 1994 – a guide for employees
IR 134	1997		Income tax and relocation packages
IR 136	1994		Income tax and company vans. A guide for employees and employers
IR 137	1994		The Enterprise Investment Scheme
IR 138	1995		Living or retiring abroad? A guide to UK tax on your UK income and pension
IR 139	1995		Income from abroad? A guide to UK tax on overseas income
IR 140	1995		Non-resident landlords, their agents and tenants
IR 141	1995		Open government
IR 144	1995		Income tax and incapacity benefit
IR 144	1995		Income tax and incapacity benefit; clear print, audio and braille versions
IR 145	1997		Low interest loans provided by employers
IR 148/CA69	1995		Are your workers employed or self-employed? A guide for tax and national insurance for contractors in the construction industry
IR 150	1996		Taxation of rents – a guide to property income
IR 152	1996		Trusts – an introduction
IR 153	1997		Tax exemption for sickness or unemployment insurance payments
IR 155	1996		PAYE settlement agreements
IR 156	1996		Our heritage. Your right to see tax exempt works of art
IR 160	1997		Inland Revenue enquiries under self-assessment
IR 161	1998		Tax relief for employees' business travel. A short guide to the tax treatment of employees' travel expenses from 6 April 1998
IR 162	1998		A better approach to local office enquiry work under self-assessment. Faster working
IR 165	1999		The individual savings account (ISA) – a guide for savers
IR 166	1999		The euro
CS1	1993		Deeds of covenant – guidance for charities
CS2	1995		Trading by charities – guidelines on the tax treatment of trades carried on by charities
—	1994		Fund-raising for charity. What to look out for on tax
—	1989		Guidelines on the tax treatment of disaster funds
—	1994		Payroll giving scheme – a guide for employees
—	1994		Payroll giving scheme – a guide for employers
—	1998		Working families tax credit and disabled person's tax credit

Pamphlet	Date	Supp	Title
CB(1)	1993		Setting up a charity in Scotland
CB(1)	1995		A'cur buidheann carthannais air chois an Alba (Gaelic)
480	1998		Expenses and benefits. A tax guide
490	1998		Employee travel. A tax and NICs guide for employers
FD/CW	1994		Double taxation relief: intercompany loans and royalties
—	1997		Digest of double taxation agreements 1997/98
PRP 2	1996		Tax relief for profit-related pay – notes for guidance
PSO1	1995		Occupational pension schemes. A guide for members of tax-approved schemes
CISFACT 5	1998		The new construction industry scheme. A handy guide
CGT 1	1998		Capital gains tax – An introduction
—	1998		Capital gains tax reform – the 1998 Finance Act
IHT 2	1998		Inheritance tax on lifetime gifts
IHT 3	1998		Inheritance tax – an introduction
IHT 8	1995		Alterations to an inheritance following a death. Inheritance tax
IHT 11	1995		Payment of inheritance tax from national savings
IHT 13	1996		Inheritance tax and penalties
IHT14	1996		Inheritance tax – the personal representatives' responsibilities
IHT15	1996		Inheritance tax – how to calculate the liability
IHT16	1996		Inheritance tax – settled property
IHT17	1996		Inheritance tax – businesses, farms and woodlands
IHT18	1996		Inheritance tax – foreign aspects
SO 1	1998		Stamp duty on buying a freehold house in England, Wales and Northern Ireland
SO 1 (Scotland)	1994		Stamp duty on buying land or buildings in Scotland
SO 2	1997		Stamp Office customer promise and service information
SO 3	1996		If things go wrong. Complaints and lost documents
SO 5	1996		Common stamp duty forms and how to complete them
SO 5 (Scotland)	1997		Common Scottish stamp duty forms and how to complete them
SO 6	1996		A short history of stamp duties
SO 7	1998		Stamp duty on buying a leasehold domestic property
SO 8	1996		Stamp duty on agreements securing short tenancies
SO 9	1996		A table of ad valorem stamp duties
SO 9 (Scotland)	1996		A table of ad valorem stamp duties for Scotland
SO 10	1996		Penalties: an explanation of penalties payable when having documents stamped late
SO 11	1997		Stamp duty and charities
SO12	1998		Stamp duty on commercial leases and agreements for leases
Collection 1		1995	Distraint
Collection 1 (Scotland)		1994	Summary Warrant
Collection 1 (N Ireland)		1995	Distraint
Collection 2		1994	Magistrates' Court proceedings
Collection 2 (Scotland)		1994	Sheriff Court proceedings
Collection 2 (N Ireland)		1994	Magistrates' Court proceedings
Collection 3		1995	County Court proceedings
Collection 3 (Scotland)		1994	Court of Session proceedings
Collection 3 (N Ireland)		1995	High Court proceedings
Collection 4		1995	Bankruptcy and winding up
Collection 4 (Scotland)		1995	Sequestration and winding up
Collection 4 (N Ireland)		1995	Bankruptcy and winding up
COP 1		1996	Mistakes by the Inland Revenue
COP 2		1995	Investigations
COP 3		1997	Inspections of employers' and contractors' records
COP 4		1997	Inspection of schemes operated by financial intermediaries
COP 5		1998	Inspection of charities' records
COP 6		1994	Collection of tax
COP 6 (Scotland)		1995	Collection of tax
COP 7		1994	Collection of amounts due from employers and contractors in the construction industry
COP 7 (Scotland)		1994	Collection of amounts due from employers and contractors in the construction industry
COP 8	1997		Special Compliance Office Investigations: cases other than suspected serious fraud
COP 9	1997		Special Compliance Office Investigations: cases of suspected serious fraud
COP 10	1998		Information and advice
COP 11	1996		Enquiries into tax returns by local tax offices
AO1	1998		How to complain about the Inland Revenue and the Valuation Office Agency
AO2	1998		How to complain about Customs and Excise
AO3	1998		How to complain about the Contributions Agency
AO4	1998		How to complain about the Contributions Unit of the Social Security Agency in Northern Ireland
RA0	1994		How to complain about the Inland Revenue – ethnic language versions
SA/BK3	1995		Self-assessment – a guide to keeping records for the self-employed
SA/BK4	1997		Self-assessment – a general guide to keeping records
SA/BK5	1998		Self-assessment – electronic version of the tax return
SA/BK6	1997		Self-assessment – penalties for late returns
SA/BK7	1997		Self-assessment – surcharges for late payment of assessment
SA/BK8	1997		Self-assessment – your guide
SAT 1	1995		Self-assessment: the new current year basis of assessment
SAT 2	1995		Self-assessment: the legal framework
SAT 3	1995		Self-assessment: what it will mean for employers
SVD 1	1999		Shares Valuation Division. An introduction
CWL 1	1998		Starting your own business? (Published with HM Customs & Excise and Contributions Agency)
CWL 2	1998		NI contributions for self-employed people. Class 2 and Class 4

Inland Revenue explanatory pamphlets — continued

Pamphlet	Date	Supp	Title
CWL 3	1997		Thinking of taking someone on? PAYE tax and NI contributions for employers
CWG 1	1998		Employer's quick guide to PAYE and NICs
CWG 2	1997		Employer's further guide to PAYE and NICs
—			Tax for you (schools)
—			Right from the start (schools video)

Business economic notes:

BEN 1	(1990)	Travel agents	BEN 14	(1990)	The pet industry
BEN 2	(1995)	Road haulage	BEN 15	(1990)	Veterinary surgeons
BEN 3	(1990)	The lodging industry	BEN 16	(1990)	Catering—general
BEN 4	(1990)	Hairdressers	BEN 17	(1990)	Catering—restaurants
BEN 5	(1990)	Waste materials reclamation and disposal	BEN 18	(1990)	Catering—fast-foods
			BEN 19	(1993)	Farming—stock valuation for income tax purposes
BEN 6	(1990)	Funeral directors			
BEN 7	(1990)	Dentists	BEN 20	(1994)	Insurance brokers and agents
BEN 8	(1990)	Florists	BEN 21	(1994)	Residential rest and nursing homes
BEN 9	(1988)	Licensed victuallers	BEN 22	(1995)	Dispensing chemists
BEN 10	(1990)	The jewellery trade	BEN 23	(1997)	Driving instructors
BEN 11	(1990)	Electrical retailers	BEN 24	(1997)	Independent fishmongers
BEN 12	(1990)	Antiques and fine art dealers	BEN 25	(1997)	Taxi cabs and private hire vehicles
BEN 13	(1990)	Fish and chip shops	BEN 26	(1997)	Confectioners, tobacconists and newsagents

Internal guidance booklets and manuals: *

Assessed Taxes
Assessment Procedures
Banking Manual
Capital Allowances Instructions
Capital Gains Manual
Claims Manual
Collection Manual
Company Taxation Manual
Complaints Handbook
Compliance and Investigation Operation Manual
(CTO) Advanced Investigation Manual (IHT)
(CTO) General Examination Manual (IHT)
Double Taxation Relief Manual
Employee Share Schemes
Employer Compliance Manual
Employers Section Manual
Employment Procedures Manual
Enforcement Manual
Enforcement Manual (Scotland)
Enquiry Handbook
European Economic Interest Groupings
General Insurance Manual
Independent Taxation Manual
Inheritance Tax Double Taxation Conventions
Insolvency Manual
Insolvency Manual (Scotland)

Inspector's Manual
Interest Review Unit Guidelines
International Tax Handbook
Investigation Handbook
Life Assurance Manual
Movements Manual (PAYE)
National Audit Group Instructions
Oil Taxation Office PRT Manual
Oil Taxation Office Ring Fence CT Manual
Oil Taxation Office Section 830 Manual
Pay and File Manual (Collection)
PAYE Instructions (Collection)
PAYE Settlement Agreement Handbook
Pension Schemes Office Manual
Personal Contact Manual
Profit Related Pay Unit Manual
Property Income Manual
Regional Office Manual
Relief
Residence Guide
Schedule D Compliance
Schedule E Manual
Self Self Assessment Manual
Shares Valuation Division Manual
Small Self Administered Schemes
Subcontractors in the Construction Industry
Trust Manual

* Copies of the manuals are available on CD-rom, with an updating service, as part of a database, from Tolley Publishing Co Ltd, Tolley House, 2 Addiscombe Road, Croydon, Surrey CR9 5AF: telephone 0181 686 9141; fax 0181 686 3155. Extracts published in looseleaf format as *Simon's Direct Tax Service*, Binders 12 and 13: prices available on application to the publishers.

All internal guidance manuals are available for inspection free of charge in Inland Revenue Tax Enquiry Centres. The inheritance tax manuals may be inspected free of charge at certain Capital Taxes Offices.

Capital gains tax

Annual exemption

Individuals, personal representatives[1] and certain trusts[2]

Exempt amount of net gains	1994-95	1995-96	1996-97	1997-98	1998-99	1999-2000
	£5,800	£6,000	£6,300	£6,500	£6,800	£7,100

[1] Year of death and following 2 years (maximum).
[2] Trusts for mentally disabled persons and those in receipt of attendance allowance or disability living allowance. Exemption divided by number of qualifying settlements created (after 9 March 1981) by one settlor, subject to a minimum of one-tenth.

Trusts[1] generally

Exempt amount of net gains	1994-95	1995-96	1996-97	1997-98	1998-99	1999-2000
	£2,900	£3,000	£3,150	£3,250	£3,400	£3,550

[1] Exemption divided by number of qualifying settlements created (after 6 June 1978) by one settlor, subject to a minimum of one-fifth.

Chattel exemption

	Disposals exemption	*Marginal relief: Maximum chargeable gain*
1989-90 to 1999-2000	£6,000	$\frac{5}{3}$ excess over £6,000

Rate of tax

1999–2000	**Individuals:** gains taxed as top slice of income: ;20% to basic rate limit, 40% above, subject to tapering in certain cases. **Trusts, personal representatives:** 34%, subject to tapering in certain cases
1998–99	**Individuals:** gains taxed at income tax rates (as top slice of income[1]), subject to tapering in certain cases **Trusts, personal representatives:** 34%, subject to tapering in certain cases
1997–98	**Individuals:** gains taxed at income tax rates (as top slice of income[1]) **Trusts, personal representatives:** 23% (34% for trusts charged to rate applicable to trusts)
1996–97	**Individuals:** gains taxed at income tax rates (as top slice of income[1]) **Trusts, personal representatives:** 24% (34% for trusts charged to rate applicable to trusts)
1988–89 to 1995–96	**Individuals:** gains taxed at income tax rates (as top slice of income[2]) **Trusts, personal representatives:** 25% (35% for trusts charged to rate applicable to trusts)

[1] Adjustment is necessary for savings income (including interest from banks and building societies, interest distributions from authorised unit trusts, interest from gilts and other securities including corporate bonds, purchased life annuities, and discounts). Adjustment is also necessary for dividends or other qualifying distributions from a UK-resident company.
[2] From 1993-94 adjustment is necessary for dividends or other qualifying distributions from UK-resident company.

Retirement relief (phased out from 6 April 1999)

Disposals after	*Minimum age*	*100% relief on gains up to*	*50% relief on gains between*	*Maximum relief*
5 April 2003	–	–	–	–
5 April 2002	50	£50,000	£50,000.01–£200,000	£125,000
5 April 2001	50	£100,000	£100,000.01–£400,000	£250,000
5 April 2000	50	£150,000	£150,000.01–£600,000	£375,000
5 April 1999	50	£200,000	£200,000.01–£800,000	£500,000
27 November 1995	50	£250,000	£250,000.01–£1,000,000	£625,000

(% determined by qualifying period. Relief also available where early retirement occurs for reasons of ill-health. Relief given after indexation allowance but before tapering relief.)

Tapering relief

Tapering relief is available for disposals made after 5 April 1998 (TCGA 1992 s 2A inserted by FA 1998 s 121). The chargeable gain is reduced according to the length of time for which the asset has been held (counting from 6 April 1998). Assets acquired before 17 March 1998 qualify for an addition of one year to the period for which they are held after 5 April 1998. The reductions available for gains on business assets are greater than for gains on non-business assets.

Business assets				Non-business assets			
Number of complete yrs after 5.4.98 for which asset held	% of gain chargeable	Equivalent tax rates:		Number of complete yrs after 5.4.98 for which asset held	% of gain chargeable	Equivalent tax rates:	
		Higher rate taxp'r	20% rate taxp'r			Higher rate taxp'r	20% rate taxp'r
0	100	40	20	0	100	40	20
1	92·5	37	18·5	1	100	40	20
2	85	34	17·0	2	100	40	20
3	77·5	31	15·5	3	95	38	19
4	70	28	14·0	4	90	36	18
5	62·5	25	12·5	5	85	34	17
6	55	22	11·0	6	80	32	16
7	47·5	19	9·5	7	75	30	15
8	40	16	8·0	8	70	28	14
9	32·5	13	6·5	9	65	26	13
10 or more	25	10	5·0	10 or more	60	24	12

Leases

Depreciation table (TCGA 1992 Sch 8 para 1)

Yrs	%	Yrs	%	Yrs	%	Yrs	%	Yrs	%	Yrs	%	Yrs	%
50 (or more)	100	42	96·593	34	91·156	27	83·816	20	72·770	13	56·167	6	31·195
49	99·657	41	96·041	33	90·280	26	82·496	19	70·791	12	53·191	5	26·722
48	99·289	40	95·457	32	89·354	25	81·100	18	68·697	11	50·038	4	21·983
47	98·902	39	94·842	31	88·371	24	79·622	17	66·470	10	46·695	3	16·959
46	98·490	38	94·189	30	87·330	23	78·055	16	64·116	9	43·154	2	11·629
45	98·059	37	93·497	29	86·226	22	76·399	15	61·617	8	39·399	1	5·983
44	97·595	36	92·761	28	85·053	21	74·635	14	58·971	7	35·414	0	0
43	97·107	35	91·981										

Formula: fraction of expenditure disallowed—

$$\frac{\left\{ \begin{array}{l}\text{Percentage for duration of lease} \\ \text{at acquisition or expenditure}\end{array}\right\} \; minus \; \left\{ \begin{array}{l}\text{Percentage for duration of} \\ \text{lease at disposal}\end{array}\right.}{\text{Percentage for duration of lease at acquisition or expenditure}}$$

Fractions of years:
Add one-twelfth of the difference between the percentage for the whole year and the next higher percentage for each additional month. Odd days under 14 are not counted; 14 odd days or more count as a month.

Short leases: premiums treated as rent (TA 1988 s 34, TCGA 1992 Sch 8 para 5)

Part of premium for grant of a short lease which is chargeable to income tax under Schedule A—

$$P - (2\% \times (n - 1) \times P)$$

Where P = amount of premium
       n = number of complete years which lease has to run when granted

Length of Lease (complete years)	Amount chargeable to CGT %	Income tax Sch A %	Length of Lease (complete years)	Amount chargeable to CGT %	Income tax Sch A %	Length of Lease (complete years)	Amount chargeable to CGT %	Income tax Sch A %
Over 50	100	0	34	66	34	17	32	68
50	98	2	33	64	36	16	30	70
49	96	4	32	62	38	15	28	72
48	94	6	31	60	40	14	26	74
47	92	8	30	58	42	13	24	76
46	90	10	29	56	44	12	22	78
45	88	12	28	54	46	11	20	80
44	86	14	27	52	48	10	18	82
43	84	16	26	50	50	9	16	84
42	82	18	25	48	52	8	14	86
41	80	20	24	46	54	7	12	88
40	78	22	23	44	56	6	10	90
39	76	24	22	42	58	5	8	92
38	74	26	21	40	60	4	6	94
37	72	28	20	38	62	3	4	96
36	70	30	19	36	64	2	2	98
35	68	32	18	34	66	1 or less	0	100

Gilt-edged securities exempt from tax on chargeable gains

The following securities have been specified for the purposes of TCGA 1992 Sch 9 and are exempt from capital gains tax. A similar exemption exists for qualifying corporate bonds issued after 13 March 1984. A 1-year qualifying limit applied to disposals before 2 July 1986. The gain accruing on the disposal of an option or contract to acquire or dispose of gilt-edged securities or qualifying corporate bonds after 1 July 1986 is also exempt from capital gains tax. (Securities redeemed before 31 March 1999 do not appear on this list.)

Readers should note that under the loan relationship provisions of FA 1996 Part IV Chapter II, the definition of 'qualifying corporate bond' for the purposes of corporation tax only has been extended (see TCGA 1992 ss 117, 117A, 117B).

* Repaid at latest date shown unless the Treasury give notice of earlier repayment.

Stocks		Redemption dates	Dividend due dates	
10½%	Treasury Stock 1999	19 May 1999	19 May	19 November
6%	Treasury Stock 1999	10 August 1999	10 February	10 August
2½%	Index-Linked Treasury Convertible Stock 1999	22 November 1999	22 May	22 November
10¼%	Conversion Stock 1999	22 November 1999	22 May	22 November
8½%	Treasury Loan 2000	28 January 2000	28 January	28 July
9%	Conversion Stock 2000	3 March 2000	3 March	3 September
9%	Conversion Stock 2000 'A'			
9%	Conversion Stock 2000 'B'			
9%	Conversion Stock 2000 'C'			
13%	Treasury Stock 2000	14 July 2000	14 January	14 July
13%	Treasury Stock 2000 'A'			
8%	Treasury Stock 2000	7 December 2000	7 June	7 December
8%	Treasury Stock 2000 'A'			
10%	Treasury Stock 2001	26 February 2001	26 February	26 August
10%	Treasury Stock 2001 'A'			
10%	Treasury Stock 2001 'B'			
14%	Treasury Stock 1998-2001*	22 May 1998/22 May 2001	22 May	22 November
9½%	Conversion Loan 2001	12 July 2001	12 January	12 July
9¾%	Conversion Stock 2001	10 August 2001	10 February	10 August
2½%	Index-Linked Treasury Stock 2001	24 September 2001	24 March	24 September
7%	Treasury Stock 2001	6 November 2001	6 May	6 November
7%	Treasury Stock 2001 'A'			
12%	Exchequer Stock 1999-2002*	22 January 1999/22 January 2002	22 January	22 July
12%	Exchequer Stock 1999-2002 'A'			
10%	Conversion Stock 2002	11 April 2002	11 April	11 October
9½%	Conversion Stock 2002	14 June 2002	14 June	14 December
9¾%	Treasury Stock 2002	27 August 2002	27 February	27 August
9¾%	Treasury Stock 2002 'A'			
9¾%	Treasury Stock 2002 'B'			
9¾%	Treasury Stock 2002 'C'			
9%	Exchequer Stock 2002	19 November 2002	19 May	19 November
9¾%	Conversion Loan 2003	7 May 2003	7 May	7 November
2½%	Index-Linked Treasury Stock 2003	20 May 2003	20 May	20 November
8%	Treasury Stock 2003	10 June 2003	10 June	10 December
8%	Treasury Stock 2003 'A'			
13¾%	Treasury Stock 2000-03*	25 July 2000/25 July 2003	25 January	25 July
13¾%	Treasury Stock 2000-03 'A'			
10%	Treasury Stock 2003	8 September 2003	8 March	8 September
10%	Treasury Stock 2003 'A'			
10%	Treasury Stock 2003 'B'			
11½%	Treasury Stock 2001-04*	19 March 2001/19 March 2004	19 March	19 September
10%	Treasury Stock 2004	18 May 2004	18 May	18 November
3½%	Funding Stock 1999-2004*	14 July 1999/14 July 2004	14 January	14 July
4⅜%	Index-Linked Treasury Stock 2004	21 October 2004	21 April	21 October
9½%	Conversion Stock 2004	25 October 2004	25 April	25 October
9½%	Conversion Stock 2004 'A'			
6¾%	Treasury Stock 2004	26 November 2004	26 May	26 November
6¾%	Treasury Stock 2004 'A'			
9½%	Conversion Stock 2005	18 April 2005	18 April	18 October
9½%	Conversion Stock 2005 'A'			
10½%	Exchequer Stock 2005	20 September 2005	20 March	20 September
12½%	Treasury Stock 2003-05*	21 November 2003/ 21 November 2005	21 May	21 November
12½%	Treasury Stock 2003-05* 'A'			
8½%	Treasury Stock 2005	7 December 2005	7 June	7 December
2%	Index-Linked Treasury Stock 2006	19 July 2006	19 January	19 July
7¾%	Treasury Stock 2006	8 September 2006	8 March	8 September
8%	Treasury Loan 2002-06*	5 October 2002/5 October 2006	5 April	5 October
8%	Treasury Loan 2002-06 'A'			
9¾%	Conversion Stock 2006	15 November 2006	15 May	15 November
7½%	Treasury Stock 2006	7 December 2006	7 June	7 December

Stocks		Redemption dates	Dividend due dates	
11¾%	Treasury Stock 2003-07*	22 January 2003/22 January 2007	22 January	22 July
11¾%	Treasury Stock 2003-07 'A'			
7¼%	Treasury Stock 2007	7 June 2007	7 June	7 December
8½%	Treasury Loan 2007	16 July 2007	16 January	16 July
8½%	Treasury Loan 2007 'A'			
8½%	Treasury Loan 2007 'B'			
8½%	Treasury Loan 2007 'C'			
13½%	Treasury Stock 2004-08*	26 March 2004/26 March 2008	26 March	26 September
9%	Treasury Loan 2008	13 October 2008	13 April	13 October
9%	Treasury Loan 2008 'A'			
9%	Treasury Loan 2008 'B'			
9%	Treasury Loan 2008 'C'			
9%	Treasury Loan 2008 'D'			
2½%	Index-Linked Treasury Stock 2009	20 May 2009	20 May	20 November
8%	Treasury Stock 2009	25 September 2009	25 March	25 September
8%	Treasury Stock 2009 'A'			
6¼%	Treasury Stock 2010	25 November 2010	25 May	25 November
9%	Conversion Loan 2011	12 July 2011	12 January	12 July
9%	Conversion Loan 2011 'A'			
9%	Conversion Loan 2011 'B'			
9%	Conversion Loan 2011 'C'			
9%	Conversion Loan 2011 'D'			
2½%	Index-Linked Treasury Stock 2011	23 August 2011	23 February	23 August
9%	Treasury Stock 2012	6 August 2012	6 February	6 August
9%	Treasury Stock 2012 'A'			
5½%	Treasury Stock 2008-12*	10 September 2008/ 10 September 2012	10 March	10 September
2½%	Index-Linked Treasury Stock 2013	16 August 2013	16 February	16 August
8%	Treasury Stock 2013	27 September 2013	27 March	27 September
7¾%	Treasury Loan 2012-15*	26 January 2012/26 January 2015	26 January	26 July
8%	Treasury Stock 2015	7 December 2015	7 June	7 December
8%	Treasury Stock 2015 'A'			
2½%	Treasury Stock 1986-2016*	15 March 1986/15 March 2016	15 March	15 September
2½%	Index-Linked Treasury Stock 2016	26 July 2016	26 January	26 July
2½%	Index-Linked Treasury Stock 2016 'A'			
8¾%	Treasury Stock 2017	25 August 2017	25 February	25 August
8¾%	Treasury Stock 2017 'A'			
12%	Exchequer Stock 2013-17*	12 December 2013/ 12 December 2017	12 June	12 December
2½%	Index-Linked Treasury Stock 2020	16 April 2020	16 April	16 October
2½%	Index-Linked Treasury Stock 2024	17 July 2024	17 January	17 July
6%	Treasury Stock 2028	7 December 2028	7 June	7 December
4⅛%	Index-Linked Treasury Stock 2030	22 July 2030	22 January	22 July
4%	Consolidated Loan	1 February 1957 or after	1 February	1 August
3½%	War Loan	1 December 1952 or after	1 June	1 December
3½%	Conversion Loan	1 April 1961 or after	1 April	1 October
3%	Treasury Stock	5 April 1966 or after	5 April	5 October
2½%	Consolidated Stock	5 April 1923 or after	5 January, 5 July	5 April, 5 October
2½%	Treasury Stock 1975 or after	1 April 1975 or after	1 April	1 October
2½%	Annuities	5 January 1905 or after	5 January, 5 July	5 April, 5 October
2¾%	Annuities	5 January 1905 or after	5 January, 5 July	5 April, 5 October

Reliefs

The following is a summary of the main reliefs and exemptions for the year 1999–2000. The legislation should be referred to for conditions and exceptions.

Charities

Gains accruing to charities which are both applicable and applied for charitable purposes	Exempt

Individuals

Annual exemption (see p 36 for earlier years)	£7,100
Chattel exemption (see p 36 for marginal relief)	£6,000
Compensation (injury to person, profession or vocation)	Exempt
Decorations for valour (acquired otherwise than for money or money's worth)	Gain exempt
Enterprise Investment Scheme (see p 72)	Gain on disposal after relevant five year period exempt to extent full relief given on shares
Foreign currency acquired for personal expenditure	Gain exempt
Gifts for public benefit, works of art, historic buildings etc	No chargeable gain/allowable loss
Gilt-edged stock (see p 38)	No chargeable gain/allowable loss
Married persons living together	No chargeable gain/allowable loss on disposals from one to the other
Motor vehicles	Gain exempt
Principal private residence	Gain exempt
If residence is partly let, exemption for the let part is limited to the smaller of—	(1) exemption on owner-occupied part and (2) £40,000
Qualifying corporate bonds	No chargeable gain (for loans made before 18 March 1998, allowable loss in certain cases if all or part of loss is irrecoverable)
Retirement relief (phased-out over 5 years beginning in 1999-2000: see p 36)	£200,000 plus 50% of gains between £200,000 and £800,000
Hold-over relief for gifts	Restricted to: (1) gifts of business assets (including unquoted shares in trading companies and holding companies of trading groups) (2) gifts of heritage property (3) gifts to heritage maintenance funds (4) gifts to political parties, and (5) gifts on which there is an immediate charge to inheritance tax. Where available, transferee's acquisition cost treated as reduced by held-over gain.
Roll-over relief on reinvestment (now forms part of a rationalised Enterprise Investment Scheme). Withdrawn for acquisitions after 5 April 1998.	(See FA 1998, s 74, Sch 13)
Venture capital trusts (see p 73)	Gain on disposal of shares by original investor exempt if company still a venture capital trust.

Reliefs — continued

Businesses

Roll-over relief for replacement of business assets

Qualifying assets:

Buildings and land both occupied and used for the purposes of the trade
Fixed plant and machinery
Ships, aircraft and hovercraft
Satellites, space stations and spacecraft
Goodwill
Milk and potato quotas
Ewe and suckler cow premium quotas

Qualifying assets are to include fish quota with effect from 21 days after regulations are laid before Parliament (IR Press Release 29/99).

The "replacement" assets must be acquired within 12 months before or 3 years after the disposal of the old asset. Both assets must be within any of the above classes. Holdover relief is available where the new asset is a depreciating asset (having a predictable useful life not exceeding 60 years).

Personal representatives

Annual exemption

Year of death and following 2 years: (See p 36 for earlier years)	£7,100

Allowable expenses

Expenses allowable for the costs of establishing title in computing chargeable gains on disposal of assets in a deceased person's estate: deaths occurring after 5 April 1993 (SP 8/94). (The Revenue accepts computations based either on the scale or on the actual allowable expenditure incurred.)

Gross value of estate	Allowable expenditure
Up to £40,000	1.75% of the probate value of the assets sold by the personal representatives
Between £40,001 and £70,000	£700, to be divided between all the assets of the estate in proportion to the probate values and allowed in those proportions on assets sold by the personal representatives
Between £70,001 and £300,000	1% of the probate value of the assets sold
Between £300,001 and £400,000	£3,000, to be divided between all the assets of the estate in proportion to the probate values and allowed in those proportions on assets sold by the personal representatives
Between £400,001 and £750,000	0.75% of the probate value of the assets sold
Exceeding £75,000	Negotiable according to the facts of the particular case

Trustees

Annual exemption see p 36.

Allowable expenses

Expenses allowable in computing chargeable gains of corporate trustees in the administration of trusts and estates: acquisition, disposals and deemed disposals after 5 April 1993 (SP 8/94). (The Revenue accepts computations based either on the scale or on the actual allowable expenditure incurred.)

Transfers of assets to beneficiaries etc	
(a) Quoted stocks and shares	
(i) One beneficiary	£20 per holding
(ii) More than one beneficiary	£20 per holding, divided equally between the beneficiaries
(b) Unquoted shares	As (a) above, plus any exceptional expenditure
(c) Other assets	As (a) above, plus any exceptional expenditure

Actual disposals and acquisitions	
(a) Quoted stocks and shares	Investment fee as charged by the trustee (where a comprehensive annual management fee is charged, the investment fee is taken to be £0.25 per £100 of the sale or purchase moneys)
(b) Unquoted shares	As (a) above, plus actual valuation costs
(c) Other assets	Investment fee (as (a) above), subject to a maximum of £60, plus actual valuation costs

Deemed disposals by trustees	
(a) Quoted stocks and shares	£6 per holding

41

Retail prices index

	Jan	Feb	Mar	Apr	May	June	July	Aug	Sept	Oct	Nov	Dec
1947	–	–	–	–	–	7·33	7·40	7·33	7·40	7·40	7·55	7·63
1948	7·63	7·78	7·78	8·33	8·33	8·49	8·33	8·33	8·33	8·33	8·41	8·41
1949	8·41	8·41	8·41	8·41	8·57	8·57	8·57	8·57	8·65	8·65	8·65	8·73
1950	8·73	8·73	8·73	8·81	8·81	8·81	8·81	8·73	8·81	8·89	8·97	8·97
1951	9·03	9·11	9·19	9·35	9·59	9·67	9·72	9·80	9·88	9·96	9·96	10·04
1952	10·20	10·28	10·28	10·44	10·44	10·65	10·65	10·04	9·96	10·11	10·11	10·11
1953	10·11	10·19	10·67	10·34	10·27	10·34	10·34	10·27	10·27	10·27	10·27	10·27
1954	10·27	10·27	10·34	10·42	10·34	10·42	10·62	10·57	10·49	10·57	10·62	10·62
1955	10·70	10·70	10·70	10·77	10·77	11·00	11·00	10·93	11·00	11·15	11·28	11·28
1956	11·25	11·25	11·38	11·56	11·53	11·51	11·48	11·51	11·48	11·56	11·58	11·63
1957	11·74	11·74	11·71	11·76	11·76	11·89	11·99	11·96	11·94	12·04	12·12	12·17
1958	12·17	12·09	12·19	12·32	12·29	12·40	12·19	12·19	12·19	12·29	12·34	12·40
1959	12·42	12·40	12·40	12·32	12·27	12·29	12·27	12·29	12·22	12·29	12·37	12·40
1960	12·37	12·37	12·34	12·40	12·40	12·47	12·50	12·42	12·42	12·52	12·60	12·62
1961	12·62	12·62	12·67	12·75	12·78	12·90	12·90	13·00	13·00	13·00	13·16	13·18
1962	13·21	13·23	13·28	13·46	13·51	13·59	13·54	13·43	13·41	13·41	13·46	13·51
1963	13·56	13·69	13·71	13·74	13·74	13·74	13·66	13·61	13·66	13·71	13·74	13·76
1964	13·84	13·84	13·89	14·02	14·14	14·20	14·20	14·25	14·25	14·27	14·37	14·42
1965	14·47	14·47	14·52	14·80	14·85	14·90	14·90	14·93	14·93	14·96	15·01	15·08
1966	15·11	15·11	15·13	15·34	15·44	15·49	15·41	15·51	15·49	15·51	15·61	15·64
1967	15·67	15·67	15·67	15·79	15·79	15·84	15·74	15·72	15·69	15·86	15·92	16·02
1968	16·07	16·15	16·20	16·50	16·50	16·58	16·58	16·60	16·63	16·70	16·76	16·96
1969	17·06	17·16	17·21	17·41	17·39	17·47	17·47	17·41	17·47	17·59	17·64	17·77
1970	17·90	18·00	18·10	18·38	18·43	18·48	18·63	18·61	18·71	18·91	19·04	19·16
1971	19·42	19·54	19·70	20·13	20·25	20·38	20·51	20·53	20·56	20·66	20·79	20·89
1972	21·01	21·12	21·19	21·39	21·50	21·62	21·70	21·88	22·00	22·31	22·38	22·48
1973	22·64	22·79	22·92	23·35	23·52	23·65	23·75	23·83	24·03	24·51	24·69	24·87
1974	25·35	25·78	26·01	26·89	27·28	27·55	27·81	27·83	28·14	28·69	29·20	29·63
1975	30·39	30·90	31·51	32·72	34·09	34·75	35·11	35·31	35·61	36·12	36·55	37·01
1976	37·49	37·97	38·17	38·91	39·34	39·54	39·62	40·18	40·71	41·44	42·03	42·59
1977	43·70	44·24	44·56	45·70	46·06	46·54	46·59	46·82	47·07	47·28	47·50	47·76
1978	48·04	48·31	48·62	49·33	49·61	49·99	50·22	50·54	50·75	50·98	51·33	51·76
1979	52·52	52·95	53·38	54·30	54·73	55·67	58·07	58·53	59·11	59·72	60·25	60·68
1980	62·18	63·07	63·93	66·11	66·72	67·35	67·91	68·06	68·49	68·92	69·48	69·86
1981	70·29	70·93	71·99	74·07	74·55	74·98	75·31	75·87	76·30	76·98	77·78	78·28
1982	78·73	78·76	79·44	81·04	81·62	81·85	81·88	81·90	81·85	82·26	82·66	82·51
1983	82·61	82·97	83·12	84·28	84·64	84·84	85·30	85·68	86·06	86·36	86·67	86·89
1984	86·84	87·20	87·48	88·64	88·97	89·20	89·10	89·94	90·11	90·67	90·95	90·87
1985	91·20	91·94	92·80	94·78	95·21	95·41	95·23	95·49	95·44	95·59	95·92	96·05
1986	96·25	96·60	96·73	97·67	97·85	97·79	97·52	97·82	98·30	98·45	99·29	99·62
1987	100·00	100·40	100·60	101·80	101·90	101·90	101·80	102·10	102·40	102·90	103·40	103·30
1988	103·30	103·70	104·10	105·80	106·20	106·60	106·70	107·90	108·40	109·50	110·00	110·30
1989	111·00	111·80	112·30	114·30	115·00	115·40	115·50	115·80	116·60	117·50	118·50	118·80
1990	119·50	120·20	121·40	125·10	126·20	126·70	126·80	128·10	129·30	130·30	130·00	129·90
1991	130·20	130·90	131·40	133·10	133·50	134·10	133·80	134·10	134·60	135·10	135·60	135·70
1992	135·60	136·30	136·70	138·80	139·30	139·30	138·80	138·90	139·40	139·90	139·70	139·20
1993	137·90	138·80	139·30	140·60	141·10	141·00	140·70	141·30	141·90	141·80	141·60	141·90
1994	141·30	142·10	142·50	144·20	144·70	144·70	144·00	144·70	145·00	145·20	145·30	146·00
1995	146·00	146·90	147·50	149·00	149·60	149·80	149·10	149·90	150·60	149·80	149·80	150·70
1996	150·20	150·90	151·50	152·60	152·90	153·00	152·40	153·10	153·80	153·80	153·90	154·40
1997	154·40	155·00	155·40	156·30	156·90	157·50	157·50	158·50	159·30	159·50	159·60	160·00
1998	159·50	160·30	160·80	162·60	163·50	163·40	163·00	163·70	164·40	164·50	164·40	164·40
1999	163·40											

Indexation allowance

For persons subject to capital gains tax, gains on disposals after 5 April 1998 of assets held on that date are indexed up to April 1998 but not beyond. No indexation allowance is available for assets acquired after 31 March 1998. Tapering relief is available for disposals after 5 April 1998, see p 37. For persons subject to corporation tax, indexation continues to be available as previously, and there is no tapering relief.

The indexation allowance is calculated as follows: allowable expenditure (or MV at 31.3.82) $\times \dfrac{RD - RI}{RI}$

RD = Retail prices index figure for month of disposal
RI = Retail prices index figure for base month (ie the month in which the allowable expenditure was incurred, or March 1982 if later).

The following indexed rise can be used when calculating the allowance—

RD — Month of disposal

RI — Base Month

Base	94 Jul	Aug	Sep	Oct	Nov	Dec	95 Jan	Feb	Mar	Apr	May	Jun	Jul	Aug	Sep	Oct	Nov	Dec	96 Jan	Feb	Mar	Apr	May	Jun	Jul	Aug	Sep	Oct	Nov	Dec	97 Jan	Feb	Mar	Apr	May	Jun	Jul	Aug	Sep	Oct	Nov	Dec	98 Jan	Feb	Mar	Apr	May	Jun	Jul	Aug	Sep	Oct	Nov	Dec	99 Jan
1982																																																							
Mar	813	821	825	828	829	838	838	849	857	876	883	886	877	887	886	886	886	897	891	899	907	921	925	926	918	927	936	936	937	944	944	951	956	967	975	983	983	995	1005	1008	1009	1014	1008	1018	1024	1047	1058	1057	1052	1061	1061	1071	1069	1069	1057
Apr	777	786	789	792	793	802	802	813	820	839	846	848	840	850	848	848	848	860	853	862	869	883	887	888	881	889	898	898	899	905	905	913	918	929	936	944	944	956	966	968	969	974	968	978	984	1006	1018	1016	1011	1019	1021	1030	1029	1029	1016
May	764	773	776	779	780	789	789	800	807	825	833	835	827	837	835	835	835	846	840	849	856	870	873	874	867	875	884	884	885	892	892	899	904	915	922	930	930	942	952	954	955	960	954	964	970	992	1003	1002	997	1006	1006	1015	1015	1014	1002
June	759	768	772	774	775	784	784	795	802	820	828	830	822	831	830	830	830	841	835	844	851	864	868	869	862	870	879	879	880	886	886	894	899	909	917	924	924	936	946	949	949	955	949	958	964	986	997	996	992	1000	1000	1010	1009	1008	996
July	759	767	771	773	775	784	783	795	802	820	827	830	821	831	830	830	830	840	834	844	850	864	867	869	861	870	878	878	879	886	886	893	898	909	916	924	923	936	945	947	949	954	948	958	963	985	996	995	991	1000	1000	1009	1009	1008	996
Aug	759	767	771	773	775	783	783	794	801	819	827	830	821	831	830	830	830	841	835	843	851	863	867	868	861	869	878	878	879	886	885	893	897	908	916	923	923	935	945	947	948	954	947	957	963	985	996	995	990	999	999	1009	1008	1007	995
Sept	759	768	772	774	775	784	784	795	802	820	828	830	822	831	831	830	830	841	835	844	851	864	868	869	862	870	879	879	880	886	886	894	898	910	917	924	924	936	946	949	949	955	949	958	965	987	998	996	991	1000	1000	1010	1009	1009	996
Oct	751	759	763	765	766	775	775	786	793	811	819	821	813	822	822	821	821	832	826	835	842	855	859	860	853	861	870	870	870	877	876	884	889	900	907	915	915	927	937	939	939	945	939	949	955	977	988	986	981	990	991	1000	1000	999	986
Nov	742	751	754	757	758	766	766	777	784	803	810	812	804	813	812	812	812	823	817	826	833	846	850	851	844	852	861	861	861	867	867	875	880	891	898	905	905	917	927	930	931	936	930	939	945	967	978	977	972	980	981	990	990	989	977
Dec	745	754	757	760	761	769	769	780	788	806	813	816	807	817	816	816	816	826	820	829	836	849	853	854	847	855	864	864	865	871	871	878	883	894	901	909	909	921	931	933	934	939	933	943	949	971	982	980	976	984	984	994	993	992	980
1983																																																							
Jan	743	752	755	758	759	767	767	778	785	804	811	813	805	815	813	813	813	824	818	827	834	847	851	852	845	853	862	862	863	869	868	876	881	892	899	907	907	919	929	931	932	937	931	940	946	968	979	978	973	982	982	992	990	990	978
Feb	736	744	748	750	751	760	760	771	778	796	803	806	797	807	806	805	806	816	810	819	826	839	843	844	837	845	854	854	855	861	860	868	873	884	891	898	898	910	920	922	924	929	922	932	938	960	971	970	965	973	973	983	982	982	969
Mar	732	741	745	747	748	757	757	767	775	793	800	802	794	803	802	802	802	813	807	815	823	835	840	841	834	842	850	850	850	857	857	865	870	880	888	895	895	907	917	919	920	925	919	929	935	956	967	966	961	969	970	979	978	978	966
Apr	709	717	720	723	724	732	732	743	750	768	775	777	769	779	777	777	777	788	782	790	797	811	814	815	808	816	825	825	826	832	831	839	844	854	862	869	869	881	891	892	894	899	892	902	908	929	940	939	934	942	943	952	951	951	939
May	701	710	713	716	717	725	725	736	743	761	768	770	762	771	770	770	770	781	775	783	790	803	807	808	801	809	817	817	818	824	823	831	836	846	854	861	861	873	882	884	885	890	884	894	900	921	932	931	926	933	934	944	942	942	931
June	697	706	709	711	713	721	721	731	739	756	763	766	757	767	766	766	766	776	771	779	786	799	803	803	796	805	813	813	814	820	819	827	832	842	849	857	857	869	878	880	881	886	880	890	895	917	927	926	921	929	929	939	938	938	926
July	688	696	700	702	703	712	712	722	729	746	753	756	748	757	756	756	756	767	761	769	776	789	793	794	787	795	803	803	804	810	809	817	822	832	839	846	846	858	867	869	870	876	869	879	885	906	917	916	911	919	919	929	927	927	916
Aug	688	696	700	702	703	712	712	722	730	747	754	757	748	757	757	757	757	767	762	769	776	790	794	794	787	796	805	805	804	810	810	818	822	833	840	847	846	859	868	870	871	876	870	880	885	907	917	916	911	919	919	929	927	927	916
Sept	673	681	685	687	688	697	697	707	714	731	738	741	733	742	740	741	741	751	745	753	760	773	777	778	771	779	787	787	788	794	792	800	806	816	823	830	830	842	851	853	854	859	853	863	868	889	899	899	894	902	902	911	911	910	899
Oct	667	675	679	681	682	691	691	701	708	725	732	735	726	736	735	735	735	745	739	747	754	767	770	772	765	773	781	781	781	787	786	794	799	810	817	824	824	835	845	847	848	853	847	856	862	883	893	892	887	895	895	905	904	904	892
Nov	662	670	673	675	677	685	685	695	702	719	726	728	720	730	729	728	729	739	733	741	748	761	764	765	759	767	775	775	775	781	780	788	793	803	810	817	817	829	838	840	841	846	840	850	855	876	887	885	881	889	889	899	897	897	885
Dec	657	665	669	671	672	680	680	691	697	714	721	724	716	725	725	724	724	734	729	737	743	756	760	761	754	762	770	770	770	777	775	783	788	799	806	813	813	824	833	836	837	841	836	845	851	871	882	880	876	884	884	894	892	892	880
1984																																																							
Jan	658	666	670	672	673	681	681	692	698	716	723	725	717	726	726	725	725	735	730	738	745	757	761	762	755	763	772	772	772	778	778	786	789	800	807	814	814	825	834	837	838	842	837	846	852	872	883	882	877	885	885	894	893	893	882
Feb	651	659	663	665	666	674	674	685	692	709	716	718	710	719	719	718	718	728	722	731	737	750	753	755	748	756	763	763	764	771	771	778	782	792	799	806	806	818	827	829	830	835	829	838	844	865	875	874	869	877	877	886	885	885	874
Mar	646	654	658	660	661	669	669	679	686	703	710	712	704	714	713	712	712	723	717	725	732	744	748	749	742	750	758	758	759	765	765	772	776	787	794	800	800	812	821	823	824	829	823	832	838	859	869	868	863	871	871	880	879	879	868
Apr	624	632	636	638	639	647	647	657	664	681	688	690	682	691	691	690	690	700	694	702	709	721	725	726	719	727	735	735	736	742	742	749	753	763	770	777	777	788	797	799	800	805	799	808	814	834	844	843	839	847	847	856	855	855	843

43

Indexation allowance — continued

RD — Month of disposal

The table below gives the indexation allowance (per £1,000, expressed in whole units) by RI Base Month (rows) against Month of disposal (columns, years 1994–1999).

RI Base Month	1994 Jul	Aug	Sept	Oct	Nov	Dec	1995 Jan	Feb	Mar	Apr	May	June	July	Aug	Sept	Oct	Nov	Dec	1996 Jan	Feb	Mar	Apr	May	June	July	Aug	Sept	Oct	Nov	Dec	1997 Jan	Feb	Mar	Apr	May	June	July	Aug	Sept	Oct	Nov	Dec	1998 Jan	Feb	Mar	Apr	May	June	July	Aug	Sept	Oct	Nov	Dec	1999 Jan
1984 May	618	626	630	632	633	641	641	651	658	675	681	684	676	685	693	684	679	694	688	696	703	715	718	720	713	721	724	729	730	735	735	742	747	757	763	770	770	781	790	793	794	798	793	802	807	828	838	837	832	840	846	849	848	848	837
June	614	622	626	628	629	637	637	647	654	670	676	679	672	681	688	680	674	689	684	692	700	711	715	716	708	716	719	724	725	730	731	738	742	752	759	766	766	777	786	788	789	794	788	797	803	825	835	834	827	835	843	844	843	843	832
July	616	624	627	630	631	639	639	649	655	672	679	681	673	682	690	681	676	691	686	694	700	713	716	718	710	718	726	726	725	734	733	744	744	754	761	768	768	779	788	791	791	796	790	799	805	826	836	835	827	837	845	846	845	845	834
Aug	601	609	612	614	616	620	623	633	640	657	663	666	658	667	675	666	662	676	670	678	685	697	700	701	695	702	710	707	708	713	713	724	724	734	741	748	748	759	768	770	771	776	773	784	793	804	814	813	809	817	824	825	824	828	817
Sept	598	606	609	611	612	620	619	630	637	653	660	662	655	663	671	662	657	672	667	675	681	693	697	697	691	699	696	707	708	713	713	720	719	730	737	732	737	748	757	759	760	765	768	779	784	804	814	813	808	813	824	825	824	828	817
Oct	596	604	607	609	610	618	618	628	635	651	657	660	652	661	669	660	656	670	665	673	680	692	695	697	689	697	701	706	707	712	711	718	717	728	735	732	732	743	752	754	755	759	762	773	778	798	808	807	802	808	819	820	819	813	802
Nov	588	596	598	602	602	605	608	615	622	638	645	647	639	648	656	647	643	657	651	657	664	678	681	682	676	677	685	691	686	691	689	704	704	714	721	728	728	739	748	751	752	756	754	765	770	790	800	799	794	800	808	809	808	808	797
Dec	585	592	594	598	599	607	607	617	623	640	646	648	641	650	657	648	644	658	653	661	667	679	683	684	677	677	684	691	686	691	689	705	710	720	727	733	733	744	753	755	756	761	758	769	774	793	802	799	798	801	809	810	809	809	796
1985 Jan	579	587	590	592	593	601	601	611	617	634	640	642	635	642	651	642	638	652	647	654	661	673	676	678	671	678	686	686	687	693	683	699	704	714	720	727	727	738	747	749	750	754	749	758	763	783	793	792	787	795	803	804	803	803	792
Feb	566	574	577	579	580	588	588	598	604	621	627	629	622	630	638	629	625	639	634	641	648	660	663	664	657	665	673	673	674	680	679	686	690	700	707	713	713	724	733	735	736	740	744	749	749	769	778	777	773	781	788	789	788	788	777
Mar	552	559	562	565	566	573	573	583	589	606	612	614	607	615	623	614	611	624	619	626	633	644	648	649	642	650	657	657	658	664	664	675	680	690	691	697	697	708	717	719	720	724	727	733	733	752	762	761	756	764	772	772	772	761	724
Apr	519	527	530	532	533	540	540	550	556	572	578	581	573	582	589	581	578	591	578	585	591	603	606	607	600	608	615	615	616	618	610	627	629	638	644	648	648	658	667	669	669	673	676	681	684	716	725	724	720	727	734	735	735	735	724
May	512	520	522	525	526	530	533	543	549	566	571	573	566	574	582	573	570	583	574	581	587	599	602	603	597	605	608	612	613	618	610	623	627	637	644	651	651	661	670	672	673	677	674	685	690	708	717	716	712	719	727	723	722	723	716
June	509	517	519	521	522	530	529	539	545	560	566	569	561	570	578	569	566	579	577	585	591	603	606	607	601	608	615	611	612	617	611	623	632	637	648	654	654	664	673	673	674	676	670	671	673	707	716	716	713	716	723	722	722	713	709
July	512	519	521	523	524	532	532	542	548	565	570	573	566	574	582	573	570	582	577	584	591	602	606	607	600	608	615	612	613	618	612	623	627	637	644	651	651	662	671	673	674	677	676	677	684	703	712	716	713	716	723	723	722	722	711
Aug	508	515	519	521	522	529	529	540	543	560	566	569	561	570	577	569	565	579	573	580	587	598	602	603	596	604	611	610	613	618	615	628	632	641	648	651	651	665	672	672	673	677	664	680	684	707	717	716	707	714	722	723	722	726	716
Sept	509	521	519	521	522	530	530	539	546	561	567	570	561	570	578	570	567	579	574	581	587	599	602	603	597	605	612	611	613	618	617	623	627	637	644	648	648	661	670	672	673	676	671	682	687	704	713	712	708	715	723	724	723	722	711
Oct	506	519	521	522	520	530	530	537	543	559	565	567	560	568	575	567	562	577	571	579	585	596	600	601	594	603	610	611	612	617	615	622	626	635	641	648	648	658	667	669	670	674	676	677	682	702	711	710	705	713	720	721	720	720	709
Nov	501	514	519	519	515	527	527	532	538	552	560	562	554	563	570	562	559	571	566	573	579	591	594	595	589	596	603	604	604	610	610	616	620	630	634	642	642	652	661	663	664	666	660	671	676	696	705	704	699	707	714	714	714	714	704
Dec	499	512	513	515	520	530	530	532	536	551	558	560	554	561	568	560	556	569	564	571	577	589	591	593	584	594	601	602	602	606	608	616	618	627	634	640	640	650	661	662	660	666	659	671	674	696	702	701	697	704	712	713	712	712	701
1986 Jan	496	509	509	521	520	533	531	526	532	548	554	556	549	557	565	556	556	566	561	568	574	585	589	590	583	591	598	599	599	604	604	610	615	624	630	636	636	647	655	657	658	662	657	665	671	689	699	698	694	701	708	709	708	708	698
Feb	491	503	503	505	511	520	511	521	527	542	549	551	543	552	559	551	551	560	555	562	568	580	583	584	578	585	592	593	593	598	598	605	609	618	624	630	630	641	649	651	652	656	651	659	664	683	692	691	687	695	702	703	702	700	691
Mar	489	501	501	502	509	509	509	519	525	540	547	549	541	550	557	549	549	558	553	560	566	578	581	582	576	583	590	591	591	596	596	607	607	616	622	628	628	639	647	649	650	654	657	665	670	688	692	691	687	695	700	700	700	683	673
Apr	474	487	487	488	478	495	495	504	510	526	532	534	526	535	542	534	534	543	538	545	551	562	566	567	560	562	567	572	573	578	578	588	591	600	606	613	613	623	631	634	635	638	641	646	646	665	674	673	669	676	684	684	683	683	673
May	472	480	482	486	476	493	492	501	508	524	530	532	525	533	540	532	532	541	537	544	549	560	563	564	558	562	562	567	570	573	576	589	589	603	604	610	610	624	620	631	633	638	639	644	644	663	672	671	666	674	681	682	681	680	671
June	477	480	480	490	483	497	493	506	513	528	534	536	528	537	542	534	533	543	540	547	554	560	566	569	560	565	565	570	572	574	574	589	591	600	606	613	613	621	629	631	632	636	644	649	644	663	672	671	667	674	679	681	680	676	676
July	472	484	484	485	474	493	492	502	508	523	529	531	525	531	540	531	531	541	535	543	548	560	563	564	556	564	562	565	568	571	571	581	587	596	604	610	610	620	628	629	631	633	633	641	646	661	670	670	666	673	681	680	670	672	671
Aug	465	477	477	478	485	493	484	490	500	516	522	524	517	525	532	524	520	533	526	532	539	551	554	556	548	557	557	562	563	566	566	578	581	590	596	602	602	612	621	623	623	627	619	638	644	660	670	670	660	663	673	672	672	672	662
Sept	463	475	475	476	465	483	483	490	496	513	519	522	514	523	530	522	517	531	526	533	539	550	553	554	546	555	557	562	563	566	565	572	577	586	594	600	600	610	618	620	621	625	627	633	633	657	662	661	656	663	670	671	670	670	670
Oct	450	462	462	463	470	478	470	480	486	502	508	510	502	510	517	509	509	518	513	520	526	537	540	541	535	542	549	549	550	553	553	565	565	575	580	586	586	596	604	606	607	611	614	619	619	638	647	646	642	649	656	657	656	656	646
Nov	445	457	458	459	463	466	466	475	481	496	502	504	497	505	512	504	499	513	508	515	520	532	535	537	528	535	542	542	545	550	550	558	560	569	575	581	581	591	599	601	602	606	601	609	614	634	640	640	636	643	650	651	650	650	640
Dec	445	457	458	459	463	466	466	475	481	496	502	504	497	505	512	504	499	513	508	515	520	532	535	537	528	535	542	542	545	550	550	558	560	569	575	581	581	591	599	601	602	606	601	609	614	634	640	640	636	643	650	651	650	650	640
1987 Jan	440	452	453	453	460	460	460	469	475	490	496	498	490	499	506	498	493	507	502	509	515	526	529	530	524	531	538	538	539	544	544	554	554	563	569	575	575	585	593	595	596	600	603	608	608	627	635	634	630	637	644	645	644	644	634
Feb	434	446	444	447	454	454	454	463	469	484	490	492	485	493	500	492	487	501	496	503	509	520	523	524	518	525	532	532	533	538	538	548	548	557	563	569	569	579	587	589	590	594	597	603	598	620	628	627	624	630	637	638	637	637	627
Mar	431	443	441	444	451	451	451	460	466	481	487	489	482	490	497	489	484	498	493	500	506	517	520	521	515	522	529	529	530	535	535	545	545	554	560	566	566	576	581	583	590	590	593	598	598	616	625	624	620	627	634	635	634	624	624

44

Indexation allowance — continued

RI Base Month (rows) — values by month of disposal (columns).

RD base	1994 Jul	1994 Aug	1994 Sep	1994 Oct	1994 Nov	1994 Dec	1995 Jan	1995 Feb	1995 Mar	1995 Apr	1995 May	1995 Jun	1995 Jul	1995 Aug	1995 Sep	1995 Oct	1995 Nov	1995 Dec	1996 Jan	1996 Feb	1996 Mar	1996 Apr	1996 May	1996 Jun	1996 Jul	1996 Aug	1996 Sep	1996 Oct	1996 Nov	1996 Dec	1997 Jan	1997 Feb	1997 Mar	1997 Apr	1997 May	1997 Jun	1997 Jul	1997 Aug	1997 Sep	1997 Oct	1997 Nov	1997 Dec	1998 Jan	1998 Feb	1998 Mar	1998 Apr	1998 May	1998 Jun	1998 Jul	1998 Aug	1998 Sep	1998 Oct	1998 Nov	1998 Dec	1999 Jan
1987																																																							
Apr	394	401	404	406	407	413	413	422	428	442	448	450	451	451	458	450	450	459	454	461	467	477	480	481	475	482	479	472	472	479	475	482	488	499	502	503	497	504	511	511	512	517	517	523	527	535	541	547	547	557	565	567	568	572	567
May	389	395	398	400	401	408	408	417	422	437	443	445	446	446	452	445	445	453	448	455	461	472	474	475	470	476	473	466	466	473	470	476	482	493	496	497	491	498	506	505	506	511	511	517	521	529	535	541	541	551	559	561	562	566	561
June	383	390	393	394	396	402	402	411	417	431	437	438	440	440	447	439	439	448	443	450	455	466	469	470	464	471	464	460	461	467	464	470	475	487	490	491	485	492	500	499	500	505	505	511	515	523	528	535	535	544	553	555	556	560	555
July	361	367	371	372	373	380	380	389	394	409	414	416	417	417	423	416	416	424	420	426	432	443	446	447	440	442	439	433	434	440	437	443	449	460	463	464	458	465	473	472	473	478	478	484	489	507	508	509	511	517	524	525	525	529	524
Aug	357	363	365	367	369	375	375	383	389	398	409	411	412	406	413	404	404	414	399	416	421	432	434	435	428	436	429	425	426	431	431	437	442	453	456	457	450	458	464	463	465	470	470	476	480	488	493	499	500	508	517	518	519	524	518
Sept	350	357	360	361	363	368	368	377	383	396	402	404	405	405	411	404	404	412	408	414	419	430	433	434	428	435	428	424	425	431	427	433	438	449	453	454	448	455	463	462	463	467	467	473	478	485	491	497	498	506	514	515	516	520	514
Oct	344	350	352	354	355	361	361	369	374	387	392	394	395	395	401	394	394	402	398	404	410	421	423	424	418	419	412	408	408	414	410	416	421	432	435	436	430	437	445	444	445	450	450	456	460	468	473	479	481	489	497	498	498	503	497
Nov	335	341	344	346	347	353	353	361	367	375	386	388	389	383	390	381	382	390	375	393	398	409	411	412	406	407	400	396	397	402	401	407	413	423	426	427	421	428	434	433	435	439	439	445	449	457	462	468	469	477	485	486	487	491	485
Dec	328	333	335	337	338	344	344	352	358	369	375	377	379	379	384	377	377	385	382	388	393	403	406	407	402	408	401	397	398	404	400	406	411	421	424	425	419	426	432	431	433	437	437	443	447	455	460	466	467	475	483	484	485	489	483
1988																																																							
Jan	315	324	327	328	329	336	336	344	349	363	368	370	371	371	377	370	370	378	374	380	385	396	398	399	393	400	393	389	390	396	392	398	403	414	417	418	412	419	425	425	426	431	431	436	441	448	454	459	460	468	476	477	478	482	476
Feb	306	312	315	316	317	324	324	332	337	351	356	358	359	359	365	358	358	366	362	368	374	384	387	388	382	389	382	378	378	384	380	386	392	402	405	406	400	407	413	412	414	418	418	424	428	436	441	447	448	456	464	465	466	470	464
Mar	300	306	309	310	311	317	317	325	330	344	349	351	352	352	358	351	351	359	355	361	367	377	380	381	375	382	375	371	372	377	374	380	384	395	398	399	393	400	405	405	406	410	410	416	420	428	433	439	440	448	455	456	457	461	455
Apr	289	295	297	299	300	306	306	314	319	332	337	339	340	340	346	339	339	347	343	349	355	365	367	368	363	369	362	358	359	365	365	390	390	398	400	402	396	396	402	401	403	407	407	413	417	421	426	432	432	440	447	448	449	453	448
May	283	289	291	293	294	300	300	308	313	327	332	333	335	335	341	334	334	342	338	344	349	359	362	363	357	363	357	353	353	359	356	380	380	388	391	392	386	387	393	391	393	397	397	402	407	414	420	426	426	434	442	443	444	448	442
June	280	286	289	291	292	298	298	305	310	324	329	331	333	333	339	332	332	340	336	342	348	357	360	361	355	362	355	351	352	357	353	377	377	385	388	389	384	384	389	388	390	395	395	400	404	411	417	423	423	431	439	440	441	445	439
July	277	283	286	288	289	295	295	303	308	322	327	328	330	330	336	329	329	337	333	339	345	355	357	358	352	359	352	348	349	354	351	375	375	382	385	386	380	381	386	385	387	391	391	397	401	408	414	420	420	428	435	436	437	441	435
Aug	271	276	278	280	282	288	288	296	301	314	319	321	322	322	328	321	321	329	325	331	337	347	349	350	344	351	344	340	340	346	342	366	366	374	376	378	372	373	378	377	378	382	382	388	392	399	405	411	411	419	426	427	428	432	426
Sept	265	271	273	275	276	283	283	291	296	309	314	316	317	317	323	316	316	324	320	326	332	341	344	345	339	346	339	335	336	341	339	363	363	370	373	374	368	369	374	373	375	379	379	384	389	396	402	408	408	416	423	424	425	429	423
Oct	259	265	267	269	270	277	277	285	289	303	308	309	311	311	316	309	310	318	314	320	325	335	338	339	333	340	333	329	330	335	332	356	356	364	366	367	361	362	367	366	368	372	372	377	382	389	394	400	400	408	415	416	417	421	415
Nov	257	262	264	266	271	277	277	285	289	302	308	309	310	310	316	309	310	318	314	320	325	335	338	339	333	340	333	329	330	335	332	356	356	363	366	367	361	362	367	366	368	372	372	377	382	389	394	400	400	408	414	415	416	420	415
Dec	254	259	261	263	264	269	264	270	275	285	287	288	283	289	288	281	280	285	285	287	293	300	300	308	316	326	333	334	336	341	342	347	351	359	360	360	353	359	367	367	370	375	375	381	385	391	397	403	403	411	417	418	420	424	416
1989																																																							
Jan	306	304	306	308	309	315	315	323	329	342	348	350	350	350	357	350	350	358	353	359	365	375	377	378	373	379	372	369	368	375	372	396	396	400	414	419	419	428	435	437	438	441	441	444	449	465	473	472	468	475	481	482	481	472	472
Feb	297	294	297	299	300	306	306	314	319	333	338	340	341	341	347	340	340	348	343	350	355	365	367	369	363	364	357	354	354	360	386	386	390	398	409	409	402	418	425	427	429	431	396	434	438	454	462	462	458	464	470	471	470	462	455
Mar	291	289	291	293	294	300	300	308	313	327	332	333	335	335	341	334	334	342	337	344	349	359	362	363	357	363	341	348	349	355	380	380	384	392	402	402	396	411	419	421	423	425	432	438	432	448	456	455	451	458	464	465	464	455	455
Apr	283	280	283	283	294	300	300	314	289	296	301	311	303	303	310	318	318	311	312	317	313	325	325	326	319	326	319	315	317	321	308	320	317	335	351	360	378	378	384	376	370	409	401	401	408	423	420	416	416	411	414	420	421	430	421
May	266	266	269	270	271	277	264	286	290	296	301	311	303	303	310	298	298	306	312	317	313	327	324	326	319	303	304	301	303	306	314	320	317	359	360	365	378	378	384	377	353	401	401	401	402	420	416	421	411	413	414	420	430	430	421
June	258	256	258	258	269	264	264	273	278	296	298	298	298	299	305	292	291	298	304	309	318	322	326	319	319	313	307	307	310	306	306	311	317	354	351	360	365	378	378	367	370	376	401	391	391	420	412	416	416	411	413	414	430	430	421
July	254	252	254	255	256	264	261	269	274	287	292	294	294	294	300	294	294	301	297	303	308	318	320	321	316	322	316	312	313	319	324	345	345	353	356	360	351	363	376	380	350	391	391	398	402	409	411	416	407	414	420	421	420	410	411
Aug	250	250	252	254	255	261	258	266	271	281	283	285	285	286	292	285	285	292	288	294	299	309	311	312	307	313	306	303	304	310	310	339	333	342	346	351	345	356	349	357	347	389	389	381	381	404	404	407	407	410	410	420	420	411	411
Sept	244	244	244	246	246	252	249	257	262	272	274	276	276	271	276	271	271	276	273	278	283	292	295	296	290	294	288	285	285	292	292	329	333	335	340	347	340	356	349	357	347	350	389	381	381	393	401	401	402	405	411	420	420	411	411
Oct	231	234	236	237	238	243	243	245	250	256	258	259	255	261	265	264	264	269	273	273	278	285	287	288	283	289	282	278	285	292	292	329	333	335	340	347	340	322	340	337	347	350	389	381	360	370	401	401	276	280	286	298	298	288	288
Nov	224	231	236	225	237	232	232	240	245	257	245	257	247	254	271	259	264	272	270	276	260	277	272	270	288	253	271	278	285	303	299	311	311	319	326	329	288	289	344	337	347	350	389	346	357	363	354	341	281	280	286	287	280	285	259
Dec	218	221	223	223	223	229	229	232	237	254	259	261	255	262	255	246	246	254	264	270	275	285	287	288	283	274	280	269	295	306	300	305	308	316	321	326	283	289	295	280	295	292	362	372	389	375	263	269	274	282	288	290	285	285	359
1990																																																							
Jan	211	213	215	215	216	222	222	229	234	247	252	254	248	254	260	254	254	261	257	263	268	277	279	280	275	281	274	275	279	291	292	297	300	308	313	318	311	326	333	335	336	339	335	341	346	361	368	367	364	370	376	377	376	376	367
Feb	198	206	208	209	211	215	215	222	227	240	245	246	247	253	246	246	254	254	250	255	260	270	272	273	268	274	266	280	280	285	285	290	293	300	305	310	319	319	325	327	328	331	327	334	338	353	360	359	356	362	368	369	368	359	359

45

Indexation allowance — continued

RD — Month of disposal

RI Base Month

	1994						1995											
1990	July	Aug	Sept	Oct	Nov	Dec	Jan	Feb	Mar	Apr	May	June	July	Aug	Sept	Oct	Nov	Dec
Mar	·186	·192	·194	·196	·197	·203	·203	·210	·215	·227	·232	·234	·228	·235	·241	·234	·234	·241
Apr	·151	·157	·159	·161	·161	·167	·167	·174	·179	·191	·196	·197	·192	·198	·204	·197	·197	·205
May	·141	·147	·149	·151	·151	·157	·157	·164	·169	·181	·185	·187	·181	·188	·193	·187	·187	·194
June	·137	·142	·144	·146	·147	·152	·152	·159	·164	·176	·181	·182	·177	·183	·189	·182	·182	·189
July	·136	·141	·144	·145	·146	·151	·151	·159	·163	·175	·180	·181	·176	·182	·188	·181	·181	·188
Aug	·124	·130	·132	·133	·134	·140	·140	·147	·151	·163	·168	·169	·164	·170	·176	·169	·169	·176
Sept	·114	·119	·121	·123	·124	·129	·129	·136	·141	·152	·157	·159	·153	·159	·165	·159	·159	·166
Oct	·105	·111	·113	·114	·115	·120	·120	·127	·132	·144	·148	·150	·144	·150	·156	·150	·150	·157
Nov	·108	·113	·115	·117	·118	·123	·123	·130	·135	·146	·151	·152	·147	·153	·158	·152	·152	·159
Dec	·109	·114	·116	·118	·119	·124	·124	·131	·135	·147	·152	·153	·148	·154	·159	·153	·153	·160
1991																		
Jan	·106	·111	·114	·115	·116	·121	·121	·128	·133	·144	·149	·151	·145	·151	·157	·151	·151	·157
Feb	·100	·105	·108	·109	·110	·115	·115	·122	·127	·138	·143	·144	·139	·145	·150	·144	·144	·151
Mar	·096	·101	·104	·105	·106	·111	·111	·118	·123	·134	·139	·140	·135	·141	·146	·140	·140	·147
Apr	·082	·087	·089	·091	·092	·097	·097	·104	·108	·119	·124	·125	·120	·126	·131	·125	·125	·132
May	·079	·084	·086	·088	·088	·094	·094	·100	·105	·116	·121	·122	·117	·123	·128	·122	·122	·129
June	·074	·079	·081	·083	·084	·089	·089	·095	·100	·111	·116	·117	·112	·118	·123	·117	·117	·124
July	·076	·081	·084	·085	·086	·091	·091	·098	·102	·114	·118	·120	·114	·120	·126	·120	·120	·126
Aug	·074	·079	·081	·083	·084	·089	·089	·095	·100	·111	·116	·117	·112	·118	·123	·117	·117	·124
Sept	·070	·075	·077	·079	·079	·085	·085	·091	·096	·107	·111	·113	·108	·114	·119	·113	·113	·120
Oct	·066	·071	·073	·075	·075	·081	·081	·087	·092	·103	·107	·109	·104	·110	·115	·109	·109	·115
Nov	·062	·067	·069	·071	·072	·077	·077	·083	·088	·099	·103	·105	·100	·105	·111	·105	·105	·111
Dec	·061	·066	·069	·070	·071	·076	·076	·083	·087	·098	·102	·104	·099	·105	·110	·104	·104	·111
1992																		
Jan	·062	·067	·069	·071	·072	·077	·077	·083	·088	·099	·103	·105	·100	·105	·111	·105	·105	·111
Feb	·056	·062	·064	·065	·066	·071	·071	·078	·082	·093	·098	·099	·094	·100	·105	·099	·099	·106
Mar	·053	·059	·061	·062	·063	·068	·068	·075	·079	·090	·094	·096	·091	·097	·102	·096	·096	·102
Apr	·037	·043	·045	·046	·047	·052	·052	·058	·063	·073	·078	·079	·074	·080	·085	·079	·079	·086
May	·034	·039	·041	·042	·043	·048	·048	·055	·059	·070	·074	·075	·070	·076	·081	·075	·075	·082
June	·034	·039	·041	·042	·043	·048	·048	·055	·059	·070	·074	·075	·070	·076	·081	·075	·075	·082
July	·037	·043	·045	·046	·047	·052	·052	·058	·063	·073	·078	·079	·074	·080	·085	·079	·079	·086
Aug	·037	·042	·044	·045	·046	·051	·051	·058	·062	·073	·077	·078	·073	·079	·084	·078	·078	·085
Sept	·033	·038	·040	·042	·042	·047	·047	·054	·058	·069	·073	·075	·070	·075	·080	·075	·075	·081
Oct	·029	·034	·036	·038	·039	·044	·044	·050	·054	·065	·069	·071	·066	·071	·076	·071	·071	·077
Nov	·031	·036	·038	·039	·040	·045	·045	·052	·056	·067	·071	·072	·067	·073	·078	·072	·072	·079
Dec	·034	·040	·042	·043	·044	·049	·049	·055	·060	·070	·075	·076	·071	·077	·082	·076	·076	·083
1993																		
Jan	·044	·049	·051	·053	·054	·059	·059	·065	·070	·080	·085	·086	·081	·087	·092	·086	·086	·093

	1996											
1990	Jan	Feb	Mar	Apr	May	June	July	Aug	Sept	Oct	Nov	Dec
Mar	·237	·243	·248	·257	·259	·260	·255	·261	·267	·267	·268	·272
Apr	·201	·206	·211	·220	·222	·223	·218	·224	·229	·229	·230	·234
May	·190	·196	·200	·209	·212	·212	·208	·213	·219	·219	·219	·223
June	·185	·191	·196	·204	·207	·208	·203	·208	·214	·214	·215	·219
July	·185	·190	·195	·203	·206	·207	·202	·207	·213	·213	·214	·218
Aug	·173	·178	·183	·191	·194	·194	·190	·195	·201	·201	·201	·205
Sept	·162	·167	·172	·180	·183	·183	·179	·184	·189	·189	·190	·194
Oct	·153	·158	·163	·171	·173	·174	·170	·175	·180	·180	·181	·185
Nov	·155	·161	·165	·174	·176	·177	·172	·178	·183	·183	·184	·188
Dec	·156	·162	·166	·175	·177	·178	·173	·179	·184	·184	·185	·189
1991												
Jan	·154	·159	·164	·172	·174	·175	·171	·176	·181	·181	·182	·186
Feb	·147	·153	·157	·166	·168	·169	·164	·170	·175	·175	·176	·180
Mar	·143	·148	·153	·161	·164	·164	·160	·165	·170	·170	·171	·175
Apr	·128	·134	·138	·147	·149	·150	·145	·150	·156	·156	·156	·160
May	·125	·130	·135	·143	·145	·146	·142	·147	·152	·152	·153	·157
June	·120	·125	·130	·138	·140	·141	·136	·142	·147	·147	·148	·151
July	·123	·128	·132	·141	·143	·143	·139	·144	·149	·149	·150	·154
Aug	·120	·125	·130	·138	·140	·141	·136	·142	·147	·147	·148	·151
Sept	·116	·121	·126	·134	·136	·137	·132	·137	·143	·143	·143	·147
Oct	·112	·117	·121	·130	·132	·132	·128	·133	·138	·138	·139	·143
Nov	·108	·113	·117	·125	·128	·128	·124	·129	·134	·134	·135	·139
Dec	·107	·112	·116	·125	·127	·127	·123	·128	·133	·133	·134	·138
1992												
Jan	·108	·113	·117	·125	·128	·128	·124	·129	·134	·134	·135	·139
Feb	·102	·107	·112	·120	·122	·123	·118	·123	·128	·128	·129	·133
Mar	·099	·104	·108	·116	·119	·119	·115	·120	·125	·125	·126	·129
Apr	·082	·087	·091	·099	·102	·102	·098	·103	·108	·108	·109	·112
May	·078	·083	·088	·095	·098	·098	·094	·099	·104	·104	·105	·108
June	·078	·083	·088	·095	·098	·098	·094	·099	·104	·104	·105	·108
July	·082	·087	·091	·099	·102	·102	·098	·103	·108	·108	·109	·112
Aug	·081	·086	·091	·099	·101	·102	·097	·102	·107	·107	·108	·112
Sept	·077	·082	·087	·095	·097	·098	·093	·098	·103	·103	·104	·108
Oct	·074	·079	·083	·091	·093	·094	·089	·094	·099	·099	·100	·104
Nov	·075	·080	·084	·092	·094	·095	·091	·096	·101	·101	·102	·105
Dec	·079	·084	·088	·096	·098	·099	·095	·100	·105	·105	·106	·109
1993												
Jan	·089	·094	·099	·107	·109	·109	·105	·110	·115	·115	·116	·120

	1997											
1990	Jan	Feb	Mar	Apr	May	June	July	Aug	Sept	Oct	Nov	Dec
Mar	·272	·277	·280	·287	·292	·297	·297	·306	·312	·314	·315	·318
Apr	·234	·239	·242	·249	·254	·259	·259	·267	·273	·275	·276	·279
May	·223	·228	·231	·239	·243	·248	·248	·256	·262	·264	·265	·268
June	·219	·223	·227	·234	·238	·243	·243	·251	·257	·259	·260	·263
July	·218	·222	·226	·233	·237	·242	·242	·250	·256	·258	·259	·262
Aug	·205	·210	·213	·220	·225	·230	·230	·237	·244	·245	·246	·249
Sept	·194	·199	·202	·209	·213	·218	·218	·226	·232	·234	·234	·237
Oct	·185	·190	·193	·200	·204	·209	·209	·216	·223	·224	·225	·228
Nov	·188	·192	·195	·202	·207	·212	·212	·219	·225	·227	·228	·231
Dec	·189	·193	·196	·203	·208	·212	·212	·220	·226	·228	·229	·232
1991												
Jan	·186	·190	·194	·200	·205	·210	·210	·217	·224	·225	·226	·229
Feb	·180	·184	·187	·194	·199	·203	·203	·211	·217	·218	·219	·222
Mar	·175	·180	·183	·189	·194	·199	·199	·206	·212	·214	·215	·218
Apr	·160	·165	·168	·174	·179	·183	·183	·191	·197	·198	·199	·202
May	·157	·161	·164	·171	·175	·180	·180	·187	·193	·195	·196	·199
June	·151	·156	·159	·166	·170	·174	·174	·182	·188	·189	·190	·193
July	·154	·158	·161	·168	·173	·177	·177	·185	·191	·192	·193	·196
Aug	·151	·156	·159	·166	·170	·174	·174	·182	·188	·189	·190	·193
Sept	·147	·152	·155	·161	·166	·170	·170	·178	·184	·185	·186	·189
Oct	·143	·147	·150	·157	·161	·166	·166	·173	·179	·181	·181	·184
Nov	·139	·143	·146	·153	·157	·162	·162	·169	·175	·176	·177	·180
Dec	·138	·142	·145	·152	·156	·161	·161	·168	·174	·175	·176	·179
1992												
Jan	·139	·143	·146	·153	·157	·162	·162	·169	·175	·176	·177	·180
Feb	·133	·137	·140	·147	·151	·156	·156	·163	·169	·170	·171	·174
Mar	·129	·134	·137	·143	·148	·152	·152	·159	·165	·167	·168	·170
Apr	·112	·117	·120	·126	·130	·135	·135	·142	·148	·149	·150	·153
May	·108	·113	·116	·122	·126	·131	·131	·138	·144	·145	·146	·149
June	·108	·113	·116	·122	·126	·131	·131	·138	·144	·145	·146	·149
July	·112	·117	·120	·126	·130	·135	·135	·142	·148	·149	·150	·153
Aug	·112	·116	·119	·125	·130	·134	·134	·141	·147	·148	·149	·152
Sept	·108	·112	·115	·121	·126	·130	·130	·137	·143	·144	·145	·148
Oct	·104	·108	·111	·117	·122	·126	·126	·133	·139	·140	·141	·144
Nov	·105	·110	·112	·119	·123	·127	·127	·135	·140	·142	·142	·145
Dec	·109	·114	·116	·123	·127	·131	·131	·139	·144	·146	·147	·149
1993												
Jan	·120	·124	·127	·133	·138	·142	·142	·149	·155	·157	·157	·160

	1998												1999
1990	Jan	Feb	Mar	Apr	May	June	July	Aug	Sept	Oct	Nov	Dec	Jan
Mar	·314	·320	·325	·339	·347	·346	·343	·348	·354	·355	·354	·354	·346
Apr	·275	·281	·285	·300	·307	·306	·303	·309	·314	·315	·314	·314	·306
May	·264	·270	·274	·288	·296	·295	·292	·297	·303	·303	·303	·303	·295
June	·259	·265	·269	·283	·290	·290	·287	·292	·298	·298	·298	·298	·290
July	·258	·264	·268	·282	·289	·289	·285	·291	·297	·297	·297	·297	·289
Aug	·245	·251	·255	·269	·276	·276	·272	·278	·283	·284	·283	·283	·276
Sept	·234	·240	·244	·258	·265	·264	·261	·266	·271	·272	·271	·271	·264
Oct	·224	·230	·234	·248	·255	·254	·251	·256	·262	·262	·262	·262	·254
Nov	·227	·233	·237	·251	·258	·257	·254	·259	·265	·265	·265	·265	·257
Dec	·228	·234	·238	·252	·259	·258	·255	·260	·266	·266	·266	·266	·258
1991													
Jan	·225	·231	·235	·249	·256	·255	·252	·257	·263	·263	·263	·263	·255
Feb	·218	·225	·228	·242	·249	·248	·245	·251	·256	·257	·256	·256	·248
Mar	·214	·220	·224	·237	·244	·244	·240	·246	·251	·252	·251	·251	·244
Apr	·198	·204	·208	·222	·228	·228	·225	·230	·235	·236	·235	·235	·228
May	·195	·201	·204	·218	·225	·224	·221	·226	·231	·232	·231	·231	·224
June	·189	·195	·199	·213	·219	·218	·216	·221	·226	·227	·226	·226	·218
July	·192	·198	·202	·215	·222	·221	·218	·223	·229	·229	·229	·229	·221
Aug	·189	·195	·199	·213	·219	·218	·216	·221	·226	·227	·226	·226	·218
Sept	·185	·191	·195	·208	·215	·214	·211	·216	·221	·222	·221	·221	·214
Oct	·181	·187	·190	·204	·210	·209	·207	·212	·217	·218	·217	·217	·209
Nov	·176	·182	·186	·199	·206	·205	·202	·207	·212	·213	·212	·212	·205
Dec	·175	·181	·185	·198	·205	·204	·201	·206	·211	·212	·211	·211	·204
1992													
Jan	·176	·182	·186	·199	·206	·205	·202	·207	·212	·213	·212	·212	·205
Feb	·170	·176	·180	·193	·200	·199	·196	·201	·206	·207	·206	·206	·199
Mar	·167	·173	·176	·189	·196	·195	·192	·198	·203	·203	·203	·203	·195
Apr	·149	·155	·159	·171	·178	·177	·174	·179	·184	·185	·184	·184	·177
May	·145	·151	·154	·167	·174	·173	·170	·175	·180	·181	·180	·180	·173
June	·145	·151	·154	·167	·174	·173	·170	·175	·180	·181	·180	·180	·173
July	·149	·155	·159	·171	·178	·177	·174	·179	·184	·185	·184	·184	·177
Aug	·148	·154	·158	·171	·177	·176	·174	·179	·184	·184	·184	·184	·176
Sept	·144	·150	·154	·166	·173	·172	·169	·174	·179	·180	·179	·179	·172
Oct	·140	·146	·149	·162	·169	·168	·165	·170	·175	·176	·175	·175	·168
Nov	·142	·147	·151	·164	·170	·170	·167	·172	·177	·178	·177	·177	·170
Dec	·146	·152	·155	·168	·175	·174	·171	·176	·181	·182	·181	·181	·174
1993													
Jan	·157	·162	·166	·179	·186	·185	·182	·187	·192	·193	·192	·192	·185

Indexation allowance — continued

RD — Month of disposal

RD Base Month	1999 Jan	1998 Dec	Nov	Oct	Sept	Aug	July	June	May	Apr	Mar	Feb	Jan	1997 Dec	Nov	Oct	Sept	Aug	July	June	May	Apr	Mar	Feb	Jan	1996 Dec	Nov	Oct	Sept	Aug	July	June	May	Apr	Mar	Feb	Jan	1995 Dec	Nov	Oct	Sept	Aug	July	June	May	Apr	Mar	Feb	Jan	1994 Dec	Nov	Oct	Sept	Aug	July
1993 Feb	·177	·184	·184	·185	·184	·179	·174	·177	·178	·171	·159	·155	·149	·153	·150	·148	·144	·142	·135	·135	·130	·126	·120	·117	·112	·112	·109	·108	·108	·103	·098	·102	·102	·099	·091	·087	·082	·086	·079	·075	·085	·080	·074	·079	·078	·073	·063	·058	·052	·052	·047	·046	·045	·043	·037
Mar	·173	·180	·180	·181	·180	·175	·170	·173	·174	·167	·154	·151	·145	·149	·146	·145	·144	·138	·131	·131	·126	·122	·116	·113	·108	·108	·105	·104	·104	·099	·094	·098	·098	·095	·088	·083	·078	·082	·075	·071	·081	·076	·070	·075	·074	·070	·059	·055	·048	·048	·043	·042	·041	·039	·034
Apr	·162	·169	·169	·170	·169	·164	·159	·162	·163	·156	·144	·140	·134	·138	·135	·134	·133	·127	·120	·120	·116	·115	·105	·102	·098	·098	·095	·094	·094	·090	·084	·088	·087	·085	·078	·073	·068	·072	·065	·065	·071	·066	·060	·065	·064	·060	·049	·045	·038	·038	·033	·033	·031	·029	·024
May	·158	·165	·165	·166	·165	·160	·155	·158	·159	·152	·140	·136	·130	·134	·131	·130	·129	·123	·116	·116	·112	·111	·101	·099	·094	·094	·091	·090	·090	·085	·080	·084	·084	·082	·074	·069	·065	·068	·062	·062	·067	·063	·057	·062	·060	·056	·045	·041	·035	·035	·030	·029	·028	·026	·021
June	·159	·166	·166	·167	·166	·161	·156	·159	·160	·153	·140	·137	·131	·135	·132	·131	·130	·124	·117	·117	·113	·112	·102	·099	·095	·095	·091	·091	·091	·086	·081	·085	·085	·082	·074	·070	·066	·069	·062	·062	·067	·063	·057	·062	·061	·057	·046	·042	·035	·033	·030	·029	·028	·026	·015
July	·161	·168	·168	·169	·168	·163	·158	·161	·160	·151	·143	·139	·137	·137	·134	·134	·132	·127	·115	·111	·115	·117	·100	·097	·097	·088	·087	·086	·091	·081	·074	·083	·078	·075	·074	·072	·068	·061	·058	·060	·066	·063	·057	·062	·063	·057	·050	·047	·041	·042	·042	·037	·036	·028	·017
Aug	·161	·168	·168	·169	·168	·163	·163	·161	·157	·151	·143	·139	·134	·128	·130	·131	·132	·124	·117	·119	·115	·117	·100	·097	·097	·088	·094	·093	·093	·084	·083	·079	·081	·075	·077	·072	·068	·061	·058	·060	·065	·063	·056	·061	·059	·054	·044	·040	·034	·033	·033	·028	·031	·020	—
Sept	·156	·163	·163	·164	·163	·163	·158	·156	·157	·151	·133	·134	·124	·128	·130	·124	·127	·117	·110	·110	·106	·101	·095	·092	·088	·085	·084	·084	·084	·079	·074	·078	·078	·075	·068	·063	·059	·064	·056	·056	·066	·061	·055	·056	·054	·050	·039	·035	·029	·029	·024	·023	·023	·018	—
Oct	·152	·159	·163	·160	·159	·154	·150	·156	·153	·146	·133	·130	·125	·129	·126	·125	·123	·118	·111	·115	·109	·108	·096	·093	·089	·089	·086	·085	·085	·080	·075	·079	·080	·076	·070	·064	·061	·064	·056	·056	·064	·056	·051	·058	·055	·052	·040	·037	·031	·030	·025	·024	·023	·020	—
Nov	·152	·159	·161	·162	·161	·156	·151	·154	·155	·148	·136	·132	·126	·130	·127	·126	·125	·119	·112	·112	·108	·107	·097	·095	·090	·090	·087	·086	·086	·081	·076	·081	·080	·078	·070	·066	·061	·064	·058	·058	·060	·056	·051	·058	·056	·052	·042	·037	·031	·029	·025	·023	·024	·022	—
Dec	·154	·159	·159	·159	·159	·154	·149	·152	·152	·146	·133	·130	·124	·128	·125	·124	·123	·117	·110	·110	·110	·101	·095	·094	·089	·089	·087	·086	·085	·079	·074	·078	·078	·075	·068	·063	·058	·061	·058	·058	·061	·056	·051	·058	·054	·054	·042	·037	·031	·024	·024	·023	·022	·020	·015
1994 Jan	·152	·156	—	—	—	—	—	—	—	—	—	—	—	·129	·122	·119	·106	·102	·102	·108	·102	·098	·096	·092	·093	·082	·078	·068	·065	·065	·063	·068	·062	·059	·061	·058	·054	·033	·027	·025	·012	·009	·009	·014	·008	·005	·005	·000	·000	—	—	—	—	—	—
Feb	·156	·150	—	—	—	—	—	—	—	—	—	—	—	·134	·128	·125	·112	·108	·108	·113	·106	·104	·103	·098	·087	·083	·073	·070	·070	·067	·076	·071	·067	·069	·064	·055	·051	·040	·034	·031	·019	·015	·013	·009	·013	·012	·006	·000	—	—	—	—	—	—	—
Mar	·150	·147	—	—	—	—	—	—	—	—	—	—	—	·138	·128	·118	·115	·111	·111	·117	·109	·107	·107	·101	·091	·088	·078	·074	·074	·072	·066	·063	·051	·047	·042	·037	·037	·035	·027	·023	·019	·015	·019	·017	·010	·004	—	—	—	—	—	—	—	—	—
Apr	·147	·133	—	—	—	—	—	—	—	—	—	—	—	·128	·115	·106	·102	·095	·088	·088	·084	·080	·078	·075	·069	·071	·067	·058	·044	·042	·057	·053	·050	·058	·051	·046	·042	·033	·026	·016	·006	·005	·000	—	·000	—	—	—	—	—	—	—	—	—	—
May	·133	·129	—	—	—	—	—	—	—	—	—	—	—	·124	·111	·102	·099	·093	·086	·089	·082	·076	·074	·071	·067	·064	·061	·054	·040	·038	·033	·033	·034	·030	·027	·023	·022	·028	·020	·010	·000	·000	—	—	—	—	—	—	—	—	—	—	—	—	—
June	·129	·129	—	—	—	—	—	—	—	—	—	—	—	·124	·111	·103	·100	·095	·088	·089	·081	·076	·074	·072	·068	·063	·060	·053	·039	·037	·033	·033	·030	·028	·026	·022	·021	·022	·020	·012	·000	—	—	—	—	—	—	—	—	—	—	—	—	—	—
July	·135	·129	—	—	—	—	—	—	—	—	—	—	—	·119	·106	·099	·091	·085	·086	·088	·080	·076	·072	·070	·067	·063	·059	·052	·038	·041	·035	·034	·035	·031	·028	·027	·017	·025	·017	·005	·000	—	—	—	—	—	—	—	—	—	—	—	—	—	—
Aug	·127	·135	—	—	—	—	—	—	—	—	—	—	—	·117	·104	·096	·093	·094	·085	·084	·081	·077	·072	·069	·067	·064	·061	·058	·037	·035	·041	·040	·035	·035	·031	·027	·021	·017	·017	·010	·000	—	—	—	—	—	—	—	—	—	—	—	—	—	—
Sept	·125	·127	—	—	—	—	—	—	—	—	—	—	—	·110	·102	·098	·084	·084	·084	·084	·077	·070	·070	·067	·063	·056	·056	·056	·039	·033	·031	·030	·027	·022	·017	·011	·022	·017	—	—	—	—	—	—	—	—	—	—	—	—	—	—	—	—	—
Oct	·125	·125	—	—	—	—	—	—	—	—	—	—	—	·110	·098	·092	·086	·086	·084	·084	·080	·076	·073	·073	·068	·064	·060	·056	·035	·032	·031	·031	·021	·019	·011	·005	·022	·017	—	—	—	—	—	—	—	—	—	—	—	—	—	—	—	—	—
Dec	·119	·116	—	—	—	—	—	—	—	—	—	—	—	·096	·093	·092	·085	·086	·079	·079	·075	·071	·067	·064	·058	·058	·054	·049	·025	·016	·025	·022	·018	·013	·005	·001	·000	·016	—	—	—	—	—	—	—	—	—	—	—	—	—	—	—	—	—
1995 Jan	·119	·119	—	—	—	—	—	—	—	—	—	—	—	·092	·081	·070	·066	·065	·058	·057	·051	·047	·036	·031	·029	·029	·022	·018	·008	·004	·003	·007	·002	·007	·003	·003	·000	—	—	—	—	—	—	—	—	—	—	—	—	—	—	—	—	—	—
Feb	·112	·110	—	—	—	—	—	—	—	—	—	—	—	·085	·076	·072	·055	·051	·046	·044	·035	·029	·024	·023	·022	·017	·012	·007	—	—	·006	—	—	·006	—	—	—	—	—	—	—	—	—	—	—	—	—	—	—	—	—	—	—	—	—
Mar	·108	·105	—	—	—	—	—	—	—	—	—	—	—	·081	·070	·065	·054	·046	·043	·038	·035	·031	·027	·011	·007	·011	·007	·001	—	—	·010	·004	—	—	—	—	—	—	—	—	—	—	—	—	—	—	—	—	—	—	—	—	—	—	—	—
Apr	·097	·097	—	—	—	—	—	—	—	—	—	—	—	·064	·064	·060	·043	·042	·037	·036	·032	·027	·016	·011	·008	·005	·001	—	—	—	—	—	—	—	—	—	—	—	—	—	—	—	—	—	—	—	—	—	—	—	—	—	—	—	—
May	·092	·092	—	—	—	—	—	—	—	—	—	—	—	·065	·069	·056	·042	·037	·034	·029	·027	·022	·011	·005	·003	—	—	—	—	—	—	—	—	—	—	—	—	—	—	—	—	—	—	—	—	—	—	—	—	—	—	—	—	—	—	—
June	·091	·091	—	—	—	—	—	—	—	—	—	—	—	·051	·051	·051	·047	·043	·038	·017	·017	·017	·011	·005	·003	—	—	—	—	—	—	—	—	—	—	—	—	—	—	—	—	—	—	—	—	—	—	—	—	—	—	—	—	—	—	—
July	·096	·103	—	—	—	—	—	—	—	—	—	—	—	·073	·078	·065	·051	·046	·043	·038	·035	·031	·020	·015	·012	—	—	—	—	—	—	—	—	—	—	—	—	—	—	—	—	—	—	—	—	—	—	—	—	—	—	—	—	—	—	—
Aug	·090	·097	—	—	—	—	—	—	—	—	—	—	—	·070	·072	·059	·046	·041	·038	·032	·030	·026	·016	·011	·008	—	—	—	—	—	—	—	—	—	—	—	—	—	—	—	—	—	—	—	—	—	—	—	—	—	—	—	—	—	—	—
Sept	·085	·091	—	—	—	—	—	—	—	—	—	—	—	·065	·067	·065	·051	·046	·043	·037	·034	·030	·020	·014	·011	—	—	—	—	—	—	—	—	—	—	—	—	—	—	—	—	—	—	—	—	—	—	—	—	—	—	—	—	—	—	—
Oct	·091	·097	—	—	—	—	—	—	—	—	—	—	—	·065	·065	·064	·046	·041	·038	·032	·030	·026	·016	·011	·007	—	—	—	—	—	—	—	—	—	—	—	—	—	—	—	—	—	—	—	—	—	—	—	—	—	—	—	—	—	—	—
Nov	·091	·097	—	—	—	—	—	—	—	—	—	—	—	·065	·068	·059	·041	·040	·035	·031	·027	·022	·012	·007	·011	—	—	—	—	—	—	—	—	—	—	—	—	—	—	—	—	—	—	—	—	—	—	—	—	—	—	—	—	—	—	—
Dec	·084	·091	—	—	—	—	—	—	—	—	—	—	—	·058	·062	·057	·045	·041	·045	·025	·021	·016	·005	·000	—	—	—	—	—	—	—	—	—	—	—	—	—	—	—	—	—	—	—	—	—	—	—	—	—	—	—	—	—	—	—

Indexation allowance — continued

RD — Month of disposal

RD — Base Month

Note: the table is printed rotated 90°. Rows are the base month (RD, grouped by year 1996, 1997, 1998); columns are the month of disposal (grouped by year 1994–1999). All disposal columns for 1994 (Aug–Dec) and 1995 (Jan–Dec), and the 1996 Jan disposal column, are "—" (dash) for every base-month row, and are omitted below for legibility.

Base year 1996

Base month	1996 Feb	Mar	Apr	May	June	July	Aug	Sept	Oct	Nov	Dec	1997 Jan	Feb	Mar	Apr	May	June	July	Aug	Sept	Oct	Nov	Dec	1998 Jan	Feb	Mar	Apr	May	June	July	Aug	Sept	Oct	Nov	Dec	1999 Jan
Jan	.005	.009	.016	.018	.019	.015	.019	.024	.024	.025	.028	.028	.032	.035	.041	.045	.049	.049	.055	.061	.062	.063	.065	.062	.067	.071	.083	.089	.088	.085	.090	.095	.095	.095	.085	.088
Feb	—	.004	.011	.013	.014	.010	.015	.019	.019	.022	.023	.023	.027	.030	.036	.040	.044	.044	.050	.056	.057	.058	.060	.057	.062	.066	.078	.084	.083	.080	.085	.090	.090	.089	.080	.083
Mar	—	—	.007	.009	.010	.006	.011	.015	.015	.016	.019	.019	.023	.026	.032	.036	.040	.040	.046	.051	.053	.053	.056	.053	.058	.066	.073	.079	.079	.076	.081	.086	.086	.085	.080	.083
Apr	—	—	—	.002	.003	.000	.003	.008	.008	.009	.012	.012	.016	.018	.024	.028	.032	.032	.039	.044	.045	.046	.048	.045	.050	.054	.066	.071	.071	.068	.073	.077	.078	.077	.065	.079
May	—	—	—	—	.001	.000	.001	.006	.006	.007	.010	.010	.014	.016	.024	.026	.030	.030	.037	.042	.043	.044	.046	.043	.048	.052	.063	.069	.069	.066	.071	.075	.076	.075	.071	.071
June	—	—	—	—	—	.000	.001	.006	.006	.007	.010	.010	.013	.016	.022	.025	.030	.030	.036	.041	.042	.043	.046	.043	.048	.051	.063	.069	.068	.065	.070	.075	.075	.075	.069	.069
July	—	—	—	—	—	—	.005	.009	.009	.010	.013	.013	.017	.020	.025	.029	.033	.033	.040	.045	.047	.047	.050	.047	.052	.053	.067	.073	.072	.070	.074	.079	.079	.075	.075	.068
Aug	—	—	—	—	—	—	—	.005	.005	.006	.009	.009	.013	.015	.021	.025	.029	.029	.035	.040	.042	.042	.045	.042	.047	.050	.067	.068	.067	.065	.069	.074	.074	.074	.074	.072
Sept	—	—	—	—	—	—	—	—	.000	.001	.004	.004	.008	.010	.016	.020	.024	.024	.031	.036	.037	.038	.040	.037	.042	.050	.057	.063	.062	.060	.064	.069	.070	.069	.069	.067
Oct	—	—	—	—	—	—	—	—	—	.001	.004	.004	.008	.010	.016	.020	.024	.024	.030	.035	.036	.037	.040	.036	.042	.046	.057	.063	.062	.059	.064	.069	.069	.069	.068	.062
Nov	—	—	—	—	—	—	—	—	—	—	.003	.003	.007	.010	.016	.019	.023	.023	.030	.035	.036	.037	.040	.036	.042	.045	.057	.062	.062	.059	.064	.065	.070	.069	.068	.062
Dec	—	—	—	—	—	—	—	—	—	—	—	.000	.004	.006	.012	.016	.020	.020	.027	.032	.033	.034	.036	.033	.038	.041	.053	.059	.058	.056	.060	.065	.065	.065	.065	.058

Base year 1997

Base month	1997 Jan	Feb	Mar	Apr	May	June	July	Aug	Sept	Oct	Nov	Dec	1998 Jan	Feb	Mar	Apr	May	June	July	Aug	Sept	Oct	Nov	Dec	1999 Jan
Jan	—	.004	.006	.012	.016	.020	.020	.027	.032	.033	.034	.036	.033	.038	.041	.053	.059	.058	.056	.060	.065	.065	.065	.058	.058
Feb	—	—	.003	.008	.012	.016	.016	.023	.028	.029	.030	.032	.029	.034	.037	.049	.055	.054	.052	.056	.061	.061	.061	.054	.054
Mar	—	—	—	.006	.010	.014	.014	.020	.028	.026	.027	.030	.026	.032	.037	.046	.051	.051	.049	.053	.058	.059	.058	.051	.051
Apr	—	—	—	—	.004	.008	.008	.014	.019	.020	.021	.024	.020	.023	.029	.040	.046	.045	.043	.047	.052	.052	.052	.045	.045
May	—	—	—	—	—	.004	.004	.010	.015	.017	.017	.020	.017	.022	.025	.036	.042	.041	.039	.043	.048	.048	.048	.041	.041
June	—	—	—	—	—	—	.000	.006	.011	.013	.013	.016	.013	.018	.021	.032	.038	.037	.035	.039	.044	.044	.044	.037	.037
July	—	—	—	—	—	—	—	.006	.011	.013	.013	.016	.013	.018	.021	.032	.038	.037	.035	.039	.044	.044	.044	.037	.037
Aug	—	—	—	—	—	—	—	—	.005	.006	.007	.009	.006	.011	.015	.026	.031	.031	.028	.033	.037	.038	.037	.031	.031
Sept	—	—	—	—	—	—	—	—	—	.001	.002	.004	.000	.005	.009	.019	.025	.024	.022	.026	.031	.031	.031	.026	.026
Oct	—	—	—	—	—	—	—	—	—	—	.001	.003	.000	.004	.008	.019	.024	.024	.021	.026	.031	.031	.031	.024	.024
Nov	—	—	—	—	—	—	—	—	—	—	—	.003	.000	.002	.005	.016	.022	.021	.019	.023	.028	.028	.028	.024	.024
Dec	—	—	—	—	—	—	—	—	—	—	—	—	.000	.002	.005	.016	.022	.021	.019	.023	.028	.028	.028	.021	.021

Base year 1998

Base month	1998 Feb	Mar	Apr	May	June	July	Aug	Sept	Oct	Nov	Dec	1999 Jan
Jan	.005	.008	.019	.020	.024	.022	.026	.031	.031	.031	.031	.024
Feb	—	.003	.014	.017	.019	.017	.021	.026	.026	.026	.026	.019
Mar	—	—	.011	.017	.016	.014	.018	.026	.023	.022	.022	.016
Apr	—	—	—	.006	.005	.002	.007	.011	.012	.011	.011	.005
May	—	—	—	—	.000	.000	.001	.006	.006	.006	.006	.000
June	—	—	—	—	—	.000	.002	.004	.007	.006	.006	.000
July	—	—	—	—	—	—	.004	.002	.005	.004	.004	.002
Aug	—	—	—	—	—	—	—	.004	.004	.004	.004	.000
Sept	—	—	—	—	—	—	—	—	.001	.000	.000	.000
Oct	—	—	—	—	—	—	—	—	—	.000	.000	.000
Nov	—	—	—	—	—	—	—	—	—	—	.000	.000
Dec	—	—	—	—	—	—	—	—	—	—	—	.000

Corporation tax

Rates of corporation tax and advance corporation tax

	1990	1991	1992	1993	1994	1995	1996	1997	1998	1999
Corporation tax (full rate)	34%*	33%	33%	33%	33%	33%	33%	31%	31%	30%§
Advance corporation tax	⅓	⅓	⅓	9/31	¼	¼	¼	¼	¼	—§§
Tax credit	25%	25%	25%	20%†	20%†	20%†	20%†	20%†	20%†	10%†

* Reduced retrospectively from 35% by FA 1991. The reduction took effect from 25 July 1991.
§ It was announced in the 1999 Budget that the rate is to remain at 30% for financial year 2000.
§§ Advance corporation tax is abolished from 6 April 1999. ACT remains at ¼ for distributions on 1 April to 5 April 1999.
† Individual shareholders not subject to tax at the higher rate will have no further tax to pay.
  In the case of charities, the reduced tax credit was phased in over four years, 1993–94 to 1996–97. In general, trustees of discretionary trusts are taxed at a flat rate on dividend income from 6 April 1993 (35% before 6 April 1996; 34% from 6 April 1996).

Small companies rate

	1993	1994	1995	1996	1997	1998	1999
Small companies rate	25%	25%	25%	24%	21%	21%	20%
Lower relevant amount*	£250,000	£300,000	£300,000	£300,000	£300,000	£300,000	£300,000
Higher relevant amount*	£1,250,000	£1,500,000	£1,500,000	£1,500,000	£1,500,000	£1,500,000	£1,500,000
Fraction	1/50	1/50	1/50	9/400	1/40	1/40	1/40

* Reduced proportionally for accounting periods of less than 12 months. Associated companies: divide limits by total number of associated companies (including the company in question).
1) Small companies rate applies to *basic profits* ("I") where *profits* ("P") do not exceed the lower relevant amount.
2) Where *profits* ("P") exceed the lower relevant amount but not the upper relevant amount, corporation tax on *basic profits* ("I") is reduced by—

$$(\text{higher relevant amount} - P) \times \frac{I}{P} \times \text{fraction}$$

For the purposes of 1) and 2) above—

P = profits as finally computed for corporation tax purposes *plus* franked investment income *excluding* franked investment income from UK companies in the same group or from UK companies owned by a consortium of which the recipient is a member (TA 1988 s 13(7) amended by FA 1998 Sch 3 para 7 for distributions made after 5 April 1999).
I = profits on which corporation tax is actually borne (income plus chargeable gains).

Note: It was announced in the 1999 Budget that for the financial year 2000, companies (other than close investment holding companies) will pay corporation tax at a new starting rate of 10% on profits up to £10,000, with marginal relief for profits between £10,000 and £50,000. Unless the small companies rate is changed for the financial year 2000, the marginal relief fraction will be 1/40.

Capital gains

A company's chargeable gains are taxed without adjustment (other than indexation for post-1982 gains) at the rate of corporation tax applying to the company's other profits. The reform of capital gains tax for individuals, trustees and personal representatives provided in the Finance Act 1998 does not extend to the capital gains of companies.

Close investment-holding companies

Charged at full rate of corporation tax (see above).

Capital allowances see p 50.
Charities, payments to see p 71.
Claims and elections see p 22.
Due date of tax see p 10.

Interest on overdue tax see p 13.
Interest on overpaid tax see p 17.
Penalties see p 18.

Capital allowances

Rates

Agricultural and forestry land

Expenditure incurred after	Rate
Initial allowance	%
11 April 1978	20
31 March 1986	Nil
31 October 1992[1]	20
31 October 1993	Nil
Writing-down allowance	
5 April 1946	10
31 March 1986	4

Note:

[1] Buildings or works constructed under a contract entered into between 1 November 1992 and 31 October 1993, and brought into use for the purposes of the farming trade by 31 December 1994.

Dredging

Expenditure incurred after	Rate
Initial allowance	%
16 January 1966	15
31 March 1986	Nil
Writing-down allowance	
5 November 1962	4

Industrial buildings and structures

Expenditure[1] incurred after	Rate
Initial allowance	%
12 November 1974[2]	50
10 March 1981[2-6]	75
13 March 1984[2/4-8]	50
31 March 1985[2/5-8]	25
31 March 1986[2/5-8]	Nil
31 October 1992[2/5/10]	20
31 October 1993[5]	Nil
Writing-down allowance	
5 November 1962[9]	4

Notes:

[1] The amount qualifying for allowance is the price paid for the relevant interest *minus* (i) the value of the land element and (ii) any value attributable to elements over and above those which would feature in a normal commercial lease negotiated in the open market: FA 1995 s 100 confirming previous practice.

[2] Qualifying hotels: expenditure incurred after 11 April 1978 and before 1 April 1986, or between 1 November 1992 and 31 October 1993 – 20% initial allowance. No initial allowance after 31 March 1986 except under certain pre-14 March 1984 contracts and as above.

[3] Small industrial workshops: expenditure incurred after 26 March 1980 and before 27 March 1983 – 100% initial allowance.

[4] Very small workshops: expenditure incurred after 26 March 1980 and before 27 March 1985 – 100% initial allowance.

[5] Enterprise zones: expenditure incurred not more than 10 years after the site was first included in the zone – 100% initial allowance. (See p 52 for list of enterprise zones.)

[6] Rates and transitional relief apply also to dwelling houses let on assured tenancies: 10 March 1982 – 31 March 1987.

[7] Expenditure qualifying for a regional development grant (where a written offer of financial assistance was made between 1 April 1980–13 March 1984) – 75%.

[8] Payments made after 13 March 1984 but before 1 April 1987 under a contract agreed before 14 March 1984 – 75%.

[9] Small industrial workshops: expenditure incurred after 26 March 1980 and before 27 March 1983 – 25% writing-down allowance.

Very small workshops: expenditure incurred after 26 March 1980 and before 27 March 1985 – 25% writing-down allowance.

Enterprise zones: expenditure incurred not more than 10 years after the site was first included in the zone (including qualifying hotels in an enterprise zone) – 25% writing-down allowance.

Qualifying hotels (other than in an enterprise zone) – 4% writing-down allowance.

Toll roads: for accounting periods or basis periods ending after 5 April 1991 4% writing-down allowance for expenditure on construction of toll roads.

[10] Building constructed under, or bought unused under, a contract entered into after 31 October 1992 and before 1 November 1993, and brought into use in qualifying trade by 31 December 1994. Balance of relief by 4% pa writing-down allowance. All or part of the initial allowance may be disclaimed. See FA 1993 s 113.

Know-how

Writing-down allowance

Expenditure incurred before 1 April 1986 spread equally over 6 years on straight line basis, ie 16⅔% pa (if not otherwise deductible as trading expense).

Expenditure incurred after 31 March 1986: annual 25% writing down allowance (reducing balance basis).

Machinery and plant

Expenditure incurred after	Rate %
First-year allowance[1]	
21 March 1972	100
13 March 1984[2/3]	75
31 March 1985[2/3]	50
31 March 1986[2/3]	Nil
31 October 1992[4]	40
31 October 1993	Nil
2 July 1997[5]	50
12 May 1998 (Northern Ireland)[7]	100
2 July 1998[6]	40
Writing-down allowance	
26 October 1970	25[1]
First-year allowance: long-life assets[8]	
25 November 1996	Nil
2 July 1997[5]	12
2 July 1998	Nil
Writing-down allowance: long-life assets	
25 November 1996	6

Notes:

[1] Special provisions apply to enable expenditure on new ships to be set off at will. Extended to expenditure on second hand ships from 1 April 1985.

[2] Payments made after 13.3.1984 but before 1.4.1987 under a contract entered into before 14.3.1984 – 100%.

[3] Expenditure qualifying for a regional development grant (where a written offer of financial assistance was made between 1 April 1980–13 March 1984) – 100%.

[4] 25% writing-down allowance on reducing balance basis on remaining expenditure. All or part of the first-year allowance may be disclaimed. Certain expenditure is excluded from the 40% allowance, ie cars (other than taxis, short-term hire cars and mobility allowance vehicles for the disabled), and most assets which are acquired from a connected person, sold and leased back, or acquired in a transaction the sole or main benefit of which is to obtain a first-year allowance: see FA 1993 ss 115-117, Sch 13.

[5] (See F(No2)A 1997 ss 42, 43.) Qualifying expenditure incurred by qualifying businesses during the year ended 1 July 1998 attracts a first-year allowance of 50% rather than the normal writing-down allowance of 25%. This does not apply to certain expenditure including that on machinery and plant for leasing, motor cars, ships or railway assets. For qualifying expenditure incurred in that year where the 6% rate of writing-down allowance – see note (6) below – would otherwise apply (ie. in the case of long-life assets), the rate of the first-year allowance is restricted to 12%. After the first year, allowances revert to the normal writing-down rate of 25%/6%. Qualifying businesses are, broadly, those which satisfy any two of the following conditions:

(a) turnover £11,200,000 or less *(b)* assets £5,600,000 or less *(c)* not more than 250 employees.

[6] (See FA 1998 s 84.) The conditions for relief during the year ending 1 July 1999 are similar to those outlined in footnote 5 above, but long-life assets do not qualify. In the 1999 Budget it was announced that the relief would be extended to expenditure incurred in the year ending 1 July 2000.

[7] (See FA 1998 s 83.) Qualifying expenditure on plant and machinery for use in Northern Ireland incurred during the four year period from 12 May 1998 to 11 May 2002 by qualifying businesses attracts a first-year allowance of 100% rather than the normal 25% writing down allowance. The conditions for relief are similar to those outlined in footnote 5 above, but long-life assets do not qualify.

[8] (See CAA 1990 ss 38A-38H.) On reducing balance basis. Applies to machinery or plant with an expected working life, when new, of 25 years or more. Applies where expenditure on long-life assets in a year is £100,000 or more in the case of individuals and of partnerships made up of individuals (where the individual or at least half the partners devotes substantially the whole of their time to carrying on the business). In this case of companies the de minimis limit is £100,000 divided by one plus the number of associated companies.

Transitional provisions apply to maintain a 25% allowance for expenditure incurred before 1 January 2001 under a contract entered into before 26 November 1996 and to expenditure on second-hand plant or machinery if old rules applied to vendor (CAA 1990 s 38H).

25% allowance for machinery or plant in building used wholly or mainly as, or for purposes ancillary to, a dwelling-house, retail shop, showroom, hotel or office, and for sea-going ships and railway assets bought before 1 January 2011. Motor cars are excluded from the new provisions.

Cars: Threshold for restriction on capital allowances for expenditure on business cars £12,000 for cars leased or purchased after 10 March 1992; £8,000 from 13 June 1979 to 10 March 1992; £5,000 from 6 April 1976 to 12 June 1979; £4,000 from 26 October 1970 to 5 April 1976.

Leased assets: subject to transitional provisions, a first-year allowance was generally not available for expenditure after 31 May 1980 on the provision of leased plant or machinery unless it was used for a qualifying purpose. Writing-down allowances are available.

(a) Teletext and viewdata receivers and adaptors: transitional provisions were extended—reduced first year allowance from 1 June 1980 to 31 May 1986.

(b) Leasing to non-residents: from 10 March 1982 writing-down allowance reduced from 25% to 10%.

(c) Ships and aircraft: first year allowance was available for overseas leasing by UK resident responsible for management etc UNLESS main purpose is to obtain first year allowance, when only 10% writing-down allowance available.

Films: from 10 March 1982 expenditure on production and purchase of film etc is treated as revenue expenditure except for certain British-made films which continue to qualify for capital allowances. From 10 March 1992, pre-production expenditure on films produced with sufficient EC content is relieved as it occurs. 100% write-off is available for expenditure incurred after 1 July 1997 and before 2 July 2000 on a qualifying British film completed after 1 July 1997. see F(No 2)A 1992 ss 41–43, F (No 2)A 1997 s 48, Statement of Practice SP1/98.

Mines, oil wells etc

Expenditure incurred after	Rate
Initial allowance	%
16 January 1966	40
31 March 1986	Nil

Amount of writing-down allowance
Expenditure incurred before 1 April 1986—

Greater of: 1) $\dfrac{A}{A+B}$ x residue of expenditure

        where A = output from source in chargeable period or its basis period,
         and B = total potential future output of source, estimated as at the end of that
                 chargeable period or its basis period.
      2) 5% residue of expenditure for full year.

Expenditure incurred after 31 March 1986: annual writing-down allowance on reducing balance basis—10% for certain pre-trading expenditure and expenditure on the acquisition of a mineral asset, otherwise 25%.

Note: Transitional provisions for expenditure incurred before 31 March 1987 under contract entered into before 16 July 1985.

Patent rights

Writing-down allowance
Expenditure incurred before 1 April 1986 spread equally over 17 years or, if less
    (a) the period for which the rights are acquired, or
    (b) 17 years less the number of complete years from the commencement of the patent to the
        acquisition.

Expenditure incurred after 31 March 1986: annual 25% writing-down allowance (reducing balance basis).

Scientific research

Expenditure incurred after	Rate
	%
Allowance in year 1	
5 November 1962	100

Note: Land and houses are excluded from 1 April 1985.

Enterprise zones

The following areas have been designated as enterprise zones. The designation applies for 10 years from the commencement date. Previous enterprise zones, the designation of which has lapsed, are not shown.

Area	Commencement date
Sunderland (Castletown and Doxford Park)	27 April 1990
Sunderland (Hylton Riverside and Southwick)	27 April 1990
Lanarkshire (Hamilton)	1 February 1993
Lanarkshire (Motherwell)	1 February 1993
Lanarkshire (Monklands)	1 February 1993
Dearne Valley	3 November 1995
East Midlands (North East Derbyshire)	3 November 1995
East Midlands (Bassetlaw)	16 November 1995
East Midlands (Ashfield)	21 November 1995
East Durham	29 November 1995
Tyne Riverside (North Tyneside)	19 February 1996
Tyne Riverside (North Tyneside and South Tyneside)	21 October 1996

Time limits for capital allowances claims see p 25.

Income tax

Lower, basic and higher rates and rate applicable to trusts

1999-2000 *Band of taxable income*

Exceeding £	Not exceeding £	Band £	Rate %	Tax on full band £	Cumulative tax £
0	1,500	1,500	10	150	150
1,500	28,000	26,500	23	6,095	6,245
28,000	—	—	40	—	—

1998-99 *Band of taxable income*

Exceeding £	Not exceeding £	Band £	Rate %	Tax on full band £	Cumulative tax £
0	4,300	4,300	20	860	860
4,300	27,100	22,800	23	5,244	6,104
27,100	—	—	40	—	—

1997-98 *Band of taxable income*

Exceeding £	Not exceeding £	Band £	Rate %	Tax on full band £	Cumulative tax £
0	4,100	4,100	20	820	820
4,100	26,100	22,000	23	5,060	5,880
26,100	—	—	40	—	—

1996-97 *Band of taxable income*

Exceeding £	Not exceeding £	Band £	Rate %	Tax on full band £	Cumulative tax £
0	3,900	3,900	20	780	780
3,900	25,500	21,600	24	5,184	5,964
25,500	—	—	40	—	—

1995-96 *Band of taxable income*

Exceeding £	Not exceeding £	Band £	Rate %	Tax on full band £	Cumulative tax £
0	3,200	3,200	20	640	640
3,200	24,300	21,100	25	5,275	5,915
24,300	—	—	40	—	—

1994-95 *Band of taxable income*

Exceeding £	Not exceeding £	Band £	Rate %	Tax on full band £	Cumulative tax £
0	3,000	3,000	20	600	600
3,000	23,700	20,700	25	5,175	5,775
23,700	—	—	40	—	—

1993-94 *Band of taxable income*

Exceeding £	Not exceeding £	Band £	Rate %	Tax on full band £	Cumulative tax £
0	2,500	2,500	20	500	500
2,500	23,700	21,200	25	5,300	5,800
23,700	—	—	40	—	—

Basic rate for 2000-2001: It was announced in the 1999 Budget that the basic rate will be reduced to 22%.

Taxation of savings: From 6 April 1996, savings income is treated as the top slice of taxable income and is chargeable only at the 20% and 40% rates (see 1999 Budget Resolution No. 17, TA 1988 s 1A). Savings income includes interest from banks and building societies, interest distributions from authorised unit trusts, interest on gilts and other securities including corporate bonds, purchased life annuities and discounts. For other than higher rate taxpayers, there will be no further tax to pay on savings income from which the 20% tax rate has been deducted. Higher rate taxpayers are liable to pay tax at 40% on that part of their savings income falling above the higher rate limit.

Taxation of dividends: UK and foreign dividends (except those foreign dividends taxed under the remittance basis) form the top slice of taxable income. From 6 April 1999, special rates apply to dividend income following the reduction of the tax credit to 10%. For other than higher rate taxpayers, the special tax rate of 10% will be offset by the tax credit and there will be no further tax to pay. Higher rate taxpayers are liable to pay tax at 32.5% on that part of their dividend income falling above the higher rate limit. From 6 April 1993 to 5 April 1999, dividend income was chargeable at the 20% and 40% rates as for savings income above.

Rate applicable to trusts: 1997–98 to 1999-2000: 34%; Schedule F trust rate: 1999-2000: 25%.

Additional rate: not charged on investment income of individuals. Additional rate on income arising to trustees of discretionary trusts: 1988–89 to 1996-97: 10%.

Table of income tax reliefs

	1999-2000	1998-99
Personal allowance (under 65)	£4,335	£4,195
Married couple's allowance[1]	£1,970 (Relief restricted to 10%)[3]	£1,900 (Relief restricted to 15%)[3]
Monthly reduction in year of marriage	£164·16	£158·33
Age allowance		
Abatement of relief by £1 for every £2 income over	£16,800	£16,200
Personal allowance (under 75)	£5,720	£5,410
Not beneficial if individual's total income exceeds	£19,570	£18,630
Married couple's allowance (elder spouse under 75)	£5,125 (Relief restricted to 10%)[3]	£3,305 (Relief restricted to 15%)[3]
Not beneficial if husband:		
under 65 and his total income exceeds	£23,110	£19,010
65-74 and his total income exceeds	£25,880	£21,440
Personal allowance (75 and over)	£5,980	£5,600
Not beneficial if individual's total income exceeds	£20,090	£19,010
Married couple's allowance (elder spouse 75 or over)	£5,195 (Relief restricted to 10%)[3]	£3,345 (Relief restricted to 15%)[3]
Not beneficial if husband:		
under 65 and his total income exceeds	£23,250	£19,090
65-74 and his total income exceeds	£26,020	£21,520
75 or over and his total income exceeds	£26,540	£21,900
Widow's bereavement allowance[1]	£1,970 (Relief restricted to 10%)[3]	£1,900 (Relief restricted to 15%)[3]
Additional relief for children[1]	£1,970 (Relief restricted to 10%)[3]	£1,900 (Relief restricted to 15%)[3]
Blind person (each)	£1,380	£1,330
Mortgage interest relief[2]		
Limit on amount available for relief	£30,000[3]	£30,000[3]
Relief restricted to	10%	10%
Life assurance relief For contracts made before 14 March 1984 *only*, given by deduction	12·5%	12·5%
NI Class 2 Small earnings exception	£3,770	£3,590
NI Class 4 *Band* *Maximum payable*	£7,530-£26,000 £18,470 @ 6% £1,108·20	£7,310-£25,220 £17,910 @ 6% £1,074·60
Lower rate of tax *Band*	10% £1,500	20% £4,300
Basic rate of tax *Band*	23% £26,500	23% £22,800

Handwritten note (beside Married couple's allowance):
ie code is 519H
1970 × 10/23 = 856
4335
5191

[1] **From 6 April 2000:** The married couple's allowance (where neither spouse is aged 65 or over at 5 April 2000), the widow's bereavement allowance and the additional relief for children will be abolished (announced in 1999 Budget).
From 6 April 2001: The children's tax credit, relief on which will be given at 10%, will be introduced for families with children (announced in 1999 Budget). It is intended that the amount of the relief will be £4,160, withdrawn at the rate of £1 of tax credit for every £15 income chargeable to income tax at the higher rate.

[2] **From 6 April 2000:** Mortgage interest relief will be withdrawn (announced in 1999 Budget).

[3] Relief for 1994–95 onwards is given as a reduction in tax liability calculated as the stated percentage of the amount of the relief.

1997-98	1996–97	1995-96	1994-95	1993-94
£4,045	£3,765	£3,525[4]	£3,445[4]	£3,445[4]
£1,830 (Relief restricted to 15%)[3]	£1,790 (Relief restricted to 15%)[3]	£1,720 (Relief restricted to 15%)[3]	£1,720 (Relief restricted to 20%)[3]	£1,720
£152·50	£149·17	£143·33	£143·33	£143·33
£15,600 £5,220	£15,200 £4,910	£14,600 £4,630	£14,200 £4,200	£14,200 £4,200
£17,950	£17,490	£16,810	£15,710	£15,710
£3,185 (Relief restricted to 15%)[3]	£3,115 (Relief restricted to 15%)[3]	£2,995 (Relief restricted to 15%)[3]	£2,665 (Relief restricted to 20%)[3]	£2,465
£18,310 £20,660 £5,400	£17,850 £20,140 £5,090	£17,150 £19,360 £4,800	£16,090 £17,600 £4,370	£15,690 £17,200 £4,370
£18,310	£17,850	£17,150	£16,050	£16,050
£3,225 (Relief restricted to 15%)[3]	£3,155 (Relief restricted to 15%)[3]	£3,035 (Relief restricted to 15%)[3]	£2,705 (Relief restricted to 20%)[3]	£2,505
£18,390 £20,740 £21,100	£17,930 £20,220 £20,580	—[5] £19,440 £19,780	—[5] £17,680 £18,020	—[5] £17,280 £17,620
£1,830 (Relief restricted to 15%)[3]	£1,790 (Relief restricted to 15%)[3]	£1,720 (Relief restricted to 15%)[3]	£1,720 (Relief restricted to 20%)[3]	£1,720
£1,830 (Relief restricted to 15%)[3]	£1,790 (Relief restricted to 15%)[3]	£1,720 (Relief restricted to 15%)[3]	£1,720 (Relief restricted to 20%)[3]	£1,720
£1,280	£1,250	£1,200	£1,200	£1,080
£30,000[3] 15%	£30,000[3] 15%	£30,000[3] 15%	£30,000[3] 20%	£30,000 25%
12·5%	12·5%	12·5%	12·5%	12·5%
£3,480	£3,430	£3,260	£3,200	£3,140
£7,010-£24,180 £17,170 @ 6% £1,030·20	£6,860-£23,660 £16,800 @ 6% £1,008	£6,640-£22,880 £16,240 @ 7·3% £1,185·52[6]	£6,490-£22,360 £15,870 @ 7·3% £1,158·51[6]	£6,340-£21,840 £15,500 @ 6·3% £976·50[6]
20% £4,100	20% £3,900	20% £3,200	20% £3,000	20% £2,500
23% £22,000	24% £21,600	25% £21,100	25% £20,700	25% £21,200

[4] Transitional relief: a married man under 65 may in certain circumstances claim a £3,540 personal allowance if his wife was 75 or over on 5 April 1990 (subject to abatement if his total income exceeds £14,200 in 1994-95 or £14,600 in 1995-96).

[5] Varies depending on personal allowance: see above and note[4]

[6] Before 6 April 1996 50% of class 4 contribution paid is deductible from total income.

Car benefits

PRIVATE USE

Basic cash equivalent
1994–95 to 1999–2000:*
35% x (list price of car plus extra qualifying accessories[1] *less* capital contributions[2] by employee[3])[4].

Adjustments from 1999-2000*
(Budget Resolution No. 25)
1 Reduce *basic cash equivalent to* –
25% where business mileage is at least 2,500[5] but less than 18,000[5] miles.
15% where business mileage is 18,000[5] miles or more[6].
2 Reduce adjusted cash equivalent in **1** by –
¼ where car is 4 years old or more at end of year of assessment.
3 Reduce adjusted cash equivalent in **2** proportionately where car is not available throughout year of assessment.
4 Reduce adjusted cash equivalent in **3** by amount of payments by employee for private use.

Adjustments for 1994-95 to 1998-99
1 Reduce *basic cash equivalent* by –
1/3 where business mileage is at least 2,500[5] but less than 18,000[5] miles
2/3 where business mileage is 18,000[5] miles or more[6].
2 Reduce *adjusted cash equivalent* in **1** by –
1/3 where car is 4 years old or more at end of year of assessment.
3 Reduce *adjusted cash equivalent* in **2** proportionately where car is not available throughout year of assessment.
4 Reduce *adjusted cash equivalent* in **3** by amount of payments by employee for private use.

[1] Excluding an accessory provided after car was made available if it was provided before 1 August 1993 or its list price was less than £100. From 6 April 1995 accessories designed for use only by disabled people are also excluded. From 1998–99 where a car is manufactured so as to be capable of running on road fuel gas, its price is proportionately reduced by so much of that price as is reasonably attributable to it being manufactured in that way. Where a new car is converted to run on road fuel gas, the equipment is not regarded as an accessory.
[2] Up to £5,000.
[3] List price as adjusted capped at £80,000.
[4] Classic cars (aged 15 years or more and with a market value of £15,000 or more at end of year of assessment): substitute market value at end of year of assessment if this is higher than adjusted list price. £80,000 cap and reduction for capital contributions apply.
[5] Mileage figures are reduced proportionately where car is not available for whole year.
[6] For second and subsequent cars there is no reduction if business mileage is under 18,000 miles; **from 1999-2000** reduce basic cash equivalent to 25% if business mileage is 18,000 miles or more (from 1994-95 to 1998-1999 the basic cash equivalent was reduced by 1/3).

	Business use up to 2,500 miles pa or additional car		Business use over 2,500 miles pa but under 18,000 miles		Business use 18,000 miles pa or over	
	Under 4 yrs old†	4 years or more†	Under 4 yrs old†	4 years or more†	Under 4 yrs old†	4 years or more†
1993-94:*						
Original market value up to £19,250						
1,400 cc or less	£3,465	£2,370	£2,310	£1,580	£1,155	£790
Over 1,400 cc up to 2,000 cc	£4,485	£3,045	£2,990	£2,030	£1,495	£1,015
Over 2,000 cc	£7,200	£4,830	£4,800	£3,220	£2,400	£1,610
No cylinder capacity						
Under £6,000	£3,465	£2,370	£2,310	£1,580	£1,155	£790
£6,000 or more, but under £8,500	£4,485	£3,045	£2,990	£2,030	£1,495	£1,015
£8,500 or more, but not more than £19,250	£7,200	£4,830	£4,800	£3,220	£2,400	£1,610
Original market value over £19,250						
Over £19,250 up to £29,000	£9,315	£6,270	£6,210	£4,180	£3,105	£2,090
Over £29,000	£15,060	£9,990	£10,040	£6,660	£5,020	£3,330

* From 6 April 1991 this table is also used to calculate the national insurance contributions payable by employers on the benefit of cars they provide for the private use of their employees, see p 85.
† At the end of the relevant year of assessment.

From 6 April 2002: The existing income tax charge based on 35% of the car's price (subject to certain reductions) is to be abolished (1999 Budget). It will be replaced by a charge on a percentage of the car's price graduated according to the level of the car's carbon dioxide emissions. Comments on the proposed change may be sent to Sara Woollard, Personal Tax Division, Room 87, New Wing, Somerset House, Strand, London WC2R 1LB by 31 May 1999 (see (1999) SWTI p 427).

FUEL		(For VAT on fuel, see p 92)
1999-2000		
Cylinder capacity: (non-diesel cars)	1,400 cc or less Over 1,400 cc up to 2,000 cc Over 2,000 cc	£1,210 £1,540 £2,270
Cylinder capacity: (diesel cars)	2,000 cc or less Over 2,000 cc	£1,540 £2,270
No internal combustion engine		£2,270
1998-99		
Cylinder capacity: (non-diesel cars)	1,400 cc or less Over 1,400 cc up to 2,000 cc Over 2,000 cc	£1,010 £1,280 £1,890
Cylinder capacity: (diesel cars)	2,000 cc or less Over 2,000 cc	£1,280 £1,890
No internal combustion engine		£1,890
1997-98		
Cylinder capacity: (non-diesel cars)	1,400 cc or less Over 1,400 cc up to 2,000 cc Over 2,000 cc	£800 £1,010 £1,490
Cylinder capacity: (diesel cars)	2,000 cc or less Over 2,000 cc	£740 £940
No internal combustion engine		£1,490
1996-97		
Cylinder capacity: (non-diesel cars)	1,400 cc or less Over 1,400 cc up to 2,000 cc Over 2,000 cc	£710 £890 £1,320
Cylinder capacity: (diesel cars)	2,000 cc or less Over 2,000 cc	£640 £820
No internal combustion engine		£1,320
1995-96:		
Cylinder capacity: (non-diesel cars)	1,400 cc or less Over 1,400 cc up to 2,000 cc Over 2,000 cc	£670 £850 £1,260
Cylinder capacity: (diesel cars)	2,000 cc or less Over 2,000 cc	£605 £780
No internal combustion engine		£1,260
1994-95:		
Cylinder capacity: (non-diesel cars)	1,400 cc or less Over 1,400 cc up to 2,000 cc Over 2,000 cc	£640 £810 £1,200
Cylinder capacity: (diesel cars)	2,000 cc or less Over 2,000 cc	£580 £750
No internal combustion engine		£1,200
1993-94:		
Cylinder capacity: (non-diesel cars)	1,400 cc or less Over 1,400 cc up to 2,000 cc Over 2,000 cc	£600 £760 £1,130
Cylinder capacity: (diesel cars)	2,000 cc or less Over 2,000 cc	£550 £710
Original market value: (if no cylinder capacity)	Under £6,000 £6,000 or more but under £8,500 £8,500 or more	£600 £760 £1,130

Fuel benefit reduced to *nil* if the employee is required to make good whole cost of private fuel.

Note: From 6 April 1991 this table is also used to calculate the national insurance contributions payable by employers on the benefit of free fuel they provide for the private use of employees, see p 85.

VANS: PRIVATE USE INCLUDING FUEL		
	Under 4 years old[1]	4 years old or more[1]
1993-94 onwards: Vehicle design weight: up to 3.5 tonnes over 3.5 tonnes	£500 —	£350 —

[1] At the end of the relevant year of assessment.

Fixed profit car scheme: tax-free allowances for business travel[1]

Business mileage	Engine size Up to 1,000cc	1,001– 1,500cc	1,501– 2,000cc	Over 2,000cc	One rate[2]
1997-98 to 1999-2000:[3,4] Up to 4,000 miles Excess over 4,000 miles	28p 17p	35p 20p	45p 25p	63p 36p	40p 22·5p
1996-97:[3] Up to 4,000 miles Excess over 4,000 miles	27p 16p	34p 19p	43p 23p	61p 33p	38.5p 21p
1995-96:[3] Up to 4,000 miles Excess over 4,000 miles	27p 15p	34p 19p	43p 23p	60p 32p	38.5p 21p
1994-95:[3] Up to 4,000 miles Excess over 4,000 miles	27p 15p	33p 19p	41p 23p	56p 31p	37p 21p
1993-94:[3] Up to 4,000 miles Excess over 4,000 miles	26p 15p	32p 18p	40p 22p	54p 30p	36p 20p
1992-93:[3] Up to 4,000 miles Excess over 4,000 miles	25p 14p	30p 17p	38p 21p	51p 27p	34p 19p

[1] From 1996–97, employees using their own car may claim these rates as a tax-free allowance or as a deduction whether or not their employer operates the scheme (1995) SWTI 1879.

[2] One rate paid irrespective of engine size.

[3] Subject to transitional relief.

[4] The rates remain unchanged for 1998-99 and 1999-2000 (IR Press Release of 8 December 1997, (1997) SWTI 1583, and 7 December 1998, (1998) SWT1 1692).

Note: It is proposed in the 1999 Budget that employees using their bicycle for business cycling will be allowed to receive a tax-free mileage rate of up to 12p per mile. Where the employee is not paid by the employer for business cycling, the employee will be able to claim tax relief on 12p per business mile (or on the balance up to 12p per mile if the employer pays less than this rate (1999) SETI 430).

Mobile telephones

From

6 April 1999 onwards: no taxable benefit

Cash equivalent of benefit from 6 April 1991 to 5 April 1999   £200

Expensive cars: restricted allowances

Writing-down allowances
(CAA 1990 s 34)

From 11 March 1992

Cars costing more than £12,000 and bought outright, on hire purchase or by way of a lease with option to purchase: writing-down allowance limited to £3,000 per annum.

Before 11 March 1992

Cars costing more than £8,000 and bought outright, on hire purchase or by way of a lease with option to purchase: writing-down allowance limited to £2,000 per annum.

Restriction on deduction for hire charge
(CAA 1990 s 35)

From 11 March 1992

If a car costing more than £12,000 is acquired under a rental lease the maximum allowable deduction in computing Schedule D Case I or II profits is —

$$\frac{£12,000 + \frac{1}{2}(P - £12,000)}{P} \times R$$

Before 11 March 1992

If a car costing more than £8,000 was acquired under a rental lease the maximum allowable deduction in computing Schedule D Case I or II profits was —

$$\frac{£8,000 + \frac{1}{2}(P - £8,000)}{P} \times R$$

P = retail price of car when new
R = annual rental

Flat rate expenses

For most classes of industry flat rate allowances for the upkeep of tools and special clothing have been agreed between the Revenue and the trade unions concerned. Alternatively, the individual employee may claim as a deduction his or her actual expenses (Concession A1). Rates for healthcare and fire service employees have been introduced. The fire service rate was agreed in 1994; those for healthcare workers are introduced for 1998-99 onwards but claims may be made for the previous 6 years (see (1999) SWTI 353).

Industry code	Industry	Occupation	Deduction from 1991–92 to 1994–95	Deduction from 1995–96
10	Agriculture	All workers	60	70
100	Aluminium	(a) Continual casting operators, process operators, de-dimplers, driers, drill punchers, dross unloaders, firemen, furnace operators and their helpers, leaders, mouldmen, pourers, remelt department labourers, roll flatteners	110	130
		(b) Cable hands, case makers, labourers, mates, truck drivers and measurers, storekeepers	50	60
		(c) Apprentices	40	45
		(d) All other workers	85	100
330	Banks	Uniformed bank employees	30	40
90	Brass and Copper	All workers	85	100
270	Building	(a) Joiners and carpenters	95	105
		(b) Cement works and roofing felt and asphalt labourers		
		(c) Labourers and navvies	45	55
		(d) All other workers	30	40
			70	85
250	Building Materials	(a) Stone-masons	70	85
		(b) Tilemakers and labourers	30	40
		(c) All other workers	45	55
190	Clothing	(a) Lacemakers, hosiery bleachers, dyers, scourers and knitters, knitwear bleachers and dyers	40	45
		(b) All other workers	25	30
150	Constructional Engineering	(a) Blacksmiths and their strikers, burners, caulkers, chippers, drillers, erectors, fitters, holders up, markers off, platers, riggers, riveters, rivet heaters, scaffolders, sheeters, template workers, turners, welders		
		(b) Banksmen, labourers, shop-helpers, slewers, straighteners	95	115
		(c) Apprentices and storekeepers	50	60
		(d) All other workers	40	45
			65	75
170	Electrical and Electricity Supply	(a) Those workers incurring laundry costs only (generally CEGB employees)	20	25
		(b) All other workers	75	90
110	Engineering	(a) Pattern makers	105	120
		(b) Labourers, supervisory and unskilled workers	50	60
		(c) Apprentices and storekeepers	40	45
		(d) Motor mechanics in garage repair shops	85	100
		(e) All other workers	85	100
Not known	Fire service (see above)	Uniformed fire fighters and fire officers	From 1988-99: 60	
220	Food	All workers	30	40
20	Forestry	All workers	60	70
240	Glass	All workers	50	60
Not known	Healthcare (see abaove)	(a) Ambulance staff on active service, (ie excluding staff who take telephone calls or provide clerical support.)	From 1998-99:	110
		(b) Nurses and midwives, chiropodists, dental nurses, occupational, speech and other therapists, orthoptists, phlebotomists, physiotherapists, radiographers.		70
		(c) Plaster room orderlies, hospital porters, ward clerks, sterile supply workers, hospital domestics, hospital catering staff		60
		(d) Laboratory staff, pharmacists, pharmacy assistants		45
280	Heating	(a) Pipe fitters and plumbers	90	100
		(b) Coverers, laggers, domestic glaziers, heating engineers and their mates	75	90
		(c) All gas workers, all other workers	60	70

Flat rate expenses — continued

Industry code	Industry	Occupation	Deduction from 1991–92 to 1994–95	Deduction from 1995–96
50	Iron Mining	(a) Fillers, miners and underground workers	85	100
		(b) All other workers	65	75
70	Iron and Steel	(a) Day labourers, general labourers, stockmen, time keepers, warehouse staff and weighmen	50	60
		(b) Apprentices	40	45
		(c) All other workers	105	120
210	Leather	(a) Curriers (wet workers), fellmongering workers, tanning operatives (wet)	45	55
		(b) All other workers	30	40
140	Particular Engineering	(a) Pattern makers	105	120
		(b) All chainmakers; cleaners, galvanisers, tinners and wire drawers in the wire drawing industry; tool-makers in the lock making industry	85	100
		(c) Apprentices and storekeepers	40	45
		(d) All other workers	50	60
355	Police Force	Uniformed police officers (ranks up to and including Chief Inspector)	45	55
160	Precious Metals	All workers	60	70
230	Printing	(a) Letterpress Section Electrical engineers (rotary presses), electrotypers, ink and roller makers, machine minders (rotary), maintenance engineers (rotary presses) and stereotypers	90	105
		(b) Bench hands (P & B), compositors (Lp), readers (Lp), T & E Section wire room operators, warehousemen (Ppr box)	25	30
			60	70
		(c) All other workers		
320	Prisons	Uniformed prison officers	45	55
300	Public Service	(i) Dock and Inland Waterways		
		(a) Dockers, dredger drivers, hopper steerers	45	55
		(b) All other workers	30	40
		(ii) Public Transport		
		(a) Garage hands (including cleaners)	45	55
		(b) Conductors and drivers	30	40
60	Quarrying	All workers	60	70
290	Railways	(See the appropriate category for craftsmen, e.g. engineers, vehicle builders etc.) All other workers	60	70
30	Seamen	(a) Carpenters (Seamen) Passenger liners	140	135
		(b) Carpenters (Seamen) Cargo vessels, tankers, coasters and ferries	110	130
		(c) Other seamen Passenger liners	nil	nil
		(d) Other seamen Cargo vessels, tankers, coasters and ferries	nil	nil
120	Shipyards	(a) Blacksmiths and their strikers, boilermakers, burners, carpenters, caulkers, drillers, furnacemen (platers), holders up, fitters, platers, plumbers, riveters, sheet iron workers, shipwrights, tubers, welders	95	115
		(b) Labourers	50	60
		(c) Apprentices and storekeepers	40	45
		(d) All other workers	65	75
200	Textile Prints	All workers	50	60
180	Textiles	(a) Carders, carding engineers, overlookers (all), technicians in spinning mills	70	85
		(b) All other workers	50	60
130	Vehicles	(a) Builders, railway wagon etc. repairers, and railway wagon lifters	90	105
		(b) Railway vehicle painters and letterers, railway wagon etc. builders' and repairers' assistants	50	60
		(c) All other workers	30	40
260	Wood & Furniture	(a) Carpenters, cabinet makers, joiners, wood carvers and woodcutting machinists	95	115
		(b) Artificial limb makers (other than in wood), organ builders and packing case makers	75	90
		(c) Coopers not providing own tools, labourers, polishers and upholsterers	40	45
		(d) All other workers	65	75

1) 'Industry code' is an industry identification term used for Inland Revenue computer purposes.
2) The expressions 'all workers' and 'all other workers' refer only to manual workers who have to bear the cost of upkeep of tools and special clothing. They do not extend to other employees such as office staff.

Loan benefits and official rate of interest

A director, or an employee earning £8,500 or more a year, who receives a loan by reason of his or her employment may be charged to tax on the cash equivalent of the benefit for the year (TA 1988 s 160, Sch 7).

From 6 April 1994, there is no charge to tax if either:
(a) all the beneficial loans provided by reason of the employment; or
(b) all the beneficial loans, excluding loans qualifying for tax relief, do not exceed £5,000.
Before 6 April 1994, there was no charge to tax if the cash equivalent did not exceed a specified limit.

	Limit
6 April 1991 to 5 April 1994	£300
6 April 1980 to 5 April 1991	£200

The cash equivalent is calculated using the difference between the interest paid (if any) and the official rate of interest. The official rate of interest for this purpose is set out below.

Date	Rate
From 6 March 1999	6.25%
6 August 1997–5 March 1999	7.25%
6 November 1996–5 August 1997	6.75%
6 June 1996–5 November 1996	7%
6 February 1996–5 June 1996	7.25%
6 October 1995–5 February 1996	7.75%
6 November 1994–5 October 1995	8%
6 January 1994–5 November 1994	7·5%
6 March 1993–5 January 1994	7·75%
6 January 1993–5 March 1993	8·25%
6 December 1992–5 January 1993	9%
6 November 1992–5 December 1992	9·75%
6 June 1992–5 November 1992	10·5%
6 March 1992–5 June 1992	10·75%
6 October 1991–5 March 1992	11·25%
6 August 1991–5 October 1991	11·75%
6 July 1991–5 August 1991	12·25%
6 May 1991–5 July 1991	12·75%
6 April 1991–5 May 1991	13·5%
6 March 1991–5 April 1991	14·5%
6 November 1990–5 March 1991	15·5%
6 November 1989–5 November 1990	16·5%
6 July 1989–5 November 1989	15·5%
6 January 1989–5 July 1989	14·5%
6 October 1988–5 January 1989	13·5%
6 August 1988–5 October 1988	12%
6 May 1988–5 August 1988	9·5%
6 December 1987–5 May 1988	10·5%
6 September 1987–5 December 1987	11·5%
6 June 1987–5 September 1987	10·5%
6 April 1987–5 June 1987	11·5%
6 October 1982–5 April 1987	12%

	1993–94	1994–95	1995–96	1996–97	1997–98
Average official rate of interest	7·688%	7·7%	7·79%	6·93%	7·08%

Note
From 6 April 1994, loans made on commercial terms by employers who lend predominantly to the general public are generally exempt.

Foreign currency loans

Currency	Date	Rate
Swiss franc	From 6 July 1994	5·5%
	6 June 1994 – 6 July 1994	5·7%
Japanese yen		

Relocation expenses and benefits

Qualifying removal benefits and expenses[1]

Date of move	Limit
After 5 April 1993	£8,000

[1] The statutory relief covers the following expenses and benefits (TA 1988 Sch 11A) —

    (a) *disposal expenses and benefits* (legal and advertising expenses in connection with the disposal of accommodation, penalty for redeeming a mortgage, auctioneers' and estate agents' fees, disconnection of public utilities, rent, maintenance and insurance costs while the property is unoccupied);

    (b) *acquisition expenses and benefits* (legal expenses in connection with the acquisition of an interest in a new main residence, loan fees, mortgage indemnity insurance costs, survey and land registry fees, stamp duty, connection of public utilities). (NB: similar expenses and benefits are covered in respect of abortive acquisitions, if the property would have been the employee's new residence but the acquisition does not proceed either for reasons outside the employee's control or because he or she reasonably declines to proceed);

    (c) *transportation of domestic belongings* (including insurance costs);

    (d) *travelling and subsistence expenses and benefits* (for temporary visits to new residence before relocation; travel from old residence to new place of work or from new residence to old place of work where date of move and relocation of work do not coincide; subsistence and travel costs of child under 19 relocating before or after parents for educational reasons; benefit of a car or van for use in connection with the relocation where it is not otherwise available for private use);

    (e) *bridging loan expenses and beneficial bridging loans* (relief is given on any charge to interest at the official rate on a beneficial loan to the extent that the aggregate value of other qualifying benefits and expenses falls short of the maximum exempt amount);

    (f) *duplicate expenses and benefits in respect of new residence* (replacement domestic items).

Employers' contributions for moves to higher cost housing areas (before 6 April 1993)[1]

Date of move	Maximum contribution £
2 February 1993–5 April 1993	13,440
1 November 1991–1 February 1993	18,060
1 June 1991–31 October 1991	20,370
1 December 1990–31 May 1991	22,680
6 April 1990–30 November 1990	24,150
1 December 1989–5 April 1990	22,890
1 February 1989–30 November 1989	21,210

[1] Exempt amounts under Concession A67. Under transitional provisions, the concessionary relief continued to be available, as an alternative to the statutory relief (see above), where the employee was committed to relocate before 6 April 1993 and actually started work at the new location before 1 August 1993.

Disturbance allowances (before 6 April 1993)[1]

Category	Maximum amount	
	1.4.91–31.3.92 £	1.4.92–5.4.93 £
Married householder	2,550	2,655
Single householder	1,550	1,615
Single non-householder	600	625

[1] Exempt amounts under Concession A5. Under transitional provisions, the concessionary relief continued to be available, as an alternative to the statutory relief (see above), where the employee was committed to relocate before 6 April 1993 and actually started work at the new location before 1 August 1993.

Approved employee share schemes

From 2000-2001: It was announced in the 1999 Budget that a new all-employee share ownership scheme will be introduced in **2000-2001**. It is proposed that employees will be allowed to allocate part of their pre-tax salary to buy shares in their employing company without income tax or national insurance contributions being payable. If the shares are held for 3 years, the employee will be subject to income tax on the amount of salary allocated to the shares, but any gains arising while the shares are in the scheme will be free of income tax, NICs and capital gains tax (see (1999) SWTI 447).

Approved profit sharing schemes
(TA 1988 ss 186, 187, Sch 9, 10)

Annual limit on shares appropriated

From 1991–92:	Greater of £3,000 or 10% of salary, up to £8,000
1989–90 and 1990–91:	Greater of £2,000 or 10% of salary, up to £6,000
1988–89:	Greater of £1,250 or 10% of salary, up to £5,000

Schedule E charge on early disposal or receipt of capital from shares

Time of disposal or capital receipt	Percentage charge[1]
Before 3rd anniversary of appropriation[2]	100%[3]

[1] Calculated on the appropriate percentage of the initial market value of the shares when appropriated (or the sales proceeds if less).

[2] If that anniversary falls on or after 29 April 1996. If the 3rd anniversary of the appropriation falls before that date but the 5th anniversary falls after it, the 100% charge arises if the disposal or capital receipt takes place before 29 April 1996. Where the 5th anniversary fell before 29 April 1996, the following charges applied:

Time of disposal or capital receipt	Percentage charge
Before 4th anniversary of appropriation	100%[4]
Between 4th and 5th anniversary of appropriation	75%[4]
After 5th anniversary of appropriation	nil

[3] The charge is reduced to 50% where the employee reaches the retirement age specified in the scheme rules or leaves the employment due to injury, disability or redundancy before the shares are sold or capital is received.

[4] The charge was reduced to 50% where the employee reached the retirement age specified in the scheme rules or left the employment due to injury, disability or redundancy within 5 years of the appropriation.

Reliefs

Where the conditions of the scheme are satisfied, no Schedule E charge arises on the employee in respect of –
   (a) the value of the shares at the time of appropriation;
   (b) any increase in the value of the shares; or
   (c) any gain on the disposal of the shares (although capital gains tax is chargeable on any gain over the market value on appropriation).

Main conditions for relief

1   Shares in a company (or its parent company) must be acquired by trustees of the scheme and allocated to employee participants.
2   All employees must be eligible to participate on similar terms (subject to a minimum service requirement of up to 5 years and material interest exclusions).
3   The annual value of shares appropriated must not exceed the statutory maximum (see above).
4   The shares used in the scheme must be fully paid up, not redeemable and not subject to special restrictions.
5   Participants must permit the scheme trustees to hold the shares for the retention period (two years from the date of appropriation, unless the participant ceases to be employed before that date by reason of injury, disability, redundancy, retirement or death).
6   Shares disposed of within a specified period are subject to a Schedule E charge (see above).

Approved savings related share option schemes
(TA 1988 ss 185, 187, Sch 9)

Monthly contributions to SAYE scheme

	Maximum £	Minimum £
1 October 1998[3]	250	5–10[2]
1 April 1996–30 September 1998[1]	250	5–10[2]
1 September 1991–31 March 1996[1]	250	10 or under
1 September 1989–31 August 1991	150	10 or under

[1] The Treasury issued a new prospectus in April 1996: Booklet IR98 para 5.4.
[2] The company may choose a minimum savings contribution between £5 and £10.
[3] The Treasury issued a new prospectus applying from 1 October 1998 (see (1998) SWTI 1118)

Approved SAYE contracts: bonus and interest payments on termination

Date of termination	Amount payable – contracts to 30 September 1998	Amount payable – contracts from 1 October
3-year contract		
After at least 1 but less than 3 years	Refund of contributions plus simple interest at 3% p.a.	Refund of contributions plus simple interest at 3% p.a.
After 3 years	Refund of contributions plus bonus of 3 months' contributions	Refund of contribuitions plus bonus of 2·75 times the monthly contributions
5-year contract		
After at least 1 but less than 5 years	Refund of contributions plus simple interest at 3% p.a.	Refund of contributions plus simple interest at 3% p.a.
After 5 years	Refund of contributions plus bonus of 9 months' contributions	Refund of contributions plus bonus of 7·5 times the monthly contributions
After at least 5 but less than 7 years	Refund of contributions plus bonus of 9 months' contributions and compound interest at 3% p.a. for period after first 5 years	Refund of contributions plus bonus of 7·5 times the monthly contributions and compound interest at 3% p.a. for period after first 5 years
After 7 years	Refund of contributions plus bonus of 18 months' contributions	Refund of contributions plus bonus of 13·5 times the monthly contributions

Reliefs

Where the conditions of the scheme are complied with, no Schedule E charge arises on the employee in respect of –

(a) the grant of an option to acquire shares;

(b) the exercise of the option; or

(c) any increase in the value of the shares.

Capital gains tax is chargeable on disposal of the shares: the CGT base cost is the consideration given by the employee for both the shares and the option.

Main conditions for relief

1 All full time employees must be eligible to participate on similar terms (subject to a minimum service requirement of up to 5 years and material interest exclusions).

2 The scheme must provide for shares to be paid for with an amount of money not exceeding the repayments, bonuses and interest payments made under a linked SAYE scheme.

3 The scheme shares must be fully paid up, not redeemable and not subject to special restrictions.

4 Subject to cessation of employment due to injury, disability, redundancy, retirement or death, share options must not be exercised before the bonus date under the SAYE scheme (3, 5 or 7 years after its commencement, see above).

5 The purchase price of the shares must be stated at the time the option is granted and must not be manifestly less than 80% of their market value.

Company share option plans

(TA 1988 ss 185, 187 and Sch 9; FA 1996 s 114 and Sch 16)

Limit on value of shares under option held by employee at any one time

From 29 April 1996	£30,000

Reliefs

Where the conditions of the scheme are complied with, no Schedule E charge arises on the employee in respect of –

(a) the grant of an option to acquire shares;

(b) the exercise of the option; or

(c) any increase in the value of the shares.

Capital gains tax is chargeable on disposal of the shares: the CGT base cost is the consideration given by the employee for both the shares and the option.

Main conditions for relief

1 There is a limit (see above) on the value of shares under option held by an employee at any one time (the value being that of the shares at the time the options are granted).

2 Options must be granted at a share price not manifestly less than the market value at the date of the grant.

3 The scheme shares must be fully paid up, not redeemable and not subject to special restrictions.

4 Only full time directors or qualifying employees may participate in the scheme.

5 Options must be exercised between 3 and 10 years after the grant, and not less than 3 years after the last exercise by the participator of an option (under the same or another approved company share option plan).

Executive share option schemes

(TA 1988 ss 185, 187, Sch 9)

NOTE: The income tax relief in respect of the grant and exercise of options under executive schemes was withdrawn with effect for options granted after 17 July 1995, subject to transitional provisions (see Revenue Press Release dated 28 November 1995). In general, options granted under an approved scheme after 16 July 1995 qualify for tax relief only if they meet the conditions for approved company share option plans (see p 65).

Limit on market value of unexercised options

Greater of £100,000 or 4 times emoluments subject to PAYE (excluding benefits).

Reliefs

Where the conditions of the scheme are satisfied, no Schedule E charge arises on the employee in respect of –
   (a) the grant or exercise of the option; or
   (b) any increase in value of the shares.
Capital gains tax is chargeable on disposal of the shares: the CGT base cost is the consideration given by the employee for both the shares and the option.

Main conditions for relief

1   The market value of shares over which a participant holds unexercised options must not exceed the statutory limit (see above).
2   The purchase price of the shares must be stated at the time the option is granted and must not be manifestly less than 85% of their market value.
3   The scheme shares must be fully paid up, not redeemable and not subject to special restrictions.
4   Only full time directors or qualifying employees may participate in the scheme.
5   Options must be exercised between 3 and 10 years after the grant, and not less than 3 years after the last exercise by the participator of an option (under the same or another approved executive scheme).

Profit-related pay schemes

(TA 1988 ss 169–184, Sch 8; FA 1997, s 61; FA 1998 s 62)

Limit on tax-free pay

Profit period beginning	Exempt amount
After 31 December 1999	no relief
1 January 1999–31 December 1999	lowest of: profit-related pay, 20% of earnings[1] and £1,000
1 January 1998–31 December 1998	lowest of: profit-related pay, 20% of earnings[1] and £2,000
31 March 1991–31 December 1997	lowest of: profit-related pay, 20% of earnings[1] and £4,000
1 April 1989–31 March 1991	lowest of: half profit-related pay, 10% of earnings[1] and £2,000
Before 1 April 1989	lowest of: half profit-related pay, 10% of earnings[1] and £1,500

[1] Emoluments within PAYE (excluding benefits) plus profit-related pay.

Main conditions for relief

1   The scheme must be registered. Schemes can only be established for private sector employments.
2   A scheme must relate to an employment unit (all or part of a business).
3   A scheme must define eligible employees and include at least 80% of the employees in the employment unit.
4   The scheme must operate by reference to defined profit periods and must define the method of calculation of the distributable pool of profit-related pay.

Payments on termination or variation of employment

Exempt lump sum payments

(a) Payments in connection with the cessation of employment on the death, injury or disability of the employee.

(b) Payments under unapproved retirement benefits schemes where the employee has been taxed on the actual or notional contributions to provide the benefit.

(c) Payments under approved retirement benefits schemes which can properly be regarded as a benefit earned by past service.

(d) Certain payments of terminal grants to members of the armed forces.

(e) Certain benefits under superannuation schemes for civil servants in Commonwealth overseas territories.

(f) Payments in respect of foreign service where the period of foreign service comprises –

   (i) 75% of the whole period of service; or

   (ii) the whole of the last 10 years of service; or

   (iii) where the period of service exceeded 20 years, one-half of that period, including any 10 of the last 20 years.

Otherwise, a proportion of the payment is exempt, as follows –

$$\frac{\text{length of foreign service}}{\text{length of total service}} \times \text{amount otherwise chargeable}$$

(g) The first £30,000 of genuine ex gratia payments (where there is no "arrangement" by the employer to make the payment).

(h) Statutory redundancy payments (included in computing £30,000 limit in (f) above).

Personal pension schemes and retirement annuities

Approval of contracts

Trades and professions for which an early retirement age has been agreed by the Revenue under TA 1988 s 620(4)(c) for the purpose of the approval of retirement annuity contracts are set out below. Under the personal pension schemes legislation, individuals may not take benefits from their pension arrangements before the age of 50. The trades and professions listed below for which the Revenue has approved an earlier retirement age of 30, 35, 40 or 45 have been approved under TA 1988 s 634(3)(b) for the purposes of personal pension schemes.

Retirement age	Profession or occupation		
30	skiers (downhill) *(personal pension schemes only)*		
35	athletes badminton players boxers cyclists dancers	footballers ice hockey players models national hunt jockeys Rugby League players Rugby Union players squash players	table tennis players tennis players (including real tennis) wrestlers
40	cricketers divers (saturation, deep sea and free swimming)	golfers motocross motorcycle riders motorcycle road racing riders	motor racing drivers speedway riders trapeze artists WPBSA snooker players
45	jockeys (flat racing)	Members of the reserve forces	

50	circus animal trainers
	croupiers
	interdealer brokers
	martial arts instructors
	moneybroker dealers
		newscasters (ITV)
		off-shore riggers (mechanical
		  fitters, pipe fitters, riggers,
		  platers, welders and
		  roustabouts)
			Royal Navy reservists
			Rugby League referees
			territorial army members

55	air pilots
	brass instrumentalists
	distant water
	  trawlermen
	firemen (part-time)
	health visitors (female)
		inshore fishermen
		midwives (female)
		moneybroker dealer
		  managers and directors
		nurses (female)
		physiotherapists (female)
			psychiatrists (who are also
			  maximum part time
			  specialists employed
			  within the NHS solely
			  in the treatment of the
			  mentally disordered)
			singers

Maximum limits for qualifying premiums

Personal pension schemes	
1989–90 to 1999–2000	
Age in years at beginning of year of assessment	*Maximum percentage*
35 and below	17½
36 to 45	20
46 to 50	25
51 to 55	30
56 to 60	35
61 or more	40

| 1993–94 earnings cap £75,000 |
| 1994–95 earnings cap £76,800 |
| 1995–96 earnings cap £78,600 |
| 1996–97 earnings cap £82,200 |
| 1997–98 earnings cap £84,000 |
| 1998–99 earnings cap £87,600 |
| 1999–2000 earnings cap £90,600 |

Retirement annuities	
1987–88 to 1999–2000	
Age in years at beginning of year of assessment	*Maximum percentage*
50 and below	17½
51 to 55	20
56 to 60	22½
61 or more	27½

[handwritten annotation:] OF TAXABLE EARNED INCOME (ie includes BIK but not dividends!)

Note *retirement annuities:* contracts for dependants or life insurance—maximum percentage 5%; *personal pension schemes:* life insurance—maximum percentage 5%.

Partnership retirement annuities

The earned income limit for a retirement annuity paid to a former partner is 50% of the average of his or her share of the partnership profits in the best 3 of the last 7 years in which he or she was a partner (TA 1988 s 628).

From 1980–81 the limit is increased by the percentage increase in the RPI from the December in the year of retirement to the December preceding the year of assessment.

From 1982–83 the former partner's share of the profits in the first 6 of the last 7 years in which he or she was a partner is increased by the percentage increase in the RPI from the December in the relevant year to the December in the seventh year.

The retail prices index is printed on p 42.

Maintenance payments

From 6 April 2000: The transitional relief for payments under pre 15 March 1988 arrangements is being ended. Payments will be treated in the same way as payments under maintenance arrangements set up on or after 15 March 1988. Tax relief will only be given after 5 April 2000 if one or both parties to the marriage is aged 65 or over at 5 April 2000 (the test that applies for the receipt of a married person's allowance after that date, see p 54).

For court orders or agreements made on or after 15 March 1988, or applied for before 15 March but made after 30 June 1988, relief is given to the payer only up to an amount equal to the married couple's allowance (**£1,970 for 1999-2000,** £1,900 for 1998-99, £1,830 for 1997-98, £1,790 for 1996–97, £1,720 from 1990–91 to 1995–96; previously the difference between the higher personal relief and the single personal relief), and provided that the payment is to *the divorced or separated spouse*. The payments are made gross and the recipient is exempt from tax in respect of them.

Before 1994–95 the relief was given as a deduction from total income. From 1994–95 onwards it is given as a reduction in tax liability calculated as the appropriate percentage of the amount of the relief.

For 1994–95, the tax relief given to the payer was limited to the 20% lower rate. From 1995–96 the tax relief was limited to 15% and for **1999-2000** it is limited to 10%.

Medical insurance premiums

From 6 April 1990 to 1 July 1997, individuals were entitled to tax relief on premiums paid under an eligible contract for private medical insurance for UK resident individuals aged 60 or over (FA 1989 s 54). For premiums paid after 5 April 1994 relief was restricted to the basic rate (23% from 6 April 1997), given by deduction from the premium; there was no higher rate relief. Until that date basic rate relief was given by deduction at source and higher rate relief had to be claimed.

Tax relief on such premiums is abolished for policies taken out, or renewed, after **1 July 1997** (except where arrangements were made before 2 July 1997 and the relevant contract was made, with the premium being at least partly paid, before 1 August 1997 or where a contract that had come to an end before 2 July 1997 is renewed before 1 August 1997 and the premium is at least partly paid by that date). See F(No2)A 1997 s 17.

National Savings Bank interest

First £70 of interest on deposits (other than investment deposits) is exempt (TA 1988 s 325).

Rent-a-room scheme

Subject to a maximum, gross annual receipts from letting furnished accommodation in the only or main home are exempt from tax. If the receipts exceed the maximum, the taxpayer can pay tax on the gross receipts after deduction of expenses or on the amount by which the receipts exceed the maximum, without relief for the actual expenses. An individual's maximum is halved if during the basis period for the year some other person received income from letting accommodation in that property. (F(No 2) A 1992 Sch 10.)

	Maximum amount
6 April 1997 onwards	£4,250
6 April 1992–5 April 1997	£3,250

Schedule E assessments

Persons domiciled in UK	Services performed			
	Wholly in UK	Partly in UK	Partly abroad	Wholly abroad
Non-resident	All	That part	None	None
Resident but not ordinarily resident	All	That part	Remittances	Remittances
Resident and ordinarily resident	All	All[1]	All[1]	All[1]
Persons domiciled outside UK	UK employer	As for person domiciled in UK.		
	Foreign employer	*Non-resident* All UK earnings. *Resident (not ordinarily resident)*—All UK earnings. (Remittances for duties performed outside UK.) *Resident (and ordinarily resident)* All earnings. (Remittances if all duties performed outside UK.)		

[1] Before 17 March 1998, exempt if qualifying period of over 364 days mostly abroad. The relief for seafarers continues after that date (FA 1998 s 63). Special relief for employees forced to return early from Kuwait or Iraq who had intended to work abroad for over 364 days.

Thresholds: PAYE and national insurance

	1992–93	1993–94	1994–95	1995–96	1996–97	1997–98	1998-99	1999-2000
PAYE: Weekly	£66·50	£66·50	£66·50	£68·00	£72·50	£78·00	£80·50	£83·00
Monthly	£287·00	£287·00	£287·00	£294·00	£314·00	£337·00	£350·00	£361·00
National Insurance: Weekly	£54·00	£56·00	£57·00	£58·00	£61·00	£62·00	£64·00	£66·00
Monthly	£234·00	£243·00	£247·00	£252·00	£265·00	£269·00	£278·00	£286·00

Uniform allowances[1]

	1992–93 £	1993–94 £	1994–95 £	From 1995–96 £
Royal Navy and Royal Marines				
RN officers of flag rank and equivalent RM officers..	1,026·72	1,043·52	1,068·94	1,071·00
RN and RM below flag rank	790·68	802·08	798·84	792·12
WRNS officers (non-seagoing)	540·12	583·56	514·20	680·52
WRNS officers (seagoing)	609·12	661·56	646·56	853·80
Women medical and dental officers RN	455·76	516·36	452·16	567.48
QARNNS officers: female officers: matron and above..	588·00	731·88	572·88	544·68
below matron	875·64	963·48	821·28	828·00
male officers:				
chief nursing officer and above	475·08	488·40	527·28	489·36
below chief nursing officer	444·00	454·92	493·56	456·48
Army				
Officers serving at mounted duty with Household Cavalry and King's Troop RHA	909·92	973·93	1,012·88	1,012·88
Male dismounted officers: colonel and above	665·75	720·95	749·78	749·78
below colonel	623·22	566·63	673·19	673·19
Household Division	—	647·30	—	—
except Household Division.	—	566·63	589·29	589·29
Female QARANC: nursing officers colonels and above	623·24	627·76	671·48	671·48
non-nursing officers colonels and above	—	—	—	—
nursing officers below colonel	606·18	645·66	652·87	652·87
non-nursing officers below colonel	—	—	—	—
Female officers: colonels and above (except QARANC above)	—	480·62	499·84	499·84
below colonel (except QARANC above)	—	469·52	488·30	488·30
WRAC women officers: colonel and above	466·35	—	—	—
below colonel	438·03	—	—	—
RAMC and RADC women officers: colonel and above	—	—	—	—
below colonel	—	—	—	—
Male officers SSVC, SSLC	167·44	179·38	186·55	186·55
Women officers SSVC, SSLC	186·54	193·47	201·20	201·20
RAF				
RAF and PMRAFNS (male):				
air officers	375·48	375·48	445·68	422·76
group captains	363·60	363·60	427·56	402·72
wing commanders and below	336·36	336·36	392·52	361·10
PMRAFNS (female): air officers	461·16	461·16	624·00	589·16
group captains	445·20	445·20	621·00	586·00
wing commanders and below	439·68	439·68	615·24	579·70
WRAF and RAF (female):	406·56	406·56	500·16	477·98
air officers				
group captains	392·64	392·64	452·40	460·74
wing commanders and below	347·52	347·52	443·40	421·69

[1] Allowances have not changed from 1995-96 pending a review of the system for the provision of allowances.

Charities

The Government has published a consultation document containing proposals to:

(a) reduce the minimum limit for gift aid payments to £100 and allow for payment by instalments (from 1 January 2001);

(b) remove the maximum limit on the payroll giving scheme and allow employers to distribute donations directly to charities;

(c) add 10% to donations made by employees under the payroll giving scheme and launch a campaign encouraging more employers to set up schemes;

(d) modernise and simplify existing VAT reliefs for charities;

(e) simplify the tax system for charities.

Comments on the proposals are invited by 31 August 1999.

Covenanted payments				
	Payee		*Period capable of exceeding*	*Limits*
Individuals:	charity[1]		3 years	none
Companies:	charity		3 years	none
Gift aid				
			Minimum	*Maximum*
Individuals:	single gifts[2]		£250[4]	none[5]
Companies:	single gifts[3] (by close companies)		£250[4]	none[5]
	single gifts by non-close companies		none	none[6]
Millennium gift aid[7]			*Minimum*	
Individuals:	single gifts[8]		£100	
Payroll giving				
				Maximum
Individuals:	from 6 April 1996			£1,200 pa[9]

[1] Non-charitable deeds of covenant made by individuals after 14 March 1988 (or made before 15 March 1988 but not received by the Revenue before 1 July 1988) have no effect for tax purposes. Certain annual payments under post-14 March 1988 arrangements continue to be treated as charges on income, eg certain interest payments, payments made in connection with the payer's trade, profession or vocation and for bona fide commercial reasons, and payments for non-taxable consideration to which the anti-avoidance provisions of TA 1988 s 125 apply. Special provisions apply to maintenance payments.

[2] The gift aid scheme was introduced with effect from 1 October 1990. It gives higher rate relief for the individual; the charity claims repayment of basic rate tax.

[3] The gift aid scheme was introduced with effect from 1 October 1990. The scheme applies to all companies. The scheme gives corporation tax relief; the charity claims repayment of basic rate income tax.

[4] From 16 March 1993. From 7 May 1992 to 15 March 1993 the limit was £400. From 1 October 1990 to 6 May 1992 the minimum limit was £600.

[5] Before 19 March 1991 a maximum of £5,000,000 applied.

[6] Before 19 March 1991 the maximum limit was £5,000,000 (from 1 October 1990) or 3% of the ordinary dividends paid by a company in the same accounting period, if greater.

[7] Introduced by FA 1998 ss 47, 48. Tax relief is given on donations to charities undertaking education and anti-poverty projects in eighty "low income countries". The charities must be registered with the Revenue. The Scheme runs from 31 July 1998 to 31 December 2000. (SI 1998 No 1868). Businesses to get tax relief for goods donated to help education projects and projects undertaken for medical purposes. It was proposed in the 1999 Budget to extend the number of charitable causes to which businesses can donate equipment and receive tax relief.

[8] Relief also for gifts by smaller instalments amounting in aggregate to £100 or more.

[9] In earlier years, the following limits applied: 1993–94 to 1995–96 £900; 1990–91 to 1992–93 £600; 1989–90 £480; 1988–89 £240; 1987–88 £120.

Inheritance tax relief see p 79.

Capital gains tax see p 39.

Reliefs for investments

Enterprise investment scheme

(Shares issued after 31 December 1993: TA 1988 ss 289-312; FA 1997 Sch 8)
(The scheme is revised from 1998-99, see FA 1998 ss 70, 71, 74, Sch 13.)

Relief on investment

Maximum investment:	From 1998–99 1994–95 1993–94	£150,000 £100,000 £40,000[1]
Minimum investment:	From 1993–94	£500
Maximum carryback to preceding year	From 1998–99 1994–95	½ amount invested between 6 April and 5 October (maximum £25,000) ½ amount invested between 6 April and 5 October (maximum £15,000)
Rate of relief	From 1993–94	20%[2]

[1] Applied to total enterprise investment and business expansion scheme investments for 1993–94.
[2] Given as a reduction in income tax liability.

Other reliefs

(a) Gains on the first disposal of shares on which EIS relief has not been withdrawn are exempt from capital gains tax.

(b) Reinvestment relief (ie deferral relief under TCGA 1992 Sch 5B) is available for gains on assets where the disposal proceeds are reinvested in eligible shares in a qualifying company. (It was announced in the 1999 Budget that CGT tapering relief will be calculated in accordance with the combined periods of ownership of the first and second investments (and any subsequent qualifying periods of reinvestment) where the shares in the first EIS company were issued after 5 April 1998 and disposed of after 5 April 1999: see (1999) SWTI 450.)

(c) A loss on the first disposal of shares from which EIS relief has not been withdrawn may be relieved against income tax or capital gains tax.

Main conditions for relief

1 The relief is available for subscriptions in cash to new ordinary fully paid-up shares in a qualifying company with no present or future right of redemption and no present or future preferential right to dividends or to the company's assets on a winding-up, throughout a five year period from the date of issue.

2 The investor must hold the shares for five years from the date of issue. He or she must not be connected with the issuing company, or receive value from it, at any time during the period beginning two years before the date of the share issue and ending five years after the share issue date.

3 The money subscribed must be used wholly for the purpose of a qualifying business activity within 12 months of the share issue date (or, where the company commences a qualifying trade within 12 months of the share issue date, within 12 months of the commencement).

4 The business activity must be carried on wholly or mainly in the UK for three years after the share issue date (or after the commencement of the trade, if later).

5 Throughout the period beginning with the share issue date and ending three years after that date (or, if later, three years after the date on which its qualifying business activity commences), the company must
   (a) be unquoted;
   (b) exist for a qualifying purpose;
   (c) have fully paid up capital; and
   (d) not be controlled by another company, or control another company (apart from a qualifying subsidiary). Under the provisions of FA 1997 Sch 8, a parent company may qualify if non-qualifying activities do not form a substantial part of the group's activities *as a whole*.

6 For shares issued after 1 July 1997, no arrangement must exist before or at the time of issue for the disposal of shares in the company, the disposal of the company's assets, the ending of the company's trade or a guarantee of the shareholders' investment.

Business expansion scheme

(Shares issued before 1 January 1994: TA 1988 ss 289–312 as originally enacted)

Relief on investment

Maximum investment:	£40,000[1]
Minimum investment:	£500
Maximum carryback to preceding year	½ amount invested between 6 April and 5 October (maximum £5,000)
Rate of relief	Up to 40%[2]

[1] Applied to total enterprise investment and business expansion scheme investments for 1993–94.
[2] Given as a deduction from total income.

Reliefs for investments — continued

Other reliefs

Capital gains relief: gains on the first disposal of shares on which BES relief has not been withdrawn are exempt from capital gains tax.
Loss relief (shares issued after 18 March 1986): none.

Main conditions for relief

As for the enterprise investment scheme (see above), except that the investor had to be UK resident and ordinarily resident in the year in which the shares were issued and the company had to be UK resident throughout the three-year period from the share issue date. There was no time limit for using the funds raised.

Venture capital trusts

(TA 1988 ss 332A, 842AA, Sch 15B; TCGA 1992 ss 151A, 151B, Sch 5C; FA 1997 Sch 9; FA 1998 ss 70, 72, 73, Sch 12)

Relief on investment

Maximum annual investment:	From 1995–96	£100,000
Rate of relief:	From 1995–96	20%[1]

[1] Given as a reduction in income tax liability. The rate of relief is an amount equal to the 'lower rate' of income tax for the year of assessment in respect of which the claim is made (TA 1988 Sch 15B para 1). The lower rate of income tax for 1999-2000 is 10%, although Sch 15B may be amended in the 1999 Finance Bill to retain a 20% rate of relief.

Other reliefs

(a) Dividends on shares within investment limit exempt from income tax (unless the investor's main purpose is tax avoidance – from 9 March 1999).
(b) Gains on share disposals exempt from capital gains tax (subject to investment limit).
(c) Reinvestment relief is available for gains on assets where the disposal proceeds are reinvested in a venture capital trust.

Main conditions for relief

1   The investment must be in new eligible shares: that is, ordinary shares which, in the five-year period from the issue date, carry no present or future preferential right to dividends or to a return of assets on the winding-up of the trust and no present or future right to redemption.
2   The investor must be an individual, aged 18 or over. He or she must hold the shares for five years from the date of issue.
3   The trust must satisfy the following conditions for approval by the Revenue –
   (a)   it must not be a close company;
   (b)   its income must be derived wholly or mainly (at least 70%) from investments in shares or securities;
   (c)   at least 70% by value of its investments must comprise "qualifying holdings" (newly issued shares in unquoted companies carrying on qualifying trades – the provisions relating to parent companies are relaxed by FA 1997);
   (d)   at least 30% by value of its qualifying holdings must comprise "eligible shares" (see above);
   (e)   it may not hold more than 15% by value of its total investment portfolio in any one company;
   (f)   each class of its shares must be quoted on the Stock Exchange;
   (g)   it must distribute at least 85% of the income derived from shares and securities and 100% of income derived from other sources in each accounting period;
   (h)   at least 10% of the total investment in any one company must be held in ordinary, non-preferential shares (accounting periods ending after 1 July 1997);
   (i)   no part of a qualifying holding may consist of securities relating to a guaranteed loan (accounting periods ending after 1 July 1997).

Reliefs for investments — continued

Personal equity plans

(Subscriptions made **before 6 April 1999**: TA 1988 s 333; FA 1998 s 76; SI 1989/469; S1 1998/1869)

Subscription limit

	General plan £	Single company plan £
From 1991–92	6,000	3,000[1]
1990–91	6,000	—
1989–90	4,800	—
[1] Available from 1 January 1992.		

Limit on investments in unit and investment trusts

	Qualifying investments £	Permitted non-qualifying investments £
From 1993–94	6,000	1,500
1992–93	6,000[1]	1,500[1]
1991–92	3,000[1]	1,500[1]
1990–91	3,000[1]	900[1]
1989–90	2,400	—

[1] For the years 1990–91 to 1992–93, the limit on investments in permitted non-qualifying holdings operated as an alternative to the limit on investments in qualifying unit and investment trusts. For 1993–94 and subsequent years, investment in one category does not preclude investment in the other category up to the respective limits.

Individuals aged 18 or over who are UK resident and ordinarily resident may subscribe to one general plan and (from January 1992) one single company plan in any tax year.

Reliefs

(a) Dividends on shares held in a plan are exempt from income tax.
(b) Interest on plan investments is exempt from income tax if reinvested; interest on cash deposits is paid gross.
(c) Gains on the disposal of assets held in a plan are exempt from capital gains tax.
(d) PEPs held at 5 April 1999 can be held outside the new ISA, but with the same tax advantages as the ISA (1998) SWTI 388; FA 1998 ss 75, 76.
(e) 10% tax credits paid until 5 April 2004 on dividends from UK equities.

Eligible investments (general plans)

(a) Ordinary shares in a UK incorporated company listed on a recognised stock exchange in an EU member state or dealt in on the USM.
(b) Units in an authorised unit trust or shares in an investment trust.
(c) Qualifying EC shares.
(d) Cash held on deposit for investment.
(e) (From 6 July 1995) UK quoted preference and convertible preference shares and EU equivalent shares.
(f) (From 6 July 1995) certain corporate bonds and convertible bonds of UK quoted companies (other than authorised credit institutions).

Eligible investments (single company plans)

(a) Ordinary shares in a UK incorporated company (or, following a reorganisation, shares representing those shares).
(b) Qualifying EC shares (or, following a reorganisation, shares representing those shares).
(c) Paired shares, one of which was issued by the designated company.
(d) Shares acquired by the investor under an approved profit sharing or savings-related share option scheme.
(e) Cash held on deposit for investment.

Reliefs for investments — continued

Tax exempt special savings accounts
(Accounts opened **before 6 April 1999**: TA 1988 ss 326A–326C; FA 1998 s 78)

Maximum deposit (from 1 January 1991)

First 12 months	£3,000[1]
Subsequent 12 month periods	£1,800
Overall limit	£9,000

[1] But the full amount of capital invested in a mature TESSA can be immediately reinvested in a new TESSA.

Reliefs

Interest and bonuses payable on the account over a five-year period from the date on which it was opened are exempt from income tax.

Main conditions for relief

1 An individual aged 18 or over may hold one TESSA.
2 The TESSA must be a bank or building society deposit account or a building society share account. From 2 January 1996 European authorised institutions may operate TESSAs (SI 1995/3239 and concession A92).
3 No capital may be withdrawn from the account during the initial five-year period.
4 After five years the account ceases to be tax exempt, but the capital (ie a maximum of £9,000) may be reinvested in full within six months in another TESSA.
5 TESSAs may be opened until 5 April 1999. Payments into them may be made under the above rules for the full five-year period. The capital in a TESSA that matures between 6 January 1999 and 5 April 1999 may be transferred into an ISA after 5 April 1999 rather than invested into another TESSA before that date. (See below.)

Individual savings accounts
(TA 1988 s 333; FA 1998 s 75; SI 1998 No 1870; SI 1998 No 1871; SI 1998 No 1869; SI 1998 No 1872)

(From 6 April 1999)

Overall annual subscription limit	1999–2000 6 April 2000 onwards	£7,000 £5,000
Cash limit	1999-2000 6 April 2000 onwards	£3,000 £1,000
Life insurance limit	6 April 1999 onwards	£1,000

Reliefs

(a) Investments under the scheme will be free from income tax and capital gains tax.
(b) 10% tax credit paid until 5 April 2004 on dividends from UK equities.
(c) Withdrawals may be made without loss of tax relief.

Main conditions for relief

1 The account can include three components:
    (a) cash (including National Savings),
    (b) life insurance,
    (c) stocks and shares.
2 Savers are subject to the subscription limits set out above. If the subscription limit is reached in a year, no further subscriptions can be made in that year, irrespective of any amounts withdrawn.
3 Accounts must be administered by a single manager or by separate managers for each component.

Inheritance tax

Delivery of accounts: due dates

Type of transfer	Due date
Chargeable lifetime transfers	Later of – (a) 12 months after the end of the month in which the transfer took place; and (b) 3 months after the date on which the person delivering the account became liable
PETs which become chargeable	12 months after the end of the month in which the transferor died
Gifts with reservation chargeable on death	12 months after the end of the month in which the death occurred
Transfers on death	Later of – (a) 12 months after the end of the month in which the death occurred; and (b) 3 months after the date on which the personal representatives first act or the person liable first has reason to believe that he is liable to deliver an account
National heritage property	6 months after the end of the month in which the chargeable event occurred

Delivery of accounts: excepted estates

Date of transfer or death	1 April 1991– 5 April 1995	6 April 1995– 5 April 1996	6 April 1996– 5 April 1998	After 5 April 1998
Excepted transfers:	*Value below:*	*Value below:*	*Value below:*	*Value below:*
Total chargeable transfers since 6 April	£10,000	£10,000	£10,000	£10,000
Total chargeable transfers during last 10 years[2]	£40,000	£40,000	£40,000	£40,000
Excepted estates:				
Total gross value	£125,000	£145,000	£180,000[1]	£200,000[1]
Total gross value of property outside UK	£15,000	£15,000	£30,000	£50,000
Total gross value of chargeable transfers of cash, quoted shares or quoted securities within 7 years before death	nil	nil	£50,000	£75,000

[1] This limit applies to the aggregate gross value of the estate and of chargeable transfers of cash, quoted shares and quoted securities within 7 years before death.

[2] This limit remains the same for applicable periods prior to 1 April 1991.

Rates of tax

6 April 1999 onwards: Death rates

Cumulative chargeable transfers (gross)	Rate on gross	Tax on band	Cumulative tax	Cumulative chargeable transfers (net)	Rate on net fraction
£	%	£	£	£	
0 – 231,000	0	0	0	0 – 231,000	nil
231,000 +	40	—	—	231,000 +	⅔

Lower rates

Cumulative chargeable transfers (gross)	Rate on gross	Tax on band	Cumulative tax	Cumulative chargeable transfers (net)	Rate on net fraction
£	%	£	£	£	
0 – 231,000	0	0	0	0 – 231,000	nil
231,000 +	20	—	—	231,000 +	¼

Rates of tax — continued

6 April 1998-5 April 1999: Death rates

Cumulative chargeable transfers (gross)	Rate on gross	Tax on band	Cumulative tax	Cumulative chargeable transfers (net)	Rate on net fraction
£	%	£	£	£	
0 – 223,000	0	0	0	0 – 223,000	nil
223,000 +	40	—	—	223,000 +	⅔

Lower rates

Cumulative chargeable transfers (gross)	Rate on gross	Tax on band	Cumulative tax	Cumulative chargeable transfers (net)	Rate on net fraction
£	%	£	£	£	
0 – 223,000	0	0	0	0 – 223,000	nil
223,000 +	20	—	—	223,000 +	¼

6 April 1997–5 April 1998 : Death rates

Cumulative chargeable transfers (gross)	Rate on gross	Tax on band	Cumulative tax	Cumulative chargeable transfers (net)	Rate on net fraction
£	%	£	£	£	
0 – 215,000	0	0	0	0 – 215,000	nil
215,000 +	40	—	—	215,000 +	⅔

Lower rates

Cumulative chargeable transfers (gross)	Rate on gross	Tax on band	Cumulative tax	Cumulative chargeable transfers (net)	Rate on net fraction
£	%	£	£	£	
0 – 215,000	0	0	0	0 – 215,000	nil
215,000 +	20	—	—	215,000 +	¼

6 April 1996–5 April 1997: Death rates

Cumulative chargeable transfers (gross)	Rate on gross	Tax on band	Cumulative tax	Cumulative chargeable transfers (net)	Rate on net fraction
£	%	£	£	£	
0 – 200,000	0	0	0	0 – 200,000	nil
200,000 +	40	—	—	200,000 +	⅔

Lower rates

Cumulative chargeable transfers (gross)	Rate on gross	Tax on band	Cumulative tax	Cumulative chargeable transfers (net)	Rate on net fraction
£	%	£	£	£	
0 – 200,000	0	0	0	0 – 200,000	nil
200,000 +	20	—	—	200,000 +	¼

6 April 1995–5 April 1996: Death rates

Cumulative chargeable transfers (gross)	Rate on gross	Tax on band	Cumulative tax	Cumulative chargeable transfers (net)	Rate on net fraction
£	%	£	£	£	
0 – 154,000	0	0	0	0 – 154,000	nil
154,000 +	40	—	—	154,000 +	⅔

Lower rates

Cumulative chargeable transfers (gross)	Rate on gross	Tax on band	Cumulative tax	Cumulative chargeable transfers (net)	Rate on net fraction
£	%	£	£	£	
0 – 154,000	0	0	0	0 – 154,000	nil
154,000 +	20	—	—	154,000 +	¼

Rates of tax — continued

10 March 1992–5 April 1995: Death rates

Cumulative chargeable transfers (gross)	Rate on gross	Tax on band	Cumulative tax	Cumulative chargeable transfers (net)	Rate on net fraction
£	%	£	£	£	
0 – 150,000	0	0	0	0 – 150,000	nil
150,000 +	40	—	—	150,000 +	$\frac{2}{3}$

Lower rates

Cumulative chargeable transfers (gross)	Rate on gross	Tax on band	Cumulative tax	Cumulative chargeable transfers (net)	Rate on net fraction
£	%	£	£	£	
0 – 150,000	0	0	0	0 – 150,000	nil
150,000 +	20	—	—	150,000 +	$\frac{1}{4}$

6 April 1991–9 March 1992: Death rates

Cumulative chargeable transfers (gross)	Rate on gross	Tax on band	Cumulative tax	Cumulative chargeable transfers (net)	Rate on net fraction
£	%	£	£	£	
0 – 140,000	0	0	0	0 – 140,000	nil
140,000 +	40	—	—	140,000 +	$\frac{2}{3}$

Lower rates

Cumulative chargeable transfers (gross)	Rate on gross	Tax on band	Cumulative tax	Cumulative chargeable transfers (net)	Rate on net fraction
£	%	£	£	£	
0 – 140,000	0	0	0	0 – 140,000	nil
140,000 +	20	—	—	140,000 +	$\frac{1}{4}$

6 April 1990–5 April 1991: Death rates

Cumulative chargeable transfers (gross)	Rate on gross	Tax on band	Cumulative tax	Cumulative chargeable transfers (net)	Rate on net fraction
£	%	£	£	£	
0 – 128,000	0	0	0	0 – 128,000	nil
128,000 +	40	—	—	128,000 +	$\frac{2}{3}$

Lower rates

Cumulative chargeable transfers (gross)	Rate on gross	Tax on band	Cumulative tax	Cumulative chargeable transfers (net)	Rate on net fraction
£	%	£	£	£	
0 – 128,000	0	0	0	0 – 128,000	nil
128,000 +	20	—	—	128,000 +	$\frac{1}{4}$

Reliefs

The following is a summary of the main reliefs and exemptions for 1999–2000 under the Inheritance Tax Act 1984.
The legislation should be referred to for conditions and exceptions.

Agricultural property
Transfer with vacant possession (or right to obtain it within 12 months); transfer on or after 1 September 1995, of land let (or treated as let) on or after that date. — **100% of agricultural value**
Any other case — **50% of agricultural value**
(Under IHTA 1984 s 124C, as inserted by FA 1997 s 94, land managed according to terms of certain Habitat Schemes is treated as farm land, and qualifies for relief after 26 Nov. 1996.)

Charges arising and transfers occurring after 9 March 1992 and before 1 September 1995:
Transfer with vacant possession (or right to obtain within 12 months) — **100% of agricultural value**
Most other cases — **50% of agricultural value**

Note: The 100% relief is extended in limited circumstances by Concession F17.

Annual exemption
From 6 April 1981 — **£3,000**

Business property
Unincorporated business
Unquoted shares (including shares in AIM or USM companies) (held for 2 years or more)[1]
Unquoted securities which alone, or together with other such securities and unquoted shares, give the transferor control of the company (held for 2 years or more)[1]
Settled property used in life tenant's business
— **100%**

Controlling holding in fully quoted companies
Land, buildings, machinery or plant used in business of company or partnership
— **50%**

[1] Tax charges arising and transfers occurring after 5 April 1996. 10 March 1992–5 April 1996 minority holding of shares or securities of up to 25% in unquoted or USM company qualified for 50% relief; larger holdings qualified for 100% relief.

Charities, gifts to
From 15 March 1983 — Exempt

Marriage gifts
Made by: parent — £5,000
remoter ancestor — £2,500
party to marriage — £2,500
other person — £1,000

Political parties, gifts to
From 15 March 1988 — Exempt

Quick succession relief
Estate increased by chargeable transfer followed by death within 5 years
Death within first year — 100%
Each additional year: decreased by — 20%

Small gifts to same person
From 6 April 1981 — £250

Spouses with separate domicile (one not being in the UK)
Total exemption — £55,000

Tapering relief
The value of the estate on death is taxed as the top slice of cumulative transfers in the 7 years before death. Transfers on or within 7 years of death are taxed on their value at the date of the gift on the death rate scale, but using the scale in force at the date of death, subject to the following taper—

Years between gift and death	Percentage of full charge at death rates
0–3	100
3–4	80
4–5	60
5–6	40
6–7	20

National insurance: State benefits

Taxable and non-taxable state benefits

State benefits of an income nature are in principle taxable in the same way as other sources of income, but the majority of such benefits are not in fact taxed.

Benefits taxed under Schedule E as earned income

(Income support[1] payments made to people who had to sign on,[2] or to certain claimants[3] involved in a trade dispute)
Incapacity benefit[4]
Industrial death benefit pensions
Invalid care allowance[5]
Jobseeker's allowance

Retirement pension[5]
Statutory maternity pay
Statutory sick pay
(Unemployment benefit[1 and 6])
Widowed mothers' allowance[5]
Widows' pension

Notes:
[1] Income support paid to unemployed people and unemployment benefit were replaced by the jobseeker's allowance in October 1996.
[2] Although taxable, income support paid to an unemployed person who is aged 60 or over, or is a lone parent with a child under 16 or is someone who has to stay at home to look after a severely disabled person, is not in fact taxed (see leaflet IR41: Income tax and the unemployed).
[3] Where the claimant is one of a married or unmarried couple and he (though not his partner) is involved in a trade dispute.
[4] Payments made during the initial 28-week period, and that part of the benefit which represents a child addition, are exempt (see below).
[5] Child dependency additions are not taxable (see (2) below).
[6] Additions for children, housing and exceptional circumstances are excluded.

Benefits which are not taxed

(1) *Short-term benefits*
Maternity allowance

(2) *Benefits in respect of children*
Child benefit
Child dependency additions paid with retirement pension, widows' benefit, incapacity benefit, invalidity benefit, invalid care allowance, severe disablement allowance, higher-rate industrial death benefit, unemployability supplement and sickness (or, formerly, unemployment benefit) if beneficiary over pension age
Child's special allowance
Guardian's allowance
One-parent benefit

(3) *Industrial injury benefits*
Constant attendance allowance
Industrial disablement benefit
Pneumoconiosis, byssinosis and miscellaneous disease benefits
Workmen's compensation supplement

(4) *War disablement benefits*
Constant attendance allowance
Disablement pension
Severe disablement allowance

(5) *Other benefits*
Attendance allowance

Christmas bonus
Council tax benefit
Disability living allowance
Disability working allowance (replaced by disabled person's tax credit from October 1999)
Earnings top-up
Family credit (replaced by working families tax credit from October 1999)
Housing benefit
Incapacity benefit (initial 28-week period *only*)
Income support (other than payments made to people who had to sign on or strikers before 7 October 1996: introduction of jobseeker's allowance. In practice, payments to an unemployed person who was (a) aged 60 or over, (b) a lone parent with a child under 16, or (c) someone staying at home to look after a severely disabled person, were not taxed: IR41.)
Invalidity benefit (replaced by incapacity benefit in April 1995)
Jobfinder's grant
Redundancy payment
Social fund payments
Vaccine damage (lump sum)
War widow's or dependant's pension
Widow's payment

Statutory maternity pay
Rates: from 12 April 1999

Higher weekly rate of statutory maternity pay	Lower weekly rate of statutory maternity pay	Daily rate of statutory maternity pay
9/10ths of employee's average weekly earnings	£59·55	—
It was proposed in the 1999 Budget to extend entitlement to women earning at least £30 per week. Paid for a maximum of 18 weeks. Earnings threshold: £66		

Statutory sick pay
Rates: from 12 April 1999

Average weekly earnings	Weekly rate of statutory sick pay	Daily rate of statutory sick pay
Under £66·00	nil	Weekly rate divided by number of qualifying days in week[1] in which day to be paid occurs
£66·00 or more	£59·55 (standard)	
[1] Commencing on the Sunday		

Benefits taxed under Schedule E

	Weekly 6.4.98 onwards £	Total 1998–99 (52 weeks) £	Weekly 12.4.99 onwards £	Total 1999-2000 (52 weeks) £
Retirement pensions				
Single person	64·70	3,364·40	66·75	3,471·00
Married couple:				
both contributors—each	64·70	3,364·40	66·75	3,471·00
wife not contributor—addition	38·70	2,012·40	39·95	2,077·40
wife not contributor—joint	103·40	5,376·80	106·70	5,548·40
Age addition (over 80)—each	0·25	13·00	0·25	13·00
Hospital downrating				
20% rate (persons with dependants)	12·95	varies	13·35	varies
40% rate (no dependants)	25·90	varies	26·70	varies
Widow's benefits				
Widows' pension—standard	64·70	3,364·40	66·75	3,471·00
Widowed mothers' allowance	64·70	3,364·40	66·75	3,471·00
Non-contributory retirement pension				
Single person (category C or D)	38·70	2,012·40	39·95	2,077·40
Married couple (category C)	61·85	3,216·20	63·85	3,320·20
Married couple (category D—over 80)	77·40	4,024·80	79·90	4,154·80
Age addition	0·25	13·00	0·25	13·00
Incapacity benefit				
Long-term	64·70	3,364·40	66·75	3,471·00
Increased for age: Higher rate	13·60	707·20	14·05	730·60
Lower rate	6·80	353·60	7·05	366·60
Short-term[1] (under pension age) higher rate	57·70	3,000·40	59·55	—
(over pension age)	62·05	3,226·60	64·05	—
Invalidity allowance when paid with retirement pension (transitional)				
Higher rate	13·60	707·20	14·05	730·60
Middle rate	8·60	447·20	8·90	462·80
Lower rate	4·30	223·60	4·45	231·40
Industrial death benefit				
Widow's pension:				
Higher permanent rate	64·70	3,364·40	66·75	3,471·00
Lower permanent rate	19·41	1,009·32	20·03	1,041·56
Invalid care allowance				
Each qualifying individual	38·70	2,012·40	39·95	2,077·40
Earnings limit	50·00	—	50·00	—
Adult dependency increase	23·15	1,203·80	23·90	1,242·80
Jobseeker's allowance				
Single: under 18	30·30	—	30·95	—
18 to 24	39·85	—	40·70	—
25 or over	50·35	—	51·40	—

[1] Lower rate (tax-free) paid up to week 28 (see below). Higher rate (taxable) paid weeks 29 to 52. New claims cannot be made by persons over pensionable age.

Child dependency additions (from 12.4.99): £9·90 a week for child for whom higher rate child benefit payable
£11·35 a week for each other child (tax free).

The Revenue generally apply the basis of 52 weeks at the new rate. In certain cases, however, it may be to the advantage of the recipient to calculate the amount actually received within the year of assessment where this includes one week at the old rate.

Tax-free rates (from 12.4.99):

Attendance allowance:	Higher rate	£52·95 a week
	Lower rate	£35·40 a week
Child benefit:	£14·40 for eldest eligible child (couple)	
	£17·10 for eldest eligible child (lone parent)	
	£9·60 (each) for other eligible children	
Disability living allowance:		
Care component:	Higher rate	£52·95 a week
	Middle rate	£35·40 a week
	Lower rate	£14·05 a week
Mobility component:	Higher rate	£37·00 a week
	Lower rate	£14·05 a week
Incapacity benefit:		
Short term (under pension age)	Lower rate	£50·35 a week
Maternity allowance:	Higher rate	£59·55 a week
	Lower rate	£51·70 a week
Widow's payment:	£1,000 lump sum	

Contributions

From 6 April 1999

Lower earnings limit: £66 a week £286 a month £3,432 a year	**Upper earnings limit:** £500 a week **(employees only)** £2,167 a month £26,000 a year

Employees from 6.4.99			**Employers from 6.4.99**	
Class 1 Contributions **standard rate**			*(Earnings above £83 a week)*	
Earnings: £ 66·00–£500·00	10%		12·2%	
Over £500	no additional liability		12·2%	
Contracted out*		SR[1,3]		MP[2,3]
Earnings: £ 66·00–£500·00	8·4%	9·2%		11·6%
Over £500	no additional liability	12·2%		12·2%
Reduced rate for married women and widows with valid certificate of election	3·85%(earnings £66 to £500)		(As above)	
Men over 65 and women over 60	Nil		(As above)	
Children under 16	Nil		Nil	

Class 2 Contributions: Self employed
Flat rate: £6·55 a week.
Share fishermen's special rate: £7·20 a week.
Small earnings exception: earnings under £3,770 a year.

Class 3 Voluntary Contributions: £6·45 a week.

Class 4 Contributions: 6% of profits or gains between £7,530 and £26,000 a year.
Exempt if pensionable age reached by beginning of year of assessment.

Notes: The employer NI contribution holiday of up to a year, which applied from 6 April 1996 (see p 83), is to be restricted to employments which began before 1 April 1999: (1998) SWTI 1705.
1 Rates apply to salary-related schemes.
2 Rates apply to money-purchase schemes.
3 The lower rates apply to earnings between the earnings threshold of £83 and the upper earnings limit of £500. A deduction is made for the rebate that would have applied to NICs on earnings between the lower earnings limit of £66 and the earnings threshold £83. The rebate is 3% for salary-related schemes and 0.6% for money-purchase schemes.

From April 2000 (announced in 1999 Budget):
Class 1: First step in alignment of NIC threshold with personal tax allowance. Zero-rate of NICs for employees' earnings between lower earnings limit and new threshold. Employers' rate to be reduced from 12.2% to 11.7%.
Class 2: Rate to be reduced from £6.35 to £2 per week.
Class 4: Rate to be increased from 6% to 7%. Lower limit to be aligned with personal tax allowance.

From April 2001 (announced in 1999 Budget):
Full alignment of employees' NIC threshold with personal tax allowance.

6 April 1998-5 April 1999

Lower earnings limit: £64 a week £278 a month £3,328 a year	**Upper earnings limit:** £485 a week **(employees only)** £2,102 a month £25,220 a year

Employees from 6.4.98			**Employers from 6.4.98**		
Class 1 Contributions **standard rate**	On first £64	Remainder	*(Rate applying to all earnings)*		
Earnings: £ 64·00–£109·99	2%	10%	3%		
£110·00–£154·99	2%	10%	5%		
£155·00–£209·99	2%	10%	7%		
£210·00–£485·00	2%	10%	10%		
Over £485	no additional liability		10%		
Contracted out*	On first £64	Remainder	On first £64	Remainder	
				SR[1]	MP[2]
Earnings: £ 64·00–£109·99	2%	8·4%	3%	Nil	1·5%
£110·00–£154·99	2%	8·4%	5%	2	3·5%
£155·00–£209·99	2%	8·4%	7%	4	5·5%
£210·00–£485·00	2%	8·4%	10%	7	8·5%
Over £485	no additional liability		10%	7% (to £485)	8·5% (to £485)
			10%	10% (over £485)	10% (over £485)
Reduced rate for married women and widows with valid certificate of election	3·85% (earnings to £485)		(As above)		
Men over 65 and women over 60	Nil		(As above)		
Children under 16	Nil		Nil		

Class 2 Contributions: Self employed
Flat rate: £6·35 a week.   Share fishermen's special rate: £7 a week.
Small earnings exception: earnings under £3,590 a year.

Class 3 Voluntary Contributions: £6·25 a week.

Class 4 Contributions: 6% of profits or gains between £7,310 and £25,220 a year.
Exempt if pensionable age reached by beginning of year of assessment.

1 Rates apply to salary-related schemes. 2 Rates apply to money-purchase schemes.

Contributions — continued

6 April 1997–5 April 1998

Lower earnings limit: £62 a week £269 a month £3,224 a year			Upper earnings limit: (employees only)	£465 a week £2,015 a month £24,180 a year		

Class 1 Contributions

	Employees from 6.4.97		Employers from 6.4.97			
standard rate	On first £62	Remainder	(Rate applying to all earnings)			
Earnings: £ 62·00–£109·99	2%	10%	3%			
£110·00–£154·99	2%	10%	5%			
£155·00–£209·99	2%	10%	7%			
£210·00–£465·00	2%	10%	10%			
Over £465	no additional liability		10%			

	On first £62	Remainder	On first £62	Remainder		
Contracted out*					SR[1]	MP[2]
Earnings: £ 62·00–£109·99	2%	8·4%	3%		Nil	1·5%
£110·00–£154·99	2%	8·4%	5%		2	3·5%
£155·00–£209·99	2%	8·4%	7%		4	5·5%
£210·00–£465·00	2%	8·4%	10%		7	8·5%
Over £465	no additional liability		{ 10% 10%		7% (to £465) 10% (over £465)	8·5% (to £465) 10% (over £465)

Reduced rate for married women and widows with valid certificate of election	3·85% (earnings to £465)	(As above)
Men over 65 and women over 60	Nil	(As above)
Children under 16	Nil	Nil

Class 2 Contributions: Self employed
Flat rate: £6·15 a week.
Share fishermen's special rate: £6·80 a week.
Small earnings exception: earnings under £3,480 a year.

Class 3 Voluntary Contributions: £6·05 a week.

Class 4 Contributions: 6% of profits or gains between £7,010 and £24,180 a year.
Exempt if pensionable age reached by beginning of year of assessment.

[1] Rates apply to salary-related schemes. [2] Rates apply to money-purchase schemes.

6 April 1996–5 April 1997

Lower earnings limit: £61 a week £265 a month £3,172 a year			Upper earnings limit: (employees only)	£455 a week £1,972 a month £23,660 a year	

Class 1 Contributions

	Employees from 6.4.96		Employers from 6.4.96	
standard rate	On first £61	Remainder	(Rate applying to all earnings)	
Earnings: £ 61·00–£109·99	2%	10%	3%	
£110·00–£154·99	2%	10%	5%	
£155·00–£209·99	2%	10%	7%	
£210·00–£455·00	2%	10%	10·2%	
Over £455	no additional liability		10·2%	

	On first £61	Remainder	On first £61	Remainder
Contracted out*				
Earnings: £ 61·00–£109·99	2%	8·2%	3%	Nil
£110·00–£154·99	2%	8·2%	5%	2%
£155·00–£209·99	2%	8·2%	7%	4%
£210·00–£455·00	2%	8·2%	10·2%	7·2%
Over £455	no additional liability		{ 10·2% 10·2% (earnings over £455)	7·2% (to £455)

Reduced rate for married women and widows with valid certificate of election	3·85% (earnings to £455)	(As above)
Men over 65 and women over 60	Nil	(As above)
Children under 16	Nil	Nil

Class 2 Contributions: Self employed
Flat rate: £6·05 a week.
Share fishermen's special rate: £7.20 a week.
Small earnings exception: earnings under £3,430 a year.

Class 3 Voluntary Contributions: £5·95 a week.

Class 4 Contributions: 6% of profits or gains between £6,860 and £23,660 a year.
Exempt if pensionable age reached by beginning of year of assessment.

* Contracted out rates apply to members of contracted out occupational schemes only.
Note: From 6 April 1996 there is an employer NI contribution holiday of up to a year for individuals taken on who have been out of work for two years or more, trainees, and certain people who work intermittently during the qualifying period, who satisfy the conditions.

6 April 1995–5 April 1996

Lower earnings limit: £58 a week £252 a month £3,016 a year	**Upper earnings limit:** £440 a week **(employees only)** £1,907 a month £22,880 a year

	Employees from 6.4.95		**Employers from 6.4.95**	
Class 1 Contributions				
standard rate	*On first £58*	*Remainder*	*(Rate applying to all earnings)*	
Earnings: £ 58·00–£104·99	2%	10%	3%	
£105·00–£149·99	2%	10%	5%	
£150·00–£204·99	2%	10%	7%	
£205·00–£440·00	2%	10%	10·2%	
Over £440	no additional liability		10·2%	
Contracted out*	*On first £58*	*Remainder*	*On first £58*	*Remainder*
Earnings: £ 58·00–£104·99	2%	8·2%	3%	Nil
£105·00–£149·99	2%	8·2%	5%	2%
£150·00–£204·99	2%	8·2%	7%	4%
£205·00–£440·00	2%	8·2%	10·2%	7·2%
Over £440	no additional liability		{10·2% 10·2%	7·2% (to £440) (earnings over £440)
Reduced rate for married women and widows with valid certificate of election	3·85% (earnings to £440)		(As above)	
Men over 65 and women over 60	Nil		(As above)	
Children under 16	Nil		Nil	

Class 2 Contributions: Self employed
Flat rate: £5·75 a week.
Share fishermen's special rate: £7·30 a week.
Small earnings exception: earnings under £3,260 a year.

Class 3 Voluntary Contributions: £5·65 a week.

Class 4 Contributions: 7·3% of profits or gains between £6,640 and £22,880 a year.
Exempt if pensionable age reached by beginning of year of assessment.

6 April 1994–5 April 1995

Lower earnings limit: £57 a week £247 a month £2,964 a year	**Upper earnings limit:** £430 a week **(employees only)** £1,864 a month £22,360 a year

	Employees from 6.4.94		**Employers from 6.4.94**	
Class 1 Contributions				
standard rate	*On first £57*	*Remainder*	*(Rate applying to all earnings)*	
Earnings: £ 57·00–£ 99·99	2%	10%	3·6%	
£100·00–£144·99	2%	10%	5·6%	
£145·00–£199·99	2%	10%	7·6%	
£200·00–£430·00	2%	10%	10·2%	
Over £430	no additional liability		10·2%	
Contracted out*	*On first £57*	*Remainder*	*On first £57*	*Remainder*
Earnings: £ 57·00–£ 99·99	2%	8·2%	3·6%	0·6%
£100·00–£144·99	2%	8·2%	5·6%	2·6%
£145·00–£199·99	2%	8·2%	7·6%	4·6%
£200·00–£430·00	2%	8·2%	10·2%	7·2%
Over £430	no additional liability		{10·2% 10·2%	7·2% (to £430) (earnings over £430)
Reduced rate for married women and widows with valid certificate of election	3·85% (earnings to £430)		(As above)	
Men over 65 and women over 60	Nil		(As above)	
Children under 16	Nil		Nil	

Class 2 Contributions: Self employed
Flat rate: £5·65 a week.
Share fishermen's special rate: £7·75 a week.
Small earnings exception: earnings under £3,200 a year.

Class 3 Voluntary Contributions: £5·55 a week.

Class 4 Contributions: 7·3% of profits or gains between £6,490 and £22,360 a year.
Exempt if pensionable age reached by beginning of year of assessment.

* Contracted out rates apply to members of contracted out occupational schemes only.

Employers' contributions: company cars and free fuel

National insurance contributions are payable by employers on the benefit of cars and free fuel provided for the private use of employees where the latter are liable to the income tax charge on cars. From 6 April 1994 the car benefit figure is calculated by reference to the list price of the car rather than by use of a table (see p 56), although a car fuel benefit table continues to be used. No contribution is payable where the employee earns less than £8,500 a year. Where contributions are payable, they are levied at the main rate (ie 12·2% from 6 April 1999). They are assessed annually and collected in arrears.

Car benefits: private use	Business use up to 2,500 miles pa or additional car		Business use over 2,500 miles pa but under 18,000 miles		Business use 18,000 miles pa or over	
	Under 4 years old	4 years or more	Under 4 years old	4 years or more	Under 4 years old	4 years or more
1994–95 onwards Calculated by reference to the list price of the car, see p 56.						
1993–94 **Original market value up to £19,250**						
1,400cc or less	£360·36	£246·48	£240·24	£164·32	£120·12	£82·16
Over 1,400cc up to 2,000cc	£466·44	£316·68	£310·96	£211·12	£155·48	£105·56
Over 2,000cc	£748·80	£502·32	£499·20	£334·88	£249·60	£167·44
No cylinder capacity						
Under £6,000	£360·36	£246·48	£240·24	£164·32	£120·12	£82·16
£6,000 or more, but under £8,500	£466·44	£316·68	£310·96	£211·12	£155·48	£105·56
£8,500 or more, but not more than £19,250	£748·80	£502·32	£499·20	£334·88	£249·60	£167·44
Original market value over £19,250						
Over £19,250 up to £29,000	£968·76	£652·08	£645·84	£434·72	£322·92	£217·36
Over £29,000	£1,566·24	£1,038·96	£1,044·16	£692·64	£522·08	£346·32

Car benefits: free fuel	
1999–2000	
Cylinder capacity: 1,400cc or less	£147·62
(non-diesel cars) Over 1,400cc up to 2,000cc	£187·88
Over 2,000cc	£276·94
Cylinder capacity: 2,000cc or less	£187·88
(diesel cars) Over 2,000cc	£276·94
No internal combustion engine —	£276·94
1998–99	
Cylinder capacity: 1,400cc or less	£101·00
(non-diesel cars) Over 1,400cc up to 2,000cc	£128·00
Over 2,000cc	£189·00
Cylinder capacity: 2,000cc or less	£128·00
(diesel cars) Over 2,000cc	£189·00
No internal combustion engine —	£189·00
1997–98	
Cylinder capacity: 1,400cc or less	£80·00
(non-diesel cars) Over 1,400cc up to 2,000cc	£101·00
Over 2,000cc	£149·00
Cylinder capacity: 2,000cc or less	£74·00
(diesel cars) Over 2,000cc	£94·00
No internal combustion engine —	£149·00
1996–97	
Cylinder capacity: 1,400cc or less	£72·42
(non-diesel cars) Over 1,400cc up to 2,000cc	£90·78
Over 2,000cc	£134·64
Cylinder capacity: 2,000cc or less	£65·28
(diesel cars) Over 2,000cc	£83·64
No internal combustion engine —	£134·64
1995–96	
Cylinder capacity: 1,400cc or less	£68·34
(non-diesel cars) Over 1,400cc up to 2,000cc	£86·70
Over 2,000cc	£128·52
Cylinder capacity: 2,000cc or less	£61·71
(diesel cars) Over 2,000cc	£79·56
No internal combustion engine —	£128·52

DSS explanatory pamphlets

Five or more copies of Benefits Agency and DSS leaflets, and Braille publications, may be obtained from:
GPA Interface, Rosepark House, Upper Newtownards Road, Belfast BT4 3NR or using fax number 01232 526 121.
Where fewer than five copies of any leaflet are required, they should be obtained from the local DSS office.
Catalogues and order forms may be obtained from the Benefits Agency Publicity Register Hotline on 0645 540 000.
Contributions Agency publications may be obtained from: Contributions Agency Publications, Room A3316, DSS
Longbenton, Newcastle upon Tyne NE98 1YX.

National Insurance

Leaflet

CA01	National insurance for employees
CA01(W)	National insurance for employees (Wales)
CA02	National insurance for self-employed people with small earnings
CA02(W)	National insurance contributions for self-employed people with small earnings (Wales)
CA04	National insurance contributions, Class 2 and Class 3: direct debit—the easier way to pay
CA04(W)	National insurance contributions, Class 2 and Class 3: direct debit—the easier way to pay (Wales)
CA07	National insurance: unpaid and late-paid contributions
CA07(W)	National insurance: unpaid and late-paid contributions (Wales)
CA08	National insurance voluntary contributions
CA08(W)	National insurance voluntary contributions (Wales)
CA09	National insurance for widows
CA10	National insurance for divorced women
CA10(W)	National insurance for divorced women (Wales)
CA11	National insurance for share fishermen
CA11(W)	National insurance for share fishermen (Wales)
CA12	Training for further employment and your NI record
CA12(W)	Training for further employment and your NI record (Wales)
CA13	National insurance contributions for married women
CA14	Termination of contracted-out employment
CA15	Cessation of contracted-out employment
CA17	Employers' guide to minimum contributions
CA23	National insurance for mariners
CA24	National insurance for masters and employers of mariners
CA25	National insurance for agencies and people finding work through agencies
CA26	National insurance for examiners and part-time lecturers, teachers and instructors
CA26(W)	National insurance for examiners and part-time lecturers, teachers and instructors (Wales)
CA29	Employer's manual (SMP) (plus supplement)
CA30	Employer's manual (SSP) (plus supplement)
CA30(W)	Employer's manual (SSP) (Wales) (plus supplement)
CA33	Cars and fuel—A manual for employers (plus supplement)
CA33(W)	Cars and fuel – A manual for employers (Wales) (plus supplement)
CA34	Class 1A NIC by APM
CA35	Statutory sick pay tables
CA35(W)	Statutory sick pay tables (Wales)
CA36	Statutory maternity pay tables
CA36(W)	Statutory maternity pay tables (Wales)
CA37	Tables – simplified deductions scheme for non-contracted out employees
CA38	National insurance tables: not contracted-out
CA38(W)	National insurance tables: not contracted-out contributions (Wales)
CA39	National insurance tables: contracted-out contributions
CA40	National insurance tables: employee-only contributions
CA42	National insurance tables: mariners and deep-sea fishing vessels
CA43	Contracted-out money-purchase – employers' minimum payments
CA44	National insurance for company directors
CA45	Employer's Charter
CA45(W)	Employer's Charter (Wales)
CA47	Contributor's Charter
CA47(W)	Contributor's Charter (Wales)
CA53	Information about NI contributions

Leaflet

CA62	Unhappy with our service? (Contributions Agency)
CA62(W)	Unhappy with our service? (Wales)
CA64	Dissatisfied with our ruling?
CA64(W)	Dissatisfied with our ruling? (Wales)
CA65	National insurance for people working for embassies, consulates and overseas employers
CA66	Surveys of NI records – a code of practice
CA69/IR 148	Are your workers employed or self-employed? – construction workers
CA72	National insurance contributions – deferring payments
CA72(W)	National insurance contributions – deferring payments (Wales)
CA80	Workers in building and construction. Help with NI for employees and self-employed, including agency workers
CWG1	Employer's quick guide to PAYE and NICs
CWG2	Employer's further guide to PAYE and NICs
CWL1	Starting your own business?
CWL2	NI contributions for self-employed people, Class 2 and Class 4
CAT1	A catalogue of information, leaflets and posters
FB23	Young people's guide to social security
FB23 Braille	Young people's guide to social security
FB23(W)	Young people's guide to social security (Wales)
FB30	Self employed?
FB30 Braille	Self-employed?
FB30(W)	Self-employed? (Wales)
NI38	Social security abroad
NI132	National insurance for employers of people working abroad
NI196	Social security benefit rates
NI196 Braille	Social security benefit rates
NI196(W)	Social security benefit rates (Wales)
NI246	How to appeal
NI246 Braille	How to appeal
NI260	A guide to reviews and appeals
PP3	Personal pensions for the self-employed
PP3(W)	Personal pensions for the self-employed (Wales)
PP3 Braille	Personal pensions for the self-employed
PP3 Audio	Personal pensions for the self-employed
NIC1	National insurance contributions holiday – Employer's leaflet
NIC1(W)	National insurance contributions holiday – Employer's leaflet (Wales)
SA4	Social security agreement with Jersey and Guernsey
SA5	Social security agreement with Australia
SA6	Social security agreement with Switzerland
SA8	Social security agreement with New Zealand
SA11	Social security agreement with Malta
SA12	Social security agreement with Cyprus
SA14	Social security agreement with Israel
SA17	Social security agreement with the republics of former Yugoslavia
SA20	Social security agreement with Canada
SA22	Social security agreement with Turkey
SA23	Social security agreement with Bermuda
SA27	Social security agreement with Jamaica
SA29	Your social security insurance, benefits and health care rights in the European Community, and in Iceland, Liechtenstein and Norway
SA33	Social security agreement with the United States of America
SA38	Social security agreement with Mauritius
SA42	Social security agreement with the Philippines
SA43	Social security agreement with Barbados

Stamp duties

Ad valorem duty

Rounding

With effect from 1 October 1999, the charging provisions will be standardised to provide for the rounding up to the nearest £5 in all cases (where duty is currently rounded up to multiples of between 50p and £12) other than for SDRT. ((1999) SWTI 444 and the Stamp Office).

Rates of duty (FA 1963 s 55; FA 1997 s 49; FA 1998 s 149; 1999 Budget Resolution No. 43)

Consideration certified as:	Conveyance or transfer on sale with certificate of value	Lease premium where rent exceeds £600 p.a.	Conveyance etc without certificate of value	Stock transfers
16 March 1999[1] onwards				
Not exceeding £60,000	Nil	1%		
£60,001–£250,000	1%	1%		
£250,001–£500,000	2·5%	2·5%	3·5%	0·5%
£500,001 or more	3·5%	3·5%		
17 March 1998[2] to 15 March 1999				
Not exceeding £60,000	Nil	1%		
£60,001–£250,000	1%	1%		
£250,001–£500,000	2%	2%	3%	0·5%
£500,001 or more	3%	3%		
8 July 1997 to 16 March 1998				
Not exceeding £60,000	Nil	1%		
£60,001–£250,000	1%	1%		
£250,001–£500,000	1·5%	1·5%	2%	0·5%
£500,001 or more	2%	2%		

[1] Unless transfer is pursuant to a contract made before 10 March 1999.
[2] Unless transfer is pursuant to a contract made before 18 March 1998.

Leases

Any agreement for a lease entered into after 19 March 1984 is chargeable to duty as if it were the actual lease irrespective of the length of the term.

Premiums. If the consideration for the lease includes a premium, this is charged to ad valorem duty in accordance with the Table above. The nil rate of duty does not apply if the average rent reserved by the lease exceeds £600 p.a.

Rent. *Leases not exceeding 7 years,* or for an indefinite term, are not chargeable to duty on the rent where this does not exceed £500 p.a. If the rent exceeds £500 p.a., the duty is—

For a lease of furnished residential
accommodation for a definite term of
less than 1 year.. £1 (£5 from 1 October 1999)[3]

Other cases ....50p per £50 or part

Leases exceeding 7 years—

Rent	Over 7 yrs up to 35 yrs	Over 35 yrs up to 100 yrs	Over 100 yrs
	£	£	£
£5 or less	0·10	0·60	1·20
Over £5 up to £10	0·20	1·20	2·40
Over £10 up to £15	0·30	1·80	3·60
Over £15 up to £20	0·40	2·40	4·80
Over £20 up to £25	0·50	3·00	6·00
Over £25 up to £50	1·00	6·00	12·00
Over £50 up to £75	1·50	9·00	18·00
Over £75 up to £100	2·00	12·00	24·00
Over £100 up to £150	3·00	18·00	36·00
Over £150 up to £200	4·00	24·00	48·00
Over £200 up to £250	5·00	30·00	60·00
Over £250 up to £300	6·00	36·00	72·00
Over £300 up to £350	7·00	42·00	84·00
Over £350 up to £400	8·00	48·00	96·00
Over £400 up to £450	9·00	54·00	108·00
Over £450 up to £500	10·00	60·00	120·00
Over £500; for every £50 or fraction of £50	1·00	6·00	12·00

Fixed duties

		From 1 October 1999[3]
Stamp Act 1891 Sch 1		
Leases (other than as described above)	£2	£5
Declaration of trust; duplicate or counterpart; exchange or partition; release or renunciation; surrender	50p	£5

CREST: For instruments executed after 30 June 1996 there is no fixed stamp duty charge on deposits of shares into CREST, although there may be a liability to SDRT: see FA 1996 s 186.

[3] The minimum fixed stamp duty of 50p is to be increased to £5 with effect from 1 October 1999 ((1999) SWTI 444 and the Stamp Office).

Value added tax

Annual accounting scheme

The taxable person must have been registered for at least one year at the date of application for authorisation (SI 1995/2518 Pt VII as amended). The taxable person must have reasonable grounds for believing that the value of taxable supplies in the year beginning at the date of application will not exceed a prescribed figure.

Taxable turnover

From 9.4.91	£300,000

Registration limits
UK taxable supplies

	Past turnover[1]		Future turnover[1]
	1 year	*Unless turnover for next year will not exceed:*	*30 days[2]*
1.12.93–29.11.94	£45,000	£43,000	£45,000
30.11.94–28.11.95	£46,000	£44,000	£46,000
29.11.95–26.11.96	£47,000	£45,000	£47,000
27.11.96–29.11.97	£48,000	£46,000	£48,000
30.11.97–31.3.98	£49,000	£47,000	£49,000
1.4.98-31.3.99	£50,000	£48,000	£50,000
1.4.99 onwards	£51,000	£49,000	£51,000

[1] Value of taxable supplies (at zero and positive rates).
[2] Where there are reasonable grounds for believing that limit will be exceeded in this period.

Supplies from other EU member states

	Cumulative total[1] from beginning of calendar year
1.1.93 onwards	£70,000

[1] Value of supplies made by persons in other EU member states to non-taxable persons in the UK.

Acquisitions from other EU member states
VATA 1994 Sch 3

	Past acquisitions[1]	Future acquisitions[1]
	Cumulative total from 1 January	*30 days[2]*
1.1.94–31.12.94	£45,000	£45,000
1.1.95–31.12.95	£46,000	£46,000
1.1.96–31.12.96	£47,000	£47,000
1.1.97–31.12.97	£48,000	£48,000
1.1.98–31.3.98	£49,000	£49,000
1.4.98–31.3.99	£50,000	£50,000
1.4.99 onwards	£51,000	£51,000

[1] Value of acquisitions of taxable goods from suppliers in other EU member states.
[2] Where there are reasonable grounds for believing that limit will be exceeded in this period.

Deregistration limits

UK taxable supplies

Future turnover	Annual limit
1.12.93–20.11.94	£43,000
30.11.94–28.11.95	£44,000
29.11.95–26.11.96	£45,000
27.11.96–29.11.97	£46,000
30.11.97–31.3.98	£47,000
1.4.98–31.3.99	£48,000
1.4.99 onwards	£49,000

Unless during the year, the person will cease making taxable supplies (or suspend making taxable supplies for 30 days or more).

Supplies from other EU member states

	Past supplies[1]	Future supplies[1]
	Supplies in preceding calendar year	*Supplies in following calendar year [2]*
1.1.93 onwards	£70,000	£70,000

[1] Value of supplies made by persons in other EU member states to non-taxable persons in the UK.
[2] Where C & E are satisfied that limit will not be exceeded in this period.

Acquisitions from other EU member states

VATA 1994 Sch 3

	Past acquisitions[1]	Future acquisitions[1]
	Acquisitions in preceding calendar year	*Acquisitions in following calendar year[2]*
1.1.94–31.12.94	£45,000	£45,000
1.1.95–31.12.95	£46,000	£46,000
1.1.96–31.12.96	£47,000	£47,000
1.1.97–31.12.97	£48,000	£48,000
1.1.98–31.3.98	£49,000	£49,000
1.4.98–31.3.99	£50,000	£50,000
1.4.99 onwards	£51,000	£51,000

[1] Value of acquisitions of taxable goods from suppliers in other EU member states.
[2] Where C & E are satisfied that limit will not be exceeded in this period.

Rate of tax

	Standard rate	VAT fraction	Reduced rate[1]	VAT fraction
1.9.97 onwards	17.5%	7/47	5%	1/21
1.4.94–31.8.97	17.5%	7/47	8%	2/27
1.4.91–31.3.94	17.5%	7/47	n/a	n/a
18.6.79–31.3.91	15%	3/23	n/a	n/a

[1] Applies to supplies of fuel and power for domestic, residential or non-business charity use. Extended to the installation of energy-saving materials under certain grant schemes from 1 July 1998: SI 1998/1375.

Penalties and surcharges

Offence	Penalty
Failure to pay tax due under the payment on account scheme on time (VATA 1994 s 59A)	(From 1.6.96) Default surcharge
Failure to submit return or pay tax due within time limit. (After 30.9.93, where a return is late but the tax is paid on time or no tax is due, a default is recorded but no surcharge arises) (VATA 1994 s 59)	Default surcharge: (defaults after 30.9.93) the greater of £30 and a specified percentage of outstanding VAT for period, depending on number of defaults in surcharge period– 1st default in period: 2% 2nd default: 5% 3rd default: 10% 4th default: 15% Further defaults: 15%
Evasion of VAT: conduct involving dishonesty (VATA 1994 s 60)	Amount of tax evaded or sought to be evaded (subject to mitigation)
Issuing incorrect certificate as to zero-rating (or, under 1999 Budget provisions, as to eligibility to receive reduced-rate fuel and power (VATA 1994 s 62)	Difference between tax actually charged and tax which should have been charged
Misdeclaration or neglect (VATA 1994 s 63)	(After 9.3.92) 15% of VAT which would have been lost if inaccuracy had not been discovered
Repeated misdeclarations (VATA 1994 s 64)	(After 30.11.93) 15% of VAT which would have been lost if second and subsequent inaccuracies within penalty period had not been discovered
Material inaccuracy in EC sales statement (VATA 1994 s 65)	£100 for each material inaccuracy in 2 year penalty period (which commences following notice of second material inaccuracy)
Failure to submit an EC sales statement (VATA 1994 s 66)	Greater of £50 and a daily penalty (for no more than 100 days) depending on number of failures in default period– 1st failure: £5 2nd failure: £10 3rd and further failures: £15
Failure to notify liability for registration or change in nature of supplies by person exempted from registration (VATA 1994 s 67) (From 1.1.96 reintroduced for failure to notify liability for registration when business transferred as going concern)	(From 1.1.95) Greater of £50 and a specified percentage of the tax for which the person would have been liable, depending on the period of failure– 9 months or less: 5% Over 9, up to 18 months: 10% Over 18 months: 15% NB: Surcharge assessments are not issued for sums of less than £200 unless the rate of the surcharge is 10% or more
Unauthorised issue of invoices (VATA 1994 s 67)	(From 1.1.95) Greater of £50 and 15% of amount shown as or representing VAT
Breach of walking possession agreement (VATA 1994 s 68)	50% of VAT due and amount recoverable
Failure to preserve records for prescribed period (VATA 1994 s 69)	£500
Breaches of regulatory provisions, including failure to notify cessation of liability or entitlement to be registered, failure to keep records and non-compliance with any regulations made under VATA 1994 (VATA 1994 s 69)	Greater of £50 and a daily penalty (for no more than 100 days) of a specified amount depending on number of failures in preceding two years– No previous failures: £5 per day 1 previous failure: £10 per day 2 or more: £15 per day
Breaches of regulatory provisions involving failure to pay VAT or submit return by due date (VATA 1994 s 69)	Greater of £50 and a daily penalty (for no more than 100 days) of a specified amount depending on number of failures in preceding two years– No previous failures: greater of £5 and $\frac{1}{6}$% of VAT due 1 previous failure: greater of £10 and $\frac{1}{3}$% of VAT due 2 or more: greater of £15 and $\frac{1}{2}$% of VAT due
Failure to comply with statutory responsibility to pay correct amount of tax on time (FA 1997 ss 51,52)	(From 1 July 1997) Distress and attachment (poinding and sale and arrestment in Scotland)
Failure to comply with VAT tribunal directions or summons (VATA 1994 Sch 12 para 10)	Up to £1,000
Failure by person to whom an attachment notice has been given and who is or becomes indebted to the defaulter to pay the required amount (FA 1997)	£250 plus £20 for each day failure continues after payment has become due

Default interest

The prescribed rate of interest for the purposes of VATA 1994 s 74 (the provisions of which were operative from 1 April 1990) has varied as follows:

	Rate
From 6 March 1999	7.5%
6 January 1999–5 March 1999	8.5%
6 July 1998–5 January 1999	9.5%
6 February 1996–5 July 1998	6.25%
6 March 1995–5 February 1996	7%
6 October 1994–5 March 1995	6·25%
6 January 1994–5 October 1994	5.5%
6 March 1993–5 January 1994	6.25%
6 December 1992–5 March 1993	7%
6 November 1992–5 December 1992	7.75%
6 October 1991–5 November 1992	9.25%
6 July 1991–5 October 1991	10.00%
6 May 1991–5 July 1991	10.75%
6 March 1991–5 May 1991	11.5%
6 November 1990–5 March 1991	12.25%
1 April 1990–5 November 1990	13%

Interest on VAT overpaid in cases of official error

(VATA 1994 s 78)

	Rate		Rate
From 6 March 1999	4%	1 May 1988–31 July 1988	9.5%
6 January 1999–5 March 1999	5%	1 December 1987–30 April 1988	11%
1 April 1997–5 January 1999	6%	1 November 1987–30 November 1987	11.25%
6 February–31 March 1997	8%	1 April 1987–31 October 1987	11.75%
16 October 1991–5 February 1993	10.25%	1 January 1987–31 March 1987	12.25%
1 April 1991–15 October 1991	12%	1 August 1986–31 December 1986	11.5%
1 November 1989–31 March 1991	14.25%	1 April 1984–31 July 1986	12%
1 January 1989–31 October 1989	13%	1 April 1983–31 March 1984	12.5%
1 November 1988–31 December 1988	12.25%	1 July 1982–31 March 1983	13%
1 August 1988–31 October 1988	11%	1 March 1982–30 June 1982	14%

Zero rating

A zero-rated supply is a taxable supply, but the rate of tax is nil.
(References are to VATA 1994 Sch 8)

Group 1—Food.
Group 2—Sewerage services and water.
Group 3—Books etc.
Group 4—Talking books for the blind and handicapped and wireless sets for the blind.
Group 5—Construction of buildings etc.
Group 6—Protected buildings.
Group 7—International services.
Group 8—Transport.
Group 9—Caravans and houseboats.
Group 10—Gold.
Group 11—Bank notes.
Group 12—Drugs, medicines, aids for the handicapped etc.
Group 13—Imports, exports etc.
Group 14—Tax-free shops.
Group 15—Charities etc.
Group 16—Clothing and footwear.

Exempt supplies

No tax is chargeable on an exempt supply, and input tax cannot be recovered except as allowed under the partial exemption provisions (SI 1995/2518 Pt XIV; VAT Notice 706).
(References are to VATA 1994 Sch 9)

Group 1—Land.
Group 2—Insurance.
Group 3—Postal services.
Group 4—Betting, gaming and lotteries.
Group 5—Finance.
Group 6—Education.
Group 7—Health and welfare.
Group 8—Burial and cremation.
Group 9—Trade unions and professional bodies.
Group 10—Sport, sports competitions and physical education.
Group 11—Works of art etc.
Group 12—Fund-raising events by charities and other qualifying bodies.
Group 13—Cultural services etc.

Partial exemption

De minimis limit for application of partial exemption rules
SI 1995/2518 reg 106

	Exempt input tax not exceeding
Tax years beginning after 30.11.94	(a) £625 per month on average; and (b) 50% of total input tax for prescribed accounting period
Periods beginning between 1.4.92 and 30.11.94	£600 per month on average
Periods beginning between 1.4.87 and 31.3.92	(a) £100 per month on average; or (b) £250 per month on average and 50% of all input tax; or (c) £500 per month on average and 25% of all input tax

Capital goods scheme

Input tax adjustment following change in taxable use of capital goods
VATA 1994 s 34, SI 1995/2518 regs 112-116 (77/388/EEC art 20), (see also (1999) SWTI 488).
From 1 April 1990

Item	*Value*	*Adjustment period*
Computer equipment	£50,000 or more	5 years
Land and buildings	£250,000 or more	10 years (5 years where interest had less than 10 years to run on acquisition)

Adjustment formula

$$\frac{\text{Total input tax on item}}{\text{Length of adjustment period}} \times \text{adjustment percentage}$$

The adjustment percentage is the percentage change in the extent to which the item is used (or treated as used) in making taxable supplies between the first interval in the adjustment period and a subsequent interval. (The first interval generally ends on the last day of the tax year in which the input tax was incurred.)

Car fuel

From 6 April 1987, VAT-inclusive scale figures are used to assess VAT due on petrol provided at below cost price for private journeys by registered traders or their employees, where the petrol has been provided from business resources. The high business-mileage discount was abolished from 1993-94.

	12 months	VAT due per car	3 months	VAT due per car	1 month	VAT due per car
1999–2000						
Diesel engine						
Cylinder capacity: 2,000cc or less	£785	£116·91	£196	£29·19	£65	£9·68
more than 2,000cc	£995	£148·19	£248	£36·93	£82	£12·21
Any other type of engine						
Cylinder capacity: 1,400cc or less	£850	£126·59	£212	£31·57	£70	£10·42
Over 1,400cc up to 2,000cc	£1,075	£160·10	£268	£39·91	£89	£13·25
Over 2,000cc	£1,585	£236·06	£396	£58·97	£132	£19·65
1998–99						
Diesel engine						
Cylinder capacity: 2,000cc or less	£785	£116·91	£196	£29·19	£65	£9·68
more than 2,000cc	£995	£148·19	£248	£36·93	£82	£12·21
Any other type of engine						
Cylinder capacity: 1,400cc or less	£850	£126·59	£212	£31·57	£70	£10·42
Over 1,400cc up to 2,000cc	£1,075	£160·10	£268	£39·91	£89	£13·25
Over 2,000cc	£1,585	£236·06	£396	£58·97	£132	£19·65
1997–98						
Diesel engine						
Cylinder capacity: 2,000cc or less	£740	£110·21	£185	£27·55	61	9·08
more than 2,000cc	£940	£140·00	£235	£35·00	78	11·61
Any other type of engine						
Cylinder capacity: 1,400cc or less	£800	£119·14	£200	£29·78	66	9·82
Over 1,400cc up to 2,000cc	£1,010	£150·42	£252	£37·53	84	12·51
Over 2,000cc	£1,490	£221·91	£372	£55·40	124	18·46
1996–97						
Diesel engine						
Cylinder capacity: 2,000cc or less	£640	£95·31	£160	£23·82	£53	£7·89
more than 2,000cc	£820	£122·12	£205	£30·53	£68	£10·12
Any other type of engine						
Cylinder capacity: 1,400cc or less	£710	£105·74	£177	£26·36	£59	£8·78
Over 1,400cc up to 2,000cc	£890	£132·55	£222	£33·06	£74	£11·02
Over 2,000cc	£1,320	£196·59	£330	£49·14	£110	£16·38

HM Customs and Excise: VAT notices

New notices no longer carry a designation of the year of issue or revision, but this is retained here as a guide to the year of publication of the latest version. Several leaflets and notices contain Update inserts, published from time to time.

Notice		Title
48		Extra-statutory concessions
400		**HM Customs and Excise Charter Standards**
700		**The VAT guide**
	700/1/97‡	Should I be registered for VAT?
	700/1W/97	Ddylwnifod wedi fy nghofrestru am TAW?
	700/1A/97	Should I be registered for VAT? Distance selling
	700/1AW/97	Ddylwnifod wedify nghofrestru am TAW? – Gweythmo bell
	700/1B/97	Should I be registered for VAT? Acquisitions
	700/1BW/97	Ddylwnifod wedify nghofrestru am TAW? – Caffaeliadau
	700/2/97	The VAT group treatment requirements
	700/3/98	Registration for VAT: Corporate bodies organised in divisions
	700/4/97	Registration for VAT: non-established taxable persons
	700/5/85	Hire-purchase and conditional sale: repossessions and transfers of agreements
	700/7/94	Business promotion schemes
	700/8/92	*Returnable containers (cancelled)*
	700/9/96	Transfer of a business as a going concern
	700/9W/96	Trosglwyddo busnes fel busnes byw
	700/10/84	*Processing and repair of goods and exchange units (cancelled)*
	700/11/98	Cancelling your registration
	700/12/95	Filling in your VAT return
	700/12W/95	Llanwi'ch ffurflen TAW
	700/13/96	*VAT publications (cancelled)*
	700/14/93	Video cassette films: rental and part-exchange
	700/15/95	The Ins and Outs of VAT
	700/15W/95	Manylion TAW
	700/17/96	Funded pension schemes
	700/18/97	Relief from VAT on bad debts
	700/21/95	Keeping records and accounts
	700/21W/95	Cadw cofnodion a chyfrifon
	700/22/89	Admissions
	700/24/94	Postage and delivery charges
	700/25/84	Taxis and hire cars
	700/26/92	*Visits by VAT officers (cancelled)*
	700/28/94	Estate agents
	700/30/89	*Default surcharge appeals (cancelled)*
	700/31/94	Pawnbrokers: disposals of pledged goods
	700/33/95	Government funded training programmes and schemes to help the unemployed
	700/34/94	Staff
	700/35/97	Business gifts
	700/36/88	*Dealer loader promotional schemes (cancelled)*
	700/41/95	Late registration penalty
	700/41W/95	Dirwy am gofrestru yn hwyr
	700/42/93	Serious misdeclaration penalty
	700/43/96	Default interest
	700/44/93	Barristers and advocates: tax point on ceasing to practise
	700/45/93	How to correct errors you find on your VAT returns
	700/45W/93	Sut i gywiro gwallau y dewch o hyd iddynt ar eich ffurflenni TAW
	700/46/93	Agricultural flat rate scheme
	700/47/93	Confidentiality in VAT matters (Tax advisers)—Statement of practice
	700/48/93	*Insolvent VAT traders—claims for input tax after deregistration (cancelled)*
	700/49/93	*Notifying Customs and Excise of insolvency (cancelled)*
	700/50/97	Default surcharge
	700/50W/97	Gordal diffyg talu
	700/51/95	VAT enquiries guide
	700/51W/95	Arweiniad ar ymholiadau TAW
	700/52/96	Notice of requirement to give security to Customs and Excise
	700/52W/96	Hysbysiad o'r angen i roi gwarant i'r Tollau Tramor o Chartref
	700/54/94	What if I don't pay?
	700/55/93	VAT input tax appeals: luxuries, amusements and entertainment
	700/56/94	Insolvency
	700/57/95	VAT—administrative agreements entered into with trade bodies
	700/58/98	Treatment of VAT repayment returns and VAT repayment supplements
	700/59/94	VAT refunds on surrendered road licences
	700/60/96	Payments on account
	700/61/97	Artificial separation of business activities: statement of practice
	700/64/96	Motoring expenses
	700/65/96	Business entertainment
	700/66/99	List of VAT business advice centres
	700/67/97	The VAT registration scheme for racehourse owners
(701)		
	701/1/95‡	Charities
	701/5/90	Clubs and associations
	701/6/97	Charity-funded equipment for medical, veterinary etc. uses
	701/7/94‡	VAT reliefs for people with disabilities
	701/8/97	Postage stamps and philatelic supplies
	701/9/85	Terminal markets: dealings with commodities
	701/10/85	Printed and similar matter
	701/12/96†	Sales of antiques, works of art etc from stately homes
	701/13/95	Gaming and amusement machines
	701/14/97	Food
	701/15/95	Food for animals

Notice		Title
	701/16/99	Sewerage services and water
	701/19/95	Fuel and power
	701/20/96†	Caravans and houseboats
	701/21/93	Gold
	701/22/95	Tools for the manufacture of goods for export
	701/23/95	Protective boots and helmets
	701/24/92	Parking facilities
	701/25/86	*Pet food (cancelled)*
	701/26/95	Betting and gaming
	701/27/97	Bingo
	701/28/97	Lotteries
	701/29/92	Finance
	701/30/97	Education and vocational training
	701/31/92	Health
(701)	701/32/97	Burial, cremation and the commemoration of the dead
	701/33/97	Trade unions, professional bodies and learned societies
	701/34/89	Competitions in sport and physical recreation
	701/35/95	Youth clubs
	701/36/97	Insurance
	701/37/94	Live animals
	701/38/93	Seeds and plants
	701/39/97	VAT liability law
	701/40/91	Abattoirs
	701/41/95	Sponsorship
	701/43/93	Financial futures and options
	701/44/98	Securities
	701/45/94	Sport and physical education
	701/46/96	Schools and school photographs
	701/47/96	Culture
	701/48/97	Corporate purchasing cards
702		**Imports**
		(Single Market supplement)
	702/3/91	*Repayment of import VAT to shipping agents and freight forwarders (cancelled)*
	702/4/94	Importing computer software
	702/6/91	Import VAT certificates
	702/7/93	Import VAT relief for goods supplied onward to another country in the European Community
	702/9/98	Warehousing and free zones
703		**Exports**
	703/1/95	Supply of freight containers for export or removal from the UK
	703/2/99	Sailaway boats supplied for export outside the European Community
	703/3/99	Sailaway boat scheme
704		**Retail exports**
	704/1/99	VAT refunds for travellers departing from the European Community
	704/2/93	Traveller's guide to the retail export scheme
	704/3/93	Guide to tax-free shopping—the VAT refund scheme (in Spanish, Arabic, Japanese and English)
705		**Personal exports of new motor vehicles to destinations outside the European Community from 1 January 1993**
705A		**VAT: Supplies of vehicles under the personal export scheme for removal from the EC**
706		**Partial exemption**
	706/1/92	Self-supply of stationery
	706/2/90	Capital goods scheme
708		**Buildings and construction**
	708/5/97	Registered social landlords (Housing Associations, etc)
709	709/1/87	Industrial, staff and public sector catering
	709/2/91	Catering and take-away food
	709/3/93	Hotels and holiday accommodation
	709/4/88	Package holidays and other holiday services
	709/5/98	Tour operators' margin scheme
	709/6/97	Travel agents
710	710/1/91	Theatrical agents and Nett Acts
	710/2/83	Agencies providing nurses and nursing auxiliaries
	710/3/83	*Private investigators: expenses charged to clients (cancelled)*
711		*Secondhand cars† (cancelled)*
	711/1/90	*VAT and the secondhand car scheme† (cancelled)*
712		***Works of art, antiques and collectors' pieces†*** *(cancelled)*
	712/2/90	*VAT: Works of art, antiques and collectors' pieces† (cancelled)*
713		***Secondhand motorcycles†*** *(cancelled)*
714		**Young children's clothing and footwear**
714A		**Young children's clothing and footwear: schedule of maximum sizes for zero-rating**
717		***Secondhand caravans and motor caravans†*** *(cancelled)*
718		**Margin scheme for secondhand goods, works of art, antiques and collectors' items**
719		**VAT refunds for DIY builders and converters**
720		***Secondhand boats and outboard motors†*** *(cancelled)*
721		***Secondhand aircraft†*** *(cancelled)*
722		***Secondhand electronic organs†*** *(cancelled)*
723		**Refunds of VAT in the European Community for EC and non-EC traders**
724		***Secondhand firearms†*** *(cancelled)*
725		**VAT: the Single Market**

Information sheets: available also at http://www.hmce.gov.uk.
(Cancelled information sheets have been deleted from the list)

† Publications having legal or quasi-legal force.   ‡ Now available in large print.

23% grossing-up table

Am't	Grossed at 23%	Am't	Grossed at 23%	Am't	Grossed at 23%	Am't	Grossed at 23%	Am't	Grossed at 23%	Am't	Grossed at 23%	Am't	Grossed at 23%	Am't	Grossed at 23%
£	£	£	£	£	£	£	£	£	£	£	£	£	£	£	£
1	1·30	71	92·21	141	183·12	211	274·03	281	364·94	351	455·84	421	546·75	491	637·66
2	2·60	72	93·51	142	184·42	212	275·32	282	366·23	352	457·14	422	548·05	492	638·96
3	3·90	73	94·81	143	185·71	213	276·62	283	367·53	353	458·44	423	549·35	493	640·26
4	5·19	74	96·10	144	187·01	214	277·92	284	368·83	354	459·74	424	550·65	494	641·56
5	6·49	75	97·40	145	188·31	215	279·22	285	370·13	355	461·04	425	551·95	495	642·86
6	7·79	76	98·70	146	189·61	216	280·52	286	371·43	356	462·34	426	553·25	496	644·16
7	9·09	77	100·00	147	190·91	217	281·82	287	372·73	357	463·64	427	554·55	497	645·45
8	10·39	78	101·30	148	192·21	218	283·12	288	374·03	358	464·94	428	555·84	498	646·75
9	11·69	79	102·60	149	193·51	219	284·42	289	375·32	359	466·23	429	557·14	499	648·05
10	12·99	80	103·90	150	194·81	220	285·71	290	376·62	360	467·53	430	558·44	500	649·35
11	14·29	81	105·19	151	196·10	221	287·01	291	377·92	361	468·83	431	559·74	510	662·34
12	15·58	82	106·49	152	197·40	222	288·31	292	379·22	362	470·13	432	561·04	520	675·32
13	16·88	83	107·79	153	198·70	223	289·61	293	380·52	363	471·43	433	562·34	530	688·31
14	18·18	84	109·09	154	200·00	224	290·91	294	381·82	364	472·73	434	563·64	540	701·30
15	19·48	85	110·39	155	201·30	225	292·21	295	383·12	365	474·03	435	564·94	550	714·29
16	20·78	86	111·69	156	202·60	226	293·51	296	384·42	366	475·32	436	566·23	560	727·27
17	22·08	87	112·99	157	203·90	227	294·81	297	385·71	367	476·62	437	567·53	570	740·26
18	23·38	88	114·29	158	205·19	228	296·10	298	387·01	368	477·92	438	568·83	580	753·25
19	24·68	89	115·58	159	206·49	229	297·40	299	388·31	369	479·22	439	570·13	590	766·23
20	25·97	90	116·88	160	207·79	230	298·70	300	389·61	370	480·52	440	571·43	600	779·22
21	27·27	91	118·18	161	209·09	231	300·00	301	390·91	371	481·82	441	572·73	610	792·21
22	28·57	92	119·48	162	210·39	232	301·30	302	392·21	372	483·12	442	574·03	620	805·19
23	29·87	93	120·78	163	211·69	233	302·60	303	393·51	373	484·42	443	575·32	630	818·18
24	31·17	94	122·08	164	212·99	234	303·90	304	394·81	374	485·71	444	576·62	640	831·17
25	32·47	95	123·38	165	214·29	235	305·19	305	396·10	375	487·01	445	577·92	650	844·16
26	33·77	96	124·68	166	215·58	236	306·49	306	397·40	376	488·31	446	579·22	660	857·14
27	35·06	97	125·97	167	216·88	237	307·79	307	398·70	377	489·61	447	580·52	670	870·13
28	36·36	98	127·27	168	218·18	238	309·09	308	400·00	378	490·91	448	581·82	680	883·12
29	37·66	99	128·57	169	219·48	239	310·39	309	401·30	379	492·21	449	583·12	690	896·10
30	38·96	100	129·87	170	220·78	240	311·69	310	402·60	380	493·51	450	584·42	700	909·09
31	40·26	101	131·17	171	222·08	241	312·99	311	403·90	381	494·81	451	585·71	710	922·08
32	41·56	102	132·47	172	223·38	242	314·29	312	405·19	382	496·10	452	587·01	720	935·06
33	42·86	103	133·77	173	224·68	243	315·58	313	406·49	383	497·40	453	588·31	730	948·05
34	44·16	104	135·06	174	225·97	244	316·88	314	407·79	384	498·70	454	589·61	740	961·04
35	45·45	105	136·36	175	227·27	245	318·18	315	409·09	385	500·00	455	590·91	750	974·03
36	46·75	106	137·66	176	228·57	246	319·48	316	410·39	386	501·30	456	592·21	760	987·01
37	48·05	107	138·96	177	229·87	247	320·78	317	411·69	387	502·60	457	593·51	770	1,000·00
38	49·35	108	140·26	178	231·17	248	322·08	318	412·99	388	503·90	458	594·81	780	1,012·99
39	50·65	109	141·56	179	232·47	249	323·38	319	414·29	389	505·19	459	596·10	790	1,025·97
40	51·95	110	142·86	180	233·77	250	324·68	320	415·58	390	506·49	460	597·40	800	1,038·96
41	53·25	111	144·16	181	235·06	251	325·97	321	416·88	391	507·79	461	598·70	810	1,051·95
42	54·55	112	145·45	182	236·36	252	327·27	322	418·18	392	509·09	462	600·00	820	1,064·94
43	55·84	113	146·75	183	237·66	253	328·57	323	419·48	393	510·39	463	601·30	830	1,077·92
44	57·14	114	148·05	184	238·96	254	329·87	324	420·78	394	511·69	464	602·60	840	1,090·91
45	58·44	115	149·35	185	240·26	255	331·17	325	422·08	395	512·99	465	603·90	850	1,103·90
46	59·74	116	150·65	186	241·56	256	332·47	326	423·38	396	514·29	466	605·19	860	1,116·88
47	61·04	117	151·95	187	242·86	257	333·77	327	424·68	397	515·58	467	606·49	870	1,129·87
48	62·34	118	153·25	188	244·16	258	335·06	328	425·97	398	516·88	468	607·79	880	1,142·86
49	63·64	119	154·55	189	245·45	259	336·36	329	427·27	399	518·18	469	609·09	890	1,155·84
50	64·94	120	155·84	190	246·75	260	337·66	330	428·57	400	519·48	470	610·39	900	1,168·83
51	66·23	121	157·14	191	248·05	261	338·96	331	429·87	401	520·78	471	611·69	910	1,181·82
52	67·53	122	158·44	192	249·35	262	340·26	332	431·17	402	522·08	472	612·99	920	1,194·81
53	68·83	123	159·74	193	250·65	263	341·56	333	432·47	403	523·38	473	614·29	930	1,207·79
54	70·13	124	161·04	194	251·95	264	342·86	334	433·77	404	524·68	474	615·58	940	1,220·78
55	71·43	125	162·34	195	253·25	265	344·16	335	435·06	405	525·97	475	616·88	950	1,233·77
56	72·73	126	163·64	196	254·55	266	345·45	336	436·36	406	527·27	476	618·18	960	1,246·75
57	74·03	127	164·94	197	255·84	267	346·75	337	437·66	407	528·57	477	619·48	970	1,259·74
58	75·32	128	166·23	198	257·14	268	348·05	338	438·96	408	529·87	478	620·78	980	1,272·73
59	76·62	129	167·53	199	258·44	269	349·35	339	440·26	409	531·17	479	622·08	990	1,285·71
60	77·92	130	168·83	200	259·74	270	350·65	340	441·56	410	532·47	480	623·38	1,000	1,298·70
61	79·22	131	170·13	201	261·04	271	351·95	341	442·86	411	533·77	481	624·68	2,000	2,597·40
62	80·52	132	171·43	202	262·34	272	353·25	342	444·16	412	535·06	482	625·97	3,000	3,896·10
63	81·82	133	172·73	203	263·64	273	354·55	343	445·45	413	536·36	483	627·27	4,000	5,194·81
64	83·12	134	174·03	204	264·94	274	355·84	344	446·75	414	537·66	484	628·57	5,000	6,493·51
65	84·42	135	175·32	205	266·23	275	357·14	345	448·05	415	538·96	485	629·87	6,000	7,792·21
66	85·71	136	176·62	206	267·53	276	358·44	346	449·35	416	540·26	486	631·17	7,000	9,090·91
67	87·01	137	177·92	207	268·83	277	359·74	347	450·65	417	541·56	487	632·47	8,000	10,389·61
68	88·31	138	179·22	208	270·13	278	361·04	348	451·95	418	542·86	488	633·77	9,000	11,688·31
69	89·61	139	180·52	209	271·43	279	362·34	349	453·25	419	544·16	489	635·06	10,000	12,987·01
70	90·91	140	181·82	210	272·73	280	363·64	350	454·55	420	545·45	490	636·36	11,000	14,285·71

34% grossing-up table

(The rate applicable to trusts remains at 34% for 1999-2000.)

Am't	Grossed at 34%	Am't	Grossed at 34%	Am't	Grossed at 34%	Am't	Grossed at 34%	Am't	Grossed at 34%	Am't	Grossed at 34%	Am't	Grossed at 34%	Am't	Grossed at 34%
£	£	£	£	£	£	£	£	£	£	£	£	£	£	£	£
1	1·52	71	107·58	141	213·64	211	319·70	281	425·76	351	531·82	421	637·88	491	743·94
2	3·03	72	109·09	142	215·15	212	321·21	282	427·27	352	533·33	422	639·39	492	745·45
3	4·55	73	110·61	143	216·67	213	322·73	283	428·79	353	534·85	423	640·91	493	746·97
4	6·06	74	112·12	144	218·18	214	324·24	284	430·30	354	536·36	424	642·42	494	748·48
5	7·58	75	113·64	145	219·70	215	325·76	285	431·82	355	537·88	425	643·94	495	750·00
6	9·09	76	115·15	146	221·21	216	327·27	286	433·33	356	539·39	426	645·45	496	751·52
7	10·61	77	116·67	147	222·73	217	328·79	287	434·85	357	540·91	427	646·97	497	753·03
8	12·12	78	118·18	148	224·24	218	330·30	288	436·36	358	542·42	428	648·48	498	754·55
9	13·64	79	119·70	149	225·76	219	331·82	289	437·88	359	543·94	429	650·00	499	756·06
10	15·15	80	121·21	150	227·27	220	333·33	290	439·39	360	545·45	430	651·52	500	757·58
11	16·67	81	122·73	151	228·79	221	334·85	291	440·91	361	546·97	431	653·03	510	772·73
12	18·18	82	124·24	152	230·30	222	336·36	292	442·42	362	548·48	432	654·55	520	787·88
13	19·70	83	125·76	153	231·82	223	337·88	293	443·94	363	550·00	433	656·06	530	803·03
14	21·21	84	127·27	154	233·33	224	339·39	294	445·45	364	551·52	434	657·58	540	818·18
15	22·73	85	128·79	155	234·85	225	340·91	295	446·97	365	553·03	435	659·09	550	833·33
16	24·24	86	130·30	156	236·36	226	342·42	296	448·48	366	554·55	436	660·61	560	848·48
17	25·76	87	131·82	157	237·88	227	343·94	297	450·00	367	556·06	437	662·12	570	863·64
18	27·27	88	133·33	158	239·39	228	345·45	298	451·52	368	557·58	438	663·64	580	878·79
19	28·79	89	134·85	159	240·91	229	346·97	299	453·03	369	559·09	439	665·15	590	893·94
20	30·30	90	136·36	160	242·42	230	348·48	300	454·55	370	560·61	440	666·67	600	909·09
21	31·82	91	137·88	161	243·94	231	350·00	301	456·06	371	562·12	441	668·18	610	924·24
22	33·33	92	139·39	162	245·45	232	351·52	302	457·58	372	563·64	442	669·70	620	939·39
23	34·85	93	140·91	163	246·97	233	353·03	303	459·09	373	565·15	443	671·21	630	954·55
24	36·36	94	142·42	164	248·48	234	354·55	304	460·61	374	566·67	444	672·73	640	969·70
25	37·88	95	143·94	165	250·00	235	356·06	305	462·12	375	568·18	445	674·24	650	984·85
26	39·39	96	145·45	166	251·52	236	357·58	306	463·64	376	569·70	446	675·76	660	1,000·00
27	40·91	97	146·97	167	253·03	237	359·09	307	465·15	377	571·21	447	677·27	670	1,015·15
28	42·42	98	148·48	168	254·55	238	360·61	308	466·67	378	572·73	448	678·79	680	1,030·30
29	43·94	99	150·00	169	256·06	239	362·12	309	468·18	379	574·24	449	680·30	690	1,045·45
30	45·45	100	151·52	170	257·58	240	363·64	310	469·70	380	575·76	450	681·82	700	1,060·61
31	46·97	101	153·03	171	259·09	241	365·15	311	471·21	381	577·27	451	683·33	710	1,075·76
32	48·48	102	154·55	172	260·61	242	366·67	312	472·73	382	578·79	452	684·85	720	1,090·91
33	50·00	103	156·06	173	262·12	243	368·18	313	474·24	383	580·30	453	686·36	730	1,106·06
34	51·52	104	157·58	174	263·64	244	369·70	314	475·76	384	581·82	454	687·88	740	1,121·21
35	53·03	105	159·09	175	265·15	245	371·21	315	477·27	385	583·33	455	689·39	750	1,136·36
36	54·55	106	160·61	176	266·67	246	372·73	316	478·79	386	584·85	456	690·91	760	1,151·52
37	56·06	107	162·12	177	268·18	247	374·24	317	480·30	387	586·36	457	692·42	770	1,166·67
38	57·58	108	163·64	178	269·70	248	375·76	318	481·82	388	587·88	458	693·94	780	1,181·82
39	59·09	109	165·15	179	271·21	249	377·27	319	483·33	389	589·39	459	695·45	790	1,196·97
40	60·61	110	166·67	180	272·73	250	378·79	320	484·85	390	590·91	460	696·97	800	1,212·12
41	62·12	111	168·18	181	274·24	251	380·30	321	486·36	391	592·42	461	698·48	810	1,227·27
42	63·64	112	169·70	182	275·76	252	381·82	322	487·88	392	593·94	462	700·00	820	1,242·42
43	65·15	113	171·21	183	277·27	253	383·33	323	489·39	393	595·45	463	701·52	830	1,257·58
44	66·67	114	172·73	184	278·79	254	384·85	324	490·91	394	596·97	464	703·03	840	1,272·73
45	68·18	115	174·24	185	280·30	255	386·36	325	492·42	395	598·48	465	704·55	850	1,287·88
46	69·70	116	175·76	186	281·82	256	387·88	326	493·94	396	600·00	466	706·06	860	1,303·03
47	71·21	117	177·27	187	283·33	257	389·39	327	495·45	397	601·52	467	707·58	870	1,318·18
48	72·73	118	178·79	188	284·85	258	390·91	328	496·97	398	603·03	468	709·09	880	1,333·33
49	74·24	119	180·30	189	286·36	259	392·42	329	498·48	399	604·55	469	710·61	890	1,348·48
50	75·76	120	181·82	190	287·88	260	393·94	330	500·00	400	606·06	470	712·12	900	1,363·64
51	77·27	121	183·33	191	289·39	261	395·45	331	501·52	401	607·58	471	713·64	910	1,378·79
52	78·79	122	184·85	192	290·91	262	396·97	332	503·03	402	609·09	472	715·15	920	1,393·94
53	80·30	123	186·36	193	292·42	263	398·48	333	504·55	403	610·61	473	716·67	930	1,409·09
54	81·82	124	187·88	194	293·94	264	400·00	334	506·06	404	612·12	474	718·18	940	1,424·24
55	83·33	125	189·39	195	295·45	265	401·52	335	507·58	405	613·64	475	719·70	950	1,439·39
56	84·85	126	190·91	196	296·97	266	403·03	336	509·09	406	615·15	476	721·21	960	1,454·55
57	86·36	127	192·42	197	298·48	267	404·55	337	510·61	407	616·67	477	722·73	970	1,469·70
58	87·88	128	193·94	198	300·00	268	406·06	338	512·12	408	618·18	478	724·24	980	1,484·85
59	89·39	129	195·45	199	301·52	269	407·58	339	513·64	409	619·70	479	725·76	990	1,500·00
60	90·91	130	196·97	200	303·03	270	409·09	340	515·15	410	621·21	480	727·27	1,000	1,515·15
61	92·42	131	198·48	201	304·54	271	410·61	341	516·67	411	622·73	481	728·79	2,000	3,030·30
62	93·94	132	200·00	202	306·06	272	412·12	342	518·18	412	624·24	482	730·30	3,000	4,545·45
63	95·45	133	201·52	203	307·58	273	413·64	343	519·70	413	625·76	483	731·82	4,000	6,060·61
64	96·97	134	203·03	204	309·09	274	415·15	344	521·21	414	627·27	484	733·33	5,000	7,575·76
65	98·48	135	204·55	205	310·61	275	416·67	345	522·73	415	628·79	485	734·85	6,000	9,090·91
66	100·00	136	206·06	206	312·12	276	418·18	346	524·24	416	630·30	486	736·36	7,000	10,606·06
67	101·52	137	207·58	207	313·64	277	419·70	347	525·76	417	631·82	487	737·88	8,000	12,121·21
68	103·03	138	209·09	208	315·15	278	421·21	348	527·27	418	633·33	488	739·39	9,000	13,636·36
69	104·55	139	210·61	209	316·67	279	422·73	349	528·79	419	634·85	489	740·91	10,000	15,151·52
70	106·06	140	212·12	210	318·18	280	424·24	350	530·30	420	636·36	490	742·42	11,000	16,666·67

17.5% VAT (tax included in amount) – VAT fraction ⁷/₄₇

Am't	VAT incl. in Am't	Am't	VAT incl. in Am't	Am't	VAT incl. in Am't	Am't	VAT incl. in Am't	Am't	VAT incl. in Am't	Am't	VAT incl. in Am't	Am't	VAT incl. in Am't
£ or p	£ or p	£ or p	£ or p	£ or p	£ or p	£ or p	£ or p	£ or p	£ or p	£ or p	£ or p	£ or p	£ or p
1	0·15	71	10·57	141	21·00	211	31·43	281	41·85	810	120·64		
2	0·30	72	10·72	142	21·15	212	31·57	282	42·00	820	122·13		
3	0·45	73	10·87	143	21·30	213	31·72	283	42·15	830	123·62		
4	0·60	74	11·02	144	21·45	214	31·87	284	42·30	840	125·11		
5	0·74	75	11·17	145	21·60	215	32·02	285	42·45	850	126·60		
6	0·89	76	11·32	146	21·74	216	32·17	286	42·60	860	128·09		
7	1·04	77	11·47	147	21·89	217	32·32	287	42·74	870	129·57		
8	1·19	78	11·62	148	22·04	218	32·47	288	42·89	880	131·06		
9	1·34	79	11·77	149	22·19	219	32·62	289	43·04	890	132·55		
10	1·49	80	11·91	150	22·34	220	32·77	290	43·19	900	134·04		
11	1·64	81	12·06	151	22·49	221	32·91	291	43·35	910	135·53		
12	1·79	82	12·21	152	22·64	222	33·06	292	43·49	920	137·02		
13	1·94	83	12·36	153	22·79	223	33·21	293	43·64	930	138·51		
14	2·09	84	12·51	154	22·94	224	33·36	294	43·79	940	140·00		
15	2·23	85	12·66	155	23·09	225	33·51	295	43·94	950	141·49		
16	2·38	86	12·81	156	23·23	226	33·66	296	44·09	960	142·98		
17	2·53	87	12·96	157	23·38	227	33·81	297	44·23	970	144·47		
18	2·68	88	13·11	158	23·53	228	33·96	298	44·38	980	145·96		
19	2·83	89	13·26	159	23·68	229	34·11	299	44·53	990	147·45		
20	2·98	90	13·40	160	23·83	230	34·26	300	44·68	1,000	148·94		
21	3·13	91	13·55	161	23·98	231	34·40	310	46·17	1,100	163·83		
22	3·28	92	13·70	162	24·13	232	34·55	320	47·66	1,200	178·72		
23	3·43	93	13·85	163	24·28	233	34·70	330	49·15	1,300	193·62		
24	3·57	94	14·00	164	24·43	234	34·85	340	50·64	1,400	208·51		
25	3·72	95	14·15	165	24·57	235	35·00	350	52·13	1,500	223·40		
26	3·87	96	14·30	166	24·72	236	35·15	360	53·62	1,600	238·30		
27	4·02	97	14·45	167	24·87	237	35·30	370	55·11	1,700	253·19		
28	4·17	98	14·60	168	25·02	238	35·45	380	56·60	1,800	268·08		
29	4·32	99	14·74	169	25·17	239	35·60	390	58·09	1,900	282·98		
30	4·47	100	14·89	170	25·32	240	35·74	400	59·57	2,000	297·87		
31	4·62	101	15·04	171	25·47	241	35·89	410	61·06	2,100	312·77		
32	4·77	102	15·19	172	25·62	242	36·04	420	62·55	2,200	327·66		
33	4·91	103	15·34	173	25·77	243	36·19	430	64·04	2,300	342·55		
34	5·06	104	15·49	174	25·91	244	36·34	440	65·53	2,400	357·45		
35	5·21	105	15·64	175	26·06	245	36·49	450	67·02	2,500	372·34		
36	5·36	106	15·79	176	26·21	246	36·64	460	68·51	2,600	387·23		
37	5·51	107	15·94	177	26·36	247	36·79	470	70·00	2,700	402·13		
38	5·66	108	16·09	178	26·51	248	36·94	480	71·49	2,800	417·02		
39	5·81	109	16·23	179	26·66	249	37·09	490	72·98	2,900	431·91		
40	5·96	110	16·38	180	26·81	250	37·23	500	74·47	3,000	446·81		
41	6·11	111	16·53	181	26·96	251	37·38	510	75·96	3,100	461·70		
42	6·26	112	16·68	182	27·11	252	37·53	520	77·45	3,200	476·60		
43	6·40	113	16·83	183	27·26	253	37·68	530	78·94	3,300	491·49		
44	6·55	114	16·98	184	27·40	254	37·83	540	80·43	3,400	506·38		
45	6·70	115	17·13	185	27·55	255	37·98	550	81·91	3,500	521·28		
46	6·85	116	17·28	186	27·70	256	38·13	560	83·40	3,600	536·17		
47	7·00	117	17·43	187	27·85	257	38·28	570	84·89	3,700	551·06		
48	7·15	118	17·57	188	28·00	258	38·43	580	86·38	3,800	565·96		
49	7·30	119	17·72	189	28·15	259	38·57	590	87·87	3,900	580·85		
50	7·45	120	17·87	190	28·30	260	38·72	600	89·36	4,000	595·74		
51	7·60	121	18·02	191	28·45	261	38·87	610	90·85	4,100	610·64		
52	7·74	122	18·17	192	28·60	262	39·02	620	92·34	4,200	625·53		
53	7·89	123	18·32	193	28·74	263	39·17	630	93·83	4,300	640·43		
54	8·04	124	18·47	194	28·89	264	39·32	640	95·32	4,400	655·32		
55	8·19	125	18·62	195	29·04	265	39·47	650	96·81	4,500	670·21		
56	8·34	126	18·77	196	29·19	266	39·62	660	98·30	4,600	685·11		
57	8·49	127	18·91	197	29·34	267	39·77	670	99·79	4,700	700·00		
58	8·64	128	19·06	198	29·49	268	39·91	680	101·28	4,800	714·89		
59	8·79	129	19·21	199	29·64	269	40·06	690	102·77	4,900	729·79		
60	8·94	130	19·36	200	29·79	270	40·21	700	104·26	5,000	744·68		
61	9·09	131	19·51	201	29·94	271	40·36	710	105·74	6,000	893·62		
62	9·23	132	19·66	202	30·09	272	40·51	720	107·23	7,000	1,042·55		
63	9·38	133	19·81	203	30·23	273	40·66	730	108·72	8,000	1,191·49		
64	9·53	134	19·96	204	30·38	274	40·81	740	110·21	9,000	1,340·42		
65	9·68	135	20·11	205	30·53	275	40·96	750	111·70	10,000	1,489·36		
66	9·83	136	20·26	206	30·68	276	41·11	760	113·19	11,000	1,638·30		
67	9·98	137	20·40	207	30·83	277	41·26	770	114·68	12,000	1,787·23		
68	10·13	138	20·55	208	30·98	278	41·40	780	116·17	13,000	1,936·17		
69	10·28	139	20·70	209	31·13	279	41·55	790	117·66	14,000	2,085·11		
70	10·43	140	20·85	210	31·28	280	41·70	800	119·15	15,000	2,234·04		

INDEX